MW01687426

SCHOOLING IN BRITISH COLUMBIA, 1849-2005:

VOICES FROM THE PAST

Thomas Fleming, Editor

THOMAS FLEMING

Thomas Fleming is a professor of educational history at the University of Victoria. He was born in Dublin and was educated in private, public, and parochial schools in Ireland and in the provinces of Saskatchewan, Alberta, and British Columbia. He studied history at the University of Victoria, where he completed B.A. and M.A. degrees, before undertaking further graduate study at Stanford University and the University of Oregon, where he earned a Ph.D. in the history of educational administration. No stranger to the real world of administration, he has managed several private-sector companies and served as Assistant to the President at both the University of Victoria and the University of British Columbia.

Dr. Fleming has written numerous articles on British Columbia school history and served as Editor-in-Chief of the 1988 British Columbia Royal Commission on Education. He co-authored the volume, *A History of Thought and Practice in Educational Administration*, a study that has become a standard reference work in the history of school management in the United States. He is also well known for his edited volume, *School Leadership: Essays on the British Columbia School Experience, 1872-1995*, as well as other books on school effectiveness, class size, and educational reform.

SCHOOLING IN BRITISH COLUMBIA, 1849-2005:

VOICES FROM THE PAST

Thomas Fleming, Editor

BENDALL BOOKS
Educational Publishers

SCHOOLING IN BRITISH COLUMBIA, 1849-2005: *Voices from the Past*
Edited by Thomas Fleming

Copyright © 2010 by Thomas Fleming. All rights reserved.

Publication of this volume was supported by funding from the British Columbia School Superintendents Association's Active Senior Membership. We also gratefully acknowledge the financial support of the Province of British Columbia, through the Ministry of Education.

Except for brief passages quoted in a review, no part of this book may be reproduced or transmitted in any form, by any means, without the permission of the publisher.

Set in Adobe Minion

Printed in Canada by Friesens Corporation

First printing: 2010

Library and Archives Canada Cataloguing in Publication

Fleming, Thomas, 1944-

Schooling in British Columbia, 1849-2005 : voices from the past
/ Thomas Fleming.

Includes index.

ISBN 978-0-9865828-0-6

1. Schools--British Columbia--History.
2. Education--British Columbia--History. I. Title.

LA418.B7S365 2010 371'.009711 C2010-907416-5

BENDALL BOOKS ***Educational Publishers***

CANADA: P.O. Box 115, Mill Bay, BC V0R 2P0

E-MAIL: Bendallbooks@islandnet.com

WEB: www.islandnet.com/bendallbooks

FAX: 250-743-2910

To Fiona McLaughlin for all the reasons

Contents

CHAPTER 2: Schools Under Construction: The Frontier Era, 1872-1898

Acknowledgements

Many people gave generously of their time in trying to add to this historical record of the province's schools. On the academic side of the ledger, special thanks are certainly due to University of British Columbia (UBC) Emeritus Professor John Calam, who has given countless hours of advice and wisdom over the past two decades about British Columbia's social and educational history during this and other historical writings—and who generously contributed a charming essay to this volume drawn from his own reminiscences as a young principal. Other educational historians also deserve thanks. Alastair Glegg and Helen Raptis at the University of Victoria (UVic) offered immensely helpful advice about the manuscript, as well as suggesting many thoughtful editorial changes. UBC Emeritus Professor J.D. Wilson similarly provided much support along with many insightful editorial suggestions. The task of assembling this edited volume of writings was lightened immeasurably by Carolyn Smyly who helped greatly with the research and who gave invaluable advice about the selection of educational materials, especially during the colonial and frontier eras.

Former school superintendents Terry McBurney and Barbara Naef also deserve credit. They gathered stories relating to schools in the 1970s and 1980s and arranged meetings with school veterans who were willing to share their experiences in schools. They also persevered with what turned out to be a long process in bringing this book to print. Appreciation is also owed to Ray Wunderlich, a former history teacher and Greater Victoria School District archivist, alas now deceased, who retrieved photographic treasures from assorted uncatalogued boxes and granted permission for their use—as did Victoria High archivist, UVic Emeritus Professor Peter Smith, also deceased, a classicist and historian par excellence who granted permission to use photographs that documented the province's first high school.

Over time, others also made important material contributions to this study. Dorothea Stafford furnished many papers and photographs belonging to herself and her husband, Harold. Dorothea's recollections of her own school days constitute an important part of this book. No less generous were Ellen Conway and her son, David, who made available papers and letters belonging to Cliff Conway, long-time director of the education department's tests and measurement branch.

More than 20 years ago, Bill Plenderleith, the school inspector who authored the Peace River plan to consolidate rural districts, likewise provided a small but valuable collection of papers and photographic records, including a brief autobiography and histories of the province's elementary curriculum and school organization. Some of these materials, along with a small part of an interview with Bill, are included in the volume. Former North Vancouver school superintendent, Bill Lucas, shared a mimeographed folder of J.B. DeLong's memoirs, a rare document of great historical interest that records one young man's development in the educational and social world of the late-nineteenth century.

Former ministry official, school superintendent, and British Columbia School Trustees Association (BCSTA) executive director, Alan Newberry, likewise did much to help provide context for this work by preserving copies of chief inspector Bill Reid's *aide memoires* on the education department's school inspectors and superintendents—several bundles of four- by eight-inch cards that he saved from extinction decades ago during one of the ministry's many reorganizations. Finally, I would like to express my gratitude to the British Columbia Ministry of Education and to the British Columbia School Superintendents Association's Active Senior Membership for the financial assistance they provided to make publication of this volume possible.

Thomas Fleming, Editor

Introduction

Since the colonial era in what is today British Columbia, people have had something to say about schools. This is not surprising because schools are easily the most accessible of all society's institutions. They are society's great meeting place and serve as a ready forum for the expression of diverse ideas, cultural values, political views and agendas, personal sentiments and beliefs, along with individual dreams and social aspirations. "Everyone's been to school," a college mate once professed, "so everyone's an expert on education and, therefore, has a view."

Of course, people's views and understandings about schools—as well as their expectations for them—change with time and have done so since the first school was established in Fort Victoria more than 150 years ago. What British Columbians have wanted from schools, and what have they said about them, are the two things that have led to this collection of writings.

Broadly speaking, this volume has attempted to chart the sentiments British Columbians have held about schools since the mid-nineteenth century, and to show the various points of view individuals have expressed about schools and their purposes since this time. Wherever possible, this collection has tried to present first-hand accounts of people's educational observations and perceptions at particular points in the past, as well as the meanings they have assigned to their own school experiences. Such accounts, to be sure, do not provide a complete rendering of events at any single moment in time, but they do provide particular angles of vision into the places schools occupy in our lives and their significance as social institutions. These stories, I hope, also bring a freshness and immediacy to our understandings of the past—a sense of being there not always found in academic or conventional historical writings.

These stories and documents also reflect time-tested traditions of storytelling as a means of inspiring curiosity and learning. I trust that these stories, textured as they are by time, circumstance, and personality, cast some small amount of light into the most important and timeless of endeavours—the task of educating the young. In assembling this collection, I have tried to present as wide a variety of voices as possible, giving individuals a chance to speak in their own words, and exercising an editorial pen only wherever necessary to provide a sense of context. On occasion, I have removed irrelevant remarks, idiosyncrasies of speech, repetitions and the like. Infrequently, I have also tried to ensure subject-verb agreement and, when necessary, reordered parts of the text to improve clarity and understanding. I have also tried to standardize the language in keeping with general grammatical conventions. At all times, my objective has been to render as complete and as accurate an account of the original stories and documents as possible without taxing readers beyond reasonable limits.

In searching to find these voices from the past, I have drawn on two kinds of sources. The first consist of customary historical materials—letters, newspaper accounts, diaries, memoranda, official documents, reports by educational experts, and assorted first-hand accounts of life in and around schools. The second is comprised of a lengthy series of transcribed interviews with former teachers, principals, and others involved in schooling.

Written records of the province's early school history proved fascinating in many respects. They illustrated, for example, that James Douglas, chief HBC factor and "father" of the first Crown Colony of Vancouver Island, was a firm believer in the value of religion in educating the young, and alarmed at the prospect of children of the "lower classes" running wild in Victoria's streets, "ignorant of their duty to God and man." Written records similarly showed that Emily Carr, arguably the province's greatest painter, sharply disagreed with the snobbish attitudes of pioneer British Columbians who insisted on behaving "more English than the English," and who ignored the fledgling public schools by enrolling children in elite private academies and European-style "finishing" schools. Early newspaper files likewise remind us that Amor de Cosmos, the brilliant and half-mad editor of one of the province's first newspapers, saw social redemption in the public schools while remaining steadfast in his opposition to any kind of religious teaching inside a publicly-supported system. Although excluded from the public schools, churchmen would exert a strong and not always positive impact on generations of aboriginal children who were obliged by the Dominion Government to attend mission schools. Some of the children's reminiscences found in this collection catalogue both the good and bad of such experiences as the Victorian Era slipped quietly into the twentieth century.

Archival and other written records similarly enable us to revisit the sparsely populated educational universe that characterized the first half of the twentieth century, when some 1,000 small and mostly impoverished schools were scattered across the province, stretched beyond their limits in trying to provide instruction across the first eight or, occasionally, 10 grades. Through letters, diaries, and inspectors' reports, we can witness the desperate state of these schools and appreciate the travails of the young female teachers who staffed them—many scarcely more than children themselves. Loneliness, homesickness, and desperation were all too often their closest companions in crudely built schoolrooms and teacherages where they trembled in fear of rough-spoken trustees or flinty-eyed school inspectors who might deem them pedagogically unfit.

But, thankfully too, the past offers its own surprises and we encounter someone like the colourful and fiery Mildred McQuillan, unrepentant about her instructional faults and unremitting in her criticism of the harsh living conditions she was forced to endure. McQuillan's diary of a teacher's life spans a four-month stint in Orange Valley near Fort Fraser at the end of the 1920s and, in its energy and blunt language, constitutes a unique declaration of one woman's independence from rural schools and rural life. Other recollections are, of course, softer and kinder in nature—notably Clare McAllister's delightful reconstruction of the intricate protocols associated with dressing for school in winter as the second decade of the twentieth century was beginning.

Supplementing such written records were a host of educational stories derived from interviews with former teachers, principals, and other educational officials who had spent long careers travelling to roadside schools. Many of them had begun their professional lives teaching in one-room schools, before becoming principals, school inspectors, superintendents, and, in some instances, senior bureaucrats in educational government. More than 50 interviews with such individuals over the past 20 years produced a rich archive of oral history that detailed educational experiences otherwise unrecorded in government's official school reports or most scholarly writings about educational history.[1] An interview with former deputy minister, Harold Campbell, for example, provided a treasure trove of school stories, not to mention a few finely drawn and, sometimes, humourous sketches of influential educational figures who shaped schools and society in twentieth-century British Columbia. Also included in the volume is a small portrait drawn in later life that recalled a rural school on northern Vancouver Island in 1910, when Campbell began his working life as a teacher.

Interviews with Campbell's contemporaries and colleagues—Bill Plenderleith, Colonel John Burnett, C.J. Frederickson, Alex Turnbull, Bernard Gillie, and Stewart Graham, among others—likewise helped illuminate the schools of the Edwardian Age and the interwar era of the 1920s and 1930s that followed. These men recalled their own boyhood in schools, the educators who taught them, their own initiations as teachers and administrators, and myriad other details relating to the social and educational norms of bygone days. Through their stories we can reconstruct the daily and weekly rhythms of school life and many of the rituals prized by teachers and pupils in eras now long beyond memory's pale. Graham's experiences as a messenger boy in educational government in the early 1920s—and, later, as a principal and school inspector—proved particularly revealing. In two lengthy interviews, he provided memorable descriptions of the legendary but remarkably different high school inspectors, J.B. DeLong and Albert Sullivan. He also recounted intriguing stories of rural life in northern British Columbia during the dark days of the Great Depression. Bernard Gillie, long influential in administrative and BCTF circles, likewise made it possible to see into the inner linings of the government's small but effective education department through his sketches of the teachers' registrar, J.L. Watson and chief inspector H.B. King, the most powerful and pedantic figure in educational government from the time of the Great Depression to the end of World War II.

An interview with Dorothea Stafford, together with her written recollections of Victoria schools in the years before the end of World War I, similarly opened up a world of schools and the details of a formal curriculum long forgotten. Stafford's later experiences as a teacher—and as a school inspector's wife who travelled the length and breadth of the province with her husband—chronicled in stories and photographs the opening of the high plains country from the 1920s to the end of World War II and the settlement of one of Canada's last great frontiers. More recently, the remembrances of educational figures who worked in and around government in the 1970s and 1980s, such as Joe Phillipson, Jack Fleming, Jim Carter, and others, help chronicle the collapse of a once-unified educational community and the eventual—and arguably tragic— politicalization of public education.

Taken as a whole, these writings and interviews touch upon many themes that resound throughout British Columbia's social and educational history—the impact of geography on provincial development, the struggle for control between central and local authorities in schools and other agencies of government, the deeply inequitable estates that have long separated rural and urban populations, longstanding traditions of social division rooted in class, race, and gender, the impact of a "boom and bust" economy on historical cycles of school creation and closure (not to mention the flood and ebb tides of educational finance), and the changing philosophical fashions in educational thought from academics and traditionalism to progressivism and vocationalism and all points in between.

One thing is apparent in the stories comprising this volume: people's reminiscences about schools are invariably as much about British Columbia's "social" history as they are about the province's "educational" history. Only rarely do people seem to confine their recollections of schools to classrooms, what they learned, or to the school's actual pedagogical work. Far more commonly, people envision schools as institutions integrally connected to larger and more complex social systems, as institutions conditioned, if not entirely determined, by the cultural and geographic environments around them. In essence, schools are not remembered as educational institutions but as something else—as centres of a community's focus or spirit, or places that encapsulate special chapters and passages in people's lives, places where relationships and friendships are found and lost, and where teachers grow up occasionally as fast as the children in their care.

Even in interviews, there appears to be avoidance of or, at least, disinterest or neglect in recounting anything to do with teaching methods or strategies, the curriculum, or how students actually performed. People willingly talk about students, along with the hardships and challenges they faced. But, almost always, it is the context surrounding schools or students that is considered to be most important. Put simply, it is the social landscape of relationships inside schools, and the topographical landscape outside them, that people remember—and describe most vividly—when they talk about schools.

It always bears remembering that the province's geography has in many respects written its history up to the closing decades of the twentieth century—particularly its educational history. The mainframe of British Columbia school history, it seems, is a network of stories about generations of young people in their teens and twenties—mostly single young women—leaving the leafy boulevards surrounding the Vancouver and Victoria normal schools and heading into the province's vast and forbidding interior in search of employment as teachers. Crushed by isolation and loneliness in mud-spattered schools and spartan teacherages, few lasted much longer than a year in these remote hamlets. The only relief most found from the grind and drudgery of rural life was planning their escape. And, escape they did, with compass points set south and west, with occasional stops along the way in the Kootenays, the Okanagan Valley, and the Fraser Valley before reaching, God willing before old age or retirement, the pedagogical Valhalla of the Lower Mainland and southern Vancouver Island.

Small wonder that educational storytellers often appear to "round up the usual suspects" when talking about the past. An understanding or, at times, a cruel inspector, a schoolmistress in distress, an errant youngster, an arrogant bureaucrat, a loutish trustee, or a kind-hearted rancher are all characters that populate tales from schools. So, too, school stories are rife with the drama of nature—deep snows, freezing rains, and raging rivers—and how these obstacles had to be overcome by children, teachers, and inspectors struggling to get to schools. Indeed, few educational stories in British Columbia ever appear complete without reference to treacherous roadways, high and sometimes impassable plateaus, or coastlines famous for their wild and dangerous beauty. There are, of course, sound reasons for these elements in storylines about schools. Provincial schools were historically small and dispersed across a vast territory with few transportation connections. Up to the middle of the twentieth century—and even beyond—many teachers worked in tiny settlements consisting of no more than a handful of families—a fact that, in itself, explains why certain central characters are common to many school stories.

Similarly, until recent decades when air travel was introduced, getting to schools in many remote parts of the province was a long and arduous process, especially in winter when trudging through a couple of miles of heavy snow might take a youngster an hour or more to get to school in some godforsaken place, or when a muddy trail of 25 miles might take a school inspector an entire day or more to cover even with the help of an automobile. Not surprising, therefore, movement, restlessness, hardship, and the tyranny of distance are recurring elements in stories about British Columbia's educational past. A quick check of the index to this volume offers ample proof of this fact: it is as much about places as people, even if the journeys between these places are taken for granted.

A word about the structure of the volume is necessary. To guide readers, the stories have been organized chronologically and divided into six chapters, each stretching across about a quarter of a century. Within each chapter, the writings are ordered by the dates the discussions refer to, rather than actual dates of publication. J.B. DeLong's "Memoirs," for example, were likely typed just before his retirement in 1946 but refer to the time when he was beginning high school more than a half-century earlier and, so, the year 1887 is entered. In instances where an exact date cannot be determined because the writing does not speak discretely to a particular year, a broader designation is applied: for example, "1880 and after" or, in another case, "The 1950s."

Chapter 1 presents materials from the establishment of Fort Victoria by the HBC in the 1840s to the final days of the colonial regime on the eve of Confederation in 1871. It examines attempts by early colonists to use schools to perpetuate a British class structure before tracing the emergence of civic demands by more democratic-minded settlers to render the "blessing of education," as newspaper editor Amor de Cosmos put it, "to the poorest as well as the richest child." Chapter 2 samples writings from the frontier era in provincial schooling when the outlines of a new public school system were first constructed and when early superintendents, such as John Jessop, tried to frame the organizational structures necessary to support schools across a vast and unsettled territory in the last half of the Victorian Age.

The great movement to build schools during the first two decades of the twentieth century is the subject of Chapter 3, a "golden age of schooling," when schools of cathedral-like proportions greatly reshaped town and city skylines. Chapter 4 presents stories of settlement and struggle amid the exuberant 1920s and the disillusionment of the Great Depression that followed. Throughout this interwar period, children and teachers in British Columbia still confronted many difficult physical challenges in a province that still very much resembled a frontier.

War's end in 1945 ushered in a new era of growth and good times that would last until 1971, as Chapter 5 illustrates. The entire governance and administrative system for British Columbia's schools was revamped during this time of consolidation and expansion. Schools and school districts grew impressively in size as hundreds of small schools and districts were closed or amalgamated. High schools, institutions once mostly reserved for elite students, now opened their doors to everyone, a move not without some difficulties as the writers in this chapter remind us.

Chapter 6, the concluding chapter in the volume, deals with the world of the schools from 1972 to 2005. More specifically, it presents materials that illustrate the emerging trends of schools in politics and politics in schools. The immense growth that marked public schooling in the last half of the twentieth century—and the great public expenditure required to support it—virtually ensured that public education could not remain forever politics free. But the intrusion of partisan politics into education has had certain costs, as the writings and interviews featured in this chapter observe. In a break with the past, British Columbians appear to have become increasingly separated from their public schools, fatigued with the fractiousness that has marked the relationship between government and the BCTF in recent decades, and increasingly disposed toward alternative kinds of educational opportunities for children in and outside public schooling.

Finally, no apology is made for the brevity of the historical forewords that precede each of these chapters, or for the short introductions used to identify the writers and sources of the materials. My intention has been to set the stage quickly and let the stories stand on their own as direct and personal statements, mostly undisturbed by the historian's hand. I believe that the stories and documents selected here are complete in themselves and that, as such, they speak explicitly and cogently to the province's educational heritage and identity.

Notes

1. I conducted more than 50 interviews with educators and former educators over a period of 15 years, including (in alphabetical order): Nelson Allen; Barry Anderson; Henry Armstrong; Robin Brayne; John Burnett; John Calam; Harold Campbell; Les Canty; Ed Carlin; Jim Carter; Joe Chell; Carlyle Clay; Alf Clinton; Jack Evans; C.J. Fredrickson; Elmer Froese; Bernard Gillie; Stewart Graham; Wilf Graham; Sue Granger; Walter Hartrick; Cory Holob; Jim Imrich; W.B. Johnson; Mike Krasnik; Fran Layton; Franklin Levirs; Duncan Lorimer; W.E. Lucas; Mary Lyon; W.A. Marchbank; Norma Mercer; John Meridith; Janet Mort; W.J. Mouat; Jerry Mussio; Barbara Naef; G.H. Nelson; Melva Nelson; Alan Newberry; Dorothy Newman; Bob Overgaard; Bill Plenderleith; Joe Phillipson; Don Smyth; Candace Soler; Mrs. Dorothea Stafford; Duane Sutherland; Bergey Thorsteinssen; R.F. Thorstenson; Alex Turnbull; and Ray Williston. Altogether, these discussions provided a wealth of details about schools and life in British Columbia during the twentieth century.

Artist's rendering of Victoria Harbour and James Bay from Church Hill in the mid-nineteenth century. **Courtesy B.C. Archives PDP02896.**

CHAPTER 1

Old Schools in a New Land: The Colonial Era, 1849-1871

European discovery and settlement on Canada's west coast was marked by a collision of cultures. With the coming of the Europeans, aboriginal cultures gave way to the traditions and institutions of the newcomers. The stories in this chapter attempt to document the educational customs that were followed before the Europeans came, as well as the efforts of the new settlers to establish forms of schooling that were familiar to them. The informal "learning by watching and doing" practiced by aboriginal peoples stood in sharp contrast to the formal educational methods brought, in particular, by the British settlers and officials of the Hudson's Bay Company who sought to create the same divisions in social class that characterized the schools of Great Britain. Through a collection of letters, reports, newspaper accounts, and personal reminiscences, we can see the early development of schools in what is today British Columbia. More than this, these stories and documents help us get a sense of early Victorian society on the Pacific Coast, already diverse in its cultural composition and the aspirations and sentiments of those who built the schools, the individuals who taught in them, and the children who attended them.

Early Times

Learning in British Columbia did not begin with textbooks and schoolrooms or with education offices or ministries. It began as soon as there were people on the land, 10,000 years ago if not longer. It began, as it began everywhere in the world, with parents or grandparents teaching youngsters what was necessary for survival.

It went further than that. The many and diverse native groups that populated the 950,000 square kilometers of what is now called British Columbia, educated their children in an oral tradition rich in music, law, legend, folklore (which had an historical component), ethics and spirituality, as well as the practical knowledge of the dangers and resources of life in mountainous, interior plateau and coastal environments.

Learning a name for every river and stream, every rock and reef, every kind of fish, fowl or flora in a complex and varied habitat, to say nothing of inherited rights and privileges, and genealogical relationships going back for generations, made excellent training for young memories. If native peoples had no concept of reading or writing, they had sufficient understanding of "rithmetic" to make them keen and adept traders with bargaining skills that astonished, and frequently irritated, the first European traders on the coast.

Winter, under leaden skies and almost incessant rain on the coast, and sub-zero temperatures on the in-land plateaus, was a time for indoor learning, never a formal process for native children so much as a daily "watch me and do as I do" experience, as natural to life as breathing. Storytelling accompanied routine tasks. It gave meaning and texture to carving, spinning, weaving, and preparing food. Storytelling accompanied births and weddings and funerals and gift giving.

"Always put the oldest child first"

James Sewid

The Kwakwaka 'wakw, speakers of the Kwak 'wala language, lived on Northern Vancouver Island and the adjacent mainland, and still live in village reserves in that area. James Sewid came from Mimkwamlis on Village Island, at the northern end of Johnstone Strait, a village now deserted. Here he tells of ways of aboriginal learning practiced long before the Europeans came, the importance of family, and the place of honour granted to first-born children:

> When I was born my grandfather called all the people together right away and gave away some blankets and other things at a potlatch which was the way of my people . . . My mother's father, Jim Bell, was from the Mamalilikulla people and I received the name Poogleedee from him, which means 'guests never leave his feasts hungry' . . .
>
> My mother and I went to stay at the mouth of the river at Vinea Sound, as we did nearly every summer. Both of my grandfathers used to always go there to fish for salmon . . . I was just a little boy but they made a little gaff hook for me to use and I did my own fishing right along with the older people . . .
>
> We stayed there for about a month and a half each summer and that was the best time of my life . . . When I wasn't helping the older people I would make little boats to play with. There was a little canoe there and I would pole it back and forth on the river . . .When the summer was over we went back to Village Island . . .
>
> It was the Indian custom to always put the oldest child first in everything they did and then the rest would follow. Since I was born to a well-to-do and very highly respected family and was the oldest son they treated me with respect . . . Sometimes in the evening we would have visits from our neighbors. The old people used to come and sit around the fire, especially when they were teaching me how to be a leader of my people when I grew up. They told me all the things about my family history on both my mother's and father's sides of the family and how the Kwakiutl people used to have wars and fight among one another. They said that I must know these things from them and not just hear it from other people.
>
> I used to love to sit around the fire and listen to the old people telling about the ways of the Indians. I remember very well how they would pound it into my head to know my relatives. That was very important. They used to tell me

who my relatives were and why I was related to different persons in different villages. When I would go to another village I knew right away that the people recognized me as their relative. The old people would just come to me and hug me. They didn't even wait for me to say anything to them but they would just say, 'I'm glad to see you because I'm your uncle or aunt or grandfather.' I thought it was very important and I really took it in when I was a little boy. I learned to respect people and when I went to a strange place I was careful not to do anything that was going to hurt them or do anything that was foolish.[1]

Schools in the Hudson's Bay Company Forts and the Crown Colonies

The informal patterns of learning characteristic of aboriginal life in what is now British Columbia greatly changed with the establishment of the first permanent settlement by Europeans. Looking to solidify its economic control in the Pacific Northwest, the Hudson's Bay Company (HBC) built a fort at the southern tip of Vancouver Island in 1842. With construction of the fort came new and formal agencies for schooling. As part of its settlement policy, the HBC provided a school for the children of company officials under the direction of an English schoolmaster, the Reverend Robert Staines, and his wife who, in 1849, assumed the task of boarding and teaching 17 boys and girls. In 1853, a second schoolmaster was engaged for the children of company employees at Nanaimo. From the beginning, the HBC's chief factor, James Douglas, was also concerned about furnishing schools for the children of other settlers, or what he would describe as the "labouring classes."

Located at the southern tip of Vancouver Island, Fort Victoria served as headquarters for the Hudson's Bay Company in Western Canada. The first schoolroom was on the second floor of one of the log buildings that comprised Fort Victoria (long since demolished). Here the fort is seen from Wharf Street. **Courtesy B.C. Archives A-04099.**

Because emigration to the new colonies in Victoria and New Westminster was slow in the early years, no organized or cohesive system of schooling seemed required. Schooling was provided in the company's quarters, in rented premises, or in the living quarters of settlers' houses. Teachers' salaries and other costs were also variously provided: the HBC paid for their own schools and the colonial government for others, supplemented by fees levied on parents. Anglican, Roman Catholic, and Methodist churches also provided schooling through the expectation that parsons would also become pedagogues as part of their duties. Entirely private schools also existed in Victoria, operated by such enterprising newcomers as John Jessop, who opened a school on a fee-for-service basis. By involving himself in local politics, Jessop would eventually become the first superintendent of education after the twin colonies of New Westminster and Vancouver Island entered Confederation in 1871 as the province of British Columbia.

Most of the early schools along Canada's west coast made a sharp distinction between social classes, and it would be some 20 years before the idea of "common schools" for all gained acceptance with the English immigrants.[2] The large influx of Americans after the gold rush of 1858 brought a demand for a more liberal and secular education, as well as an expectation that in a democratic society equality of opportunity in schooling would be expressed in free education for children of all "classes." However, in the decades before Confederation, arguments raged in the legislative councils of the colonies and in the editorial columns of the local press about the relative merits of secular and non-secular schooling. Between 1849, when the first HBC school opened in Fort Victoria, and 1872, when support for public schooling was assumed as a provincial responsibility, the development of schooling is chronicled in the letters, diaries and reminiscences of early colonial officials and educators.

1849: The HBC's first schoolmaster and schoolmistress

James Anderson

James Robert Anderson was the son of Alexander Caulfield Anderson, a factor in the HBC and a close friend of James Douglas. Young Anderson was born on June 19, 1841 at Fort Nisqually at the end of Puget Sound near the Cowlitz River route to Fort Vancouver. When James was nine years old, he was sent by fur-brigade route via Fort Hope to Fort Langley and from there to Victoria by canoe, a trip he did not expect to survive. He was enrolled in the HBC boarding school under the none-too-tender care of the schoolmaster, the Reverend Robert Staines, and his wife.[3] His memoirs, written later in life, provide a remarkably vivid account of early life in the colony and his impressions of British Columbia's first schoolmaster and schoolmistress:

James Anderson attended the first HBC school on what is today Canada's west coast.
Courtesy B.C. Archives G-07220.

The school was presided over by the Reverend R.J. Staines (Cambridge) and Mrs. Staines . . . Mr. Staines, of rather uncertain temper, and disposed at times to be unduly severe in administering corporal punishment was nevertheless a good student and teacher in natural history and personally I can conscientiously say I was never cruelly or even severely chastised, corporally; as in all truthfulness I must admit some of the other boys were. I can even at this distant day recall the many lessons imparted to me in the field and which have influenced my after life.

Commenting further on his character I now realize that whilst he was of uncertain temper, he was endowed with qualities calculated to win the respect and even the love of those who were *en rapport* with him . . . Mrs. Staines was a much more energetic person, she it was who really kept the school going and in spite of many undoubtedly adverse circumstances managed comparatively most creditably.

The school building like those of the others within the fort yard was constructed of squared logs not very carefully put together. The garret we occupied was not lined, simply the bare logs with interstices; where the roof joined the wall was a veritable runway for the numerous rats which infested the building. These disgusting rodents not content with making use of our dormitory as a place of meeting, and generally disputing our rights in the boldest manner, actually attempted to share our meals. One bold marauder got into my bed and was purloining a crust of bread I had secreted when I discovered his presence and with a quick movement I pinned him to the side of the bed with my blanket-covered arm. A bounty of a shilling a dozen was offered by Mr. Staines but with our inadequate means of catching rats; having to manufacture our own traps; we did not earn many shillings.

We were allowed one tallow dip at night which we economized by placing salt round the wick: this expedient was the means of economizing the tallow at the expense of the light. The establishment consisted, as nearly as I can remember, of an English servant named Field and his wife, and a native boy called Peter—between them the meals were somehow cooked in a way and served. Water was obtained from wells and brought to the school in a barrel set on wheels.[4] The sole means of heating the school was a box stove in the room wherein we had our meals and lessons and devilish cold it was for those who on account of their youth were jostled to one side by the bigger ones.

Mrs. Staines first action on the arrival of a new pupil was a close inspection of person and wardrobe and a general examination as to proficiency in the three 'R's' and other accomplishments. What funny looking guys we must have been in our odd makeshift costumes. When my sister appeared on the scene, she was costumed in a print gown which as nearly as I can remember was made like a bag with holes for the head and arms, and tied round the waist, moccasins and a poke bonnet like a coal scuttle . . . My suit of leather shirt and trousers, cloth cap with a peak and moccasins was not considered so unfashionable but the shirt was changed for a moleskin blouse belted below the waist and decorated with enormous white buttons like saucers. This was the costume considered *de rigueur* for the boys.

Sunday at the Staines' school is to this day a day of terror to me. After morning prayers we had breakfast such as it was, bread and treacle and tea without milk. Church at 11 a.m. in the mess hall to which we were summoned by the ringing of the Fort bell, then dinner, potatoes and meat, sometimes fish, then a dreary afternoon learning the Collects;[5] how I hated them . . . The only redeeming feature of Sunday was the evening spent by invitation in the Staines' private apartment when we would be regaled with one sweet each after prayer and then after singing 'Lord dismiss us' we were dismissed to bed. And what beds! The hard boards, an Indian mat, a Hudson's Bay blanket and over ourselves another blanket. We were hardy young beggars and did not mind it. The garret we occupied was not lined, simply the bare logs with interstices . . . and through which the fresh air had unimpeded access even in the coldest weather; perhaps it was better for us, but the trouble was that in cold weather our scant supply of water would freeze and then we did not trouble to wash and there being no one to superintend, we simply continued so until the weather abated. We did not bathe because we had no facilities for doing so. I may qualify this however by stating that when opportunity offered and the weather was favorable we would bathe in the harbour . . .

Our amusement consisted of marbles, cricket, rounders, shinny, horse racing, fighting Indian boys, worrying Indian dogs, some surreptitious shooting with our antiquated flint-lock musket, besides any occasional mischief such as boys alone are capable of conceiving . . . A favorite amusement was catching dogfish and after fastening a billet of wood with about a foot of line to the tail letting him go. It afforded us great joy to witness his futile attempts to dive . . . We often had boxing matches arranged with Indian boys with bare fists; bloody noses being consequently the result and usually ending by the flight of the savage pursued by his adversary. Our knowledge of the noble art of self-defense was limited. The Indian boy had not the slightest knowledge in the art of boxing and was therefore at a great disadvantage. The Indian dogs would swim over from the Indian village opposite the fort and get after Mrs. Finlayson's fowls so of course we naturally hailed the chance of exercising our cruelty by chasing and stoning the dogs, sometimes we being lucky enough to corner one and killing him. To this day I look with regret on the horrid cruelty we were guilty of regarding these poor dumb animals. The dogs I refer to were handsome white animals resembling a Pomeranian but larger with long wooly hair which was regularly shorn and woven into blankets and articles of clothing, so that the dogs were of economic value to the natives and we were therefore doubly blamable.[6]

1850: Letter to Alexander Anderson

James Douglas

Among the most prominent of the newcomers who shaped the character of schooling in Fort Victoria was James Douglas, head of the HBC's operations and the son of a Glasgow merchant who had business interests in Guyana (originally Guiana). His date of birth is unknown, but he was likely born around 1800 to a Creole mother. Douglas was educated in Scotland and, with his brother, joined the Northwest Company in 1819, and worked at various fur trade posts around Lake Superior, the prairies, and the Peace River before the union of the North West Company and the HBC in 1821. He had travelled the length of the northwest coast from Alaska to Monterey in California before eventually deciding in 1842 that the south end of Vancouver Island provided the best site for a trading fort. All Vancouver Island was transferred by Royal grant to the HBC in 1849, under the direction of the first governor, Richard Blanshard, whom Douglas would succeed as governor in 1851.

After a long and illustrious career during which he saw the fort become a British colony, with strong British and American elements, and the colony become part of the Dominion of Canada, Douglas was made "an ordinary member of the Civil Division of the Second Class of Knight Commander of the Most Honourable Order of the Bath." He died in 1877. In 1850, Douglas wrote this note to Alexander Anderson, father of James, outlining the social and educational conditions of the school at Fort Victoria:

> The school is progressing but not numerously attended. Six boys and 11 girls is all the force we can yet muster. The children are boarding with Mr. Staines who is very kind to them; they are not so well accommodated as I wish but we shall go on improving . . .[7]

1850: "Not exactly the man I would choose"

James Douglas

In a letter of 1850 to Archibald Barclay, HBC secretary in London, James Douglas once more described the new school at Fort Victoria:

> The school is going on as well as can be expected under the circumstances, more assistance in the way of servants of respectable character is required than we have at our command; so many children give a great deal of trouble and I often wonder how Mrs. Staines can stand the fag of looking after them. She is invaluable and receives less assistance than she ought from her husband who is rather lazy at times. The children have greatly improved in their personal appearance and one thing I particularly love in Staines is the attention he bestows on their religious training. Had I a selection to make he is not exactly the man I would choose, but it must be admitted we might find a man worse qualified for the charge of the school.[8]

1850: The girls at Fort Victoria School

John Sebastian Helmcken

Born into a German-speaking community within the poor Whitechapel district of London, England, John Sebastian Helmcken worked his way through apprenticeships as a chemist and a medical pupil before gaining admission to Guy's Hospital to complete his training. He arrived in Victoria in 1850 to take up the position of

HBC doctor and soon married Cecilia, a daughter of James Douglas. In 1856, when Vancouver Island became a crown colony with an elected assembly, he entered political life and served as Speaker in the first Legislative Assembly. In 1870, with Joseph Trutch and R.W. Carrall, he negotiated the terms of British Columbia's entry into the Dominion of Canada. His memoirs, written in 1892, provided a brief summary of early school conditions and the settlement at Fort Victoria:

> The school and residence of the parson and Mrs. Staines was a very large portion of Bachelors' Hall building—the ladies slept upstairs over our heads, and the little mischiefs used to play pranks, occasionally pouring water upon us through the cracks or holes in the flooring, for our ceiling was not sealed. By the same token our proceedings may have annoyed them too for occasionally Bachelors' Hall was pretty noisy . . . There were a good many in Bachelors' Hall—all young men.[9]
>
> I stand today upon the same spot, but oh! how changed. Of the 20 or 30 met before, but two or three answer to the call. Of the fields, naught remain. The forest has been removed and the bleak winds unhindered now rush in to what was before a genial, sheltered place . . The Indians, once half a thousand, have disappeared, homes occupy the fields; telegraph and telephone wires make the streets hideous; there is great hurry and scurry, but I doubt whether there is more happiness and content now than was enjoyed by the few but hospitable and kind-hearted Hudson's Bay Company residents in 1850.[10]

1851: "A good sound English education and nothing more"

James Douglas

In a letter of October 8, 1851 to Archibald Barclay at the HBC in London, Douglas brings up the establishment of "common schools" which he refers to here as "elementary" schools. These schools were intended for the children of settlers not directly employed by the company but whose occupation and permanent residence in the colony were necessary to maintain British sovereignty:

> I will also take the liberty of calling the attention of the governor and committee to the subject of education by recommending the establishment of one or two elementary schools in the colony to give a proper moral and religious training to the children of settlers who are at present growing up in ignorance, and the utter neglect of all their duties to God and to society.

That remark applies with peculiar force to the children of Protestant parents; the Roman Catholic families in this country having had until lately a very able and zealous teacher in the Reverend Mr. Lamffrit [variously spelled Lempfrit], a French Priest of the Société des Oblats, who is now living with the Indians in the Cowitchen Valley [today Cowichan]. One school at Victoria and one at Esquimalt will provide for the present wants of the settlements, and a fixed salary of £50 a year to be paid by the Colony with an annual payment by the parents of a certain sum not to exceed 30 shillings for each child with a free house and garden is the plan and amount of remuneration I would propose to the committee. In regard to the character of the teachers, I would venture to recommend a middle-aged married couple for each school, of strictly religious principles, capable of giving a good sound English education and nothing more, these schools being intended for the children of the labouring and poorer classes; and children of promising talents, or whom their parents wish to educate further, may pursue their studies and acquire the other branches of knowledge at the company's school conducted by the Reverend Mr. Staines. I would also recommend that a good supply of schoolbooks from the alphabet upwards, with slates and pencils be sent out with the teachers, as there are very few in this country.

I observe with much satisfaction that the governor and committee approve of the establishment of schools for the children of labourers and smaller settlers and I shall lose no time in selecting sites for the school houses and grounds, and taking the other preparatory steps toward that object . . .[11]

It was not long before Governor Douglas put his plans into effect. By March 1852, he had opened a day-school for boys in Victoria and also a girls' day-school at Colwood Farm. A year later, the Council decided to open two more schools—one at Maple Point [later to be known as Craigflower] and one in Victoria about a mile from the fort, known as the "Colonial School." On March 18, 1852, Douglas described the appointment of a schoolmaster for the Victoria boys' school in the following terms:

Mr. Charles Bailey, the young man who acted as school master for the emigrants during the outward voyage of the *Tory*, having conducted himself with great propriety since his arrival here, and not being particularly useful as a mere labourer, I have opened a day-school for boys, the children of the company's labouring servants at this place, who are growing up in ignorance of their duties as men and Christians. It is now attended by 18 boys who are making fair progress in learning. The parents furnish books and stationery and pay £1 annually for each child which goes into a fund for the support of the schoolmaster and he also receives his wages and provisions from the company who are put to no other expense for the institution.[12]

1853: A company school in Nanaimo

James Douglas

Twelve dwelling houses, a forge, one lumber store, and a bastion are finished, or in progress, but we have still a great deal to accomplish before house accommodations are provided for the expected reinforcement of miners from England, but everything in our power shall be done, to make them comfortable, when they arrive in this count . . .

While at Nanaimo, I had much conversation with the miners, and other married servants of the company, on the subject of opening an elementary school, for their children, who have been much neglected, and are growing up in ignorance of their duties as Christians and as men. Seeing that they all expressed an ardent wish to have the means of educating their children, I transferred Mr. Baillie [variously spelled Bailey], who has for some time been employed as teacher of the Victoria day school, but who is not now required here, to the establishment of Nanaimo where he has since opened school . . .

I will also take the liberty of suggesting to the governor and committee the propriety of sending out a clergyman for Nanaimo. The expense of that appointment will be richly repaid by its influence improving the morals of the people, and the saving in police charges, while in many other respects it will redound to the honour and advantage of the company. I beg also to inform the governor and committee that Mr. Langford is desirous of opening a young lady's school at his establishment with the view of bettering his circumstances; a Miss Scott, who has had much experience as a teacher, to join him in this country, provided she can obtain a free passage in any of the company's ships. May I take the liberty of asking the aid of the governor and committee in promoting that important object so far as to allow that lady a free passage in the 'Norman Morrison' to this country should she feel disposed to undertake the voyage. This would be a great boon to the country and another proof of the deep interest felt by their honours in the progress of education.[13]

1853: Remembering Craigflower

Thomas Russell

Victorian Thomas Russell wrote the following letter in 1903 to commemorate the educational legacy of his brother-in-law, Kenneth McKenzie, whose original house, named "Craigflower," still stands on the Gorge waterway across from the early schoolhouse built on the opposite shore:

> It is only fair to the memory of my brother-in-law, the late Kenneth McKenzie, to state that when leaving Scotland for Vancouver Island in charge of a number of families, young men and women, he was not unmindful of the great responsibility and trust placed in his hands, namely the education of not only the bairns that were going with him, who had gathered hips and haws on Scotland's bonny braes, but the other bairnies that might be expected after our arrival, hence he made it a condition that a schoolmaster should be engaged at the expense of the company before leaving.
>
> Mr. Barr was engaged to fill the position, himself and his wife arriving with us in the ship Norman Morrison on January 16, 1853. At the time of our arrival at Fort Victoria the late Sir James Douglas was governor of the colony, and head

In the rich farmlands surrounding the Gorge waterway outside Fort Victoria, Craigflower School was erected in 1854-1855 by HBC bailiff, Kenneth McKenzie, for his own children and the children of his employees. It is the oldest existing schoolhouse west of the Great Lakes and served as a school for many years. It stands today as one of the province's most important heritage buildings. **Courtesy City of Vancouver Archives P353.**

of the Hudson's Bay Company, and having full control over all matters and no schoolmaster being at the Fort, Mr. Douglas retained Mr. Barr temporarily for that section—hence we had to locate at Craigflower without a teacher. An afternoon class was established for the benefit of the children who had been at school before leaving, until a master could arrive, which occurred in the fall of 1854.

In the fall of 1854 the ship Princess Royal arrived bringing with her our much-wished-for schoolmaster, Mr. Charles Clarke and wife. Shortly after their arrival the school was opened with due form and ceremony, the enrollment consisting of eight boys and six girls from our own little party.

The school gradually grew in strength and continued to flourish under Mr. Clarke . . . Mr. Clarke resigned his position as teacher in 1859, returning to England in the same ship on which he arrived.[14]

1854: Recruiting the Reverend Edward Cridge

Alexander Robinson

By 1854, Robert Staines' interest was diverted from teaching school to political affairs in the new settlement and he found himself increasingly critical of Governor Douglas. Staines attempted to return to England carrying a petition from the settlers of the Sooke area to HBC headquarters in London but was drowned when his ship was lost in a storm off Cape Flattery. In an essay on the history of provincial schooling written 60 years later, superintendent of education Alexander Robinson provided the following passage that contains the terms of employment the HBC set out for Staines' replacement Edward Cridge. Reverend Cridge accepted these terms before sailing from England on September 13, 1854:

The Hudson's Bay Company is desirous of sending out a clergyman to Vancouver Island to be stationed in the vicinity of Victoria, the principal establishment in the island. He will have charge of a district or parish and, in addition, will hold the appointment of chaplain of the Hudson's Bay Company and will attend to the spiritual wants of the free settlers and of the officers, clerks and servants of the Hudson's Bay Company stationed at Victoria and at the various farms in the neighbourhood.

The church is in progress of construction, in the vicinity of the fort, and will probably be completed by the time the clergyman may be expected to arrive

> at the island. The Hudson's Bay Company proposes that the remuneration for these services shall consist: first, of a parsonage and glebe [a parcel of land used to support a priest or minister] of 100 acres, of which 30 acres will be cleared and put into a cultivable shape; secondly, of a stipend of £300 per annum charged, with the sanction of the Colonial Office, on the fund arising from the sales of land—of which funds the company are trustees; thirdly, of an allowance of £100 per annum from the fur branch of the company, for acting as a chaplain to the company and attending to the wants of the servants.
>
> Until the house is finished, quarters will be provided for the clergyman in the fort. And till the land is put into a proper state of cultivation, rations will be allowed to him and his family, as provided for the officers of the company. When the land is taken possession of by him, he will be expected to provide for himself.
>
> The company think it very desirable that the clergyman should, as is done at Red River by the Bishop of Rupert's Land, take charge of a boarding-school, of a superior class, for the children of their officers, and would wish that he would take out with him a gentleman and his wife capable of keeping a school of this nature. The fur-trade branch would find a schoolhouse and residence for the master and his family and will vote an annual grant of £100 in aid of the school. Should they give satisfaction to the gentlemen in the country they might expect from 30 to 40 pupils, and the usual payment for each pupil would be £20 per annum for board, lodging and education.
>
> A free passage will be allowed from London to Vancouver Island for the clergyman, his family and servants and also to the schoolmaster and his family. It is understood that the engagement shall be for five years, at the expiration of which a free passage home will be granted, should the clergyman wish to return; or on the contrary, a fresh engagement may be entered into. It is also to be understood that in the event of misconduct, the engagement may at any time be cancelled, on the recommendation of the Governor of Vancouver Island, and with the sanction of the Secretary of State for the Colonies.[15]

The part of the agreement stipulating that a schoolmaster and his wife should accompany Cridge appears not to have been carried into effect. Mrs. Cridge, however, opened a private school for the children of HBC officials and had the unique honour of having organized the first Sunday school in British Columbia. Partly subsidized public schools, but not altogether "free" public schools, were opened in Victoria, Craigflower and Nanaimo under Cridge as acting superintendent of education.[16]

1856: A report on Victoria schools and schoolmasters

Edward Cridge

In his capacity as colonial chaplain to the Council of Vancouver Island, Cridge wrote two reports in 1856, one on the school in Victoria and its master, Mr. Barr, and another on the school at Craigflower and its master, Mr. Clark. Noteworthy in his assessments are the uneven progress of youngsters, public concern about the irregularity of one teacher's attendance, the central part that Scriptures played in the school curriculum of the day, and the absence of schooling for young working-class women. Cridge's concern with educating "the labouring class" underscored a deeply ingrained consciousness about class distinctions held within certain quarters in the colonial community, especially by senior HBC officials such as Douglas, as well as the belief that government or some other agency would have to play a role in educating the children of families who were unable to afford schooling:

1. Report on the Victoria School, Mr. Barr, Master, up to August 1856.

A private examination was held before the committee in July, when the children were examined jointly by the master and myself—13 children present. (Some of the children answered with intelligence, and showed a fair understanding of their subjects as far as they went. The chief deficiency noticed was a want of accuracy and grounding in the elementary parts. The subjects taught are reading, writing, arithmetic, history, a little geography and grammar. Owing to domestic circumstances the master preferred not having a public examination this year.)

The number of children on the books is 17 all of whom are boys. Their ages vary from six to 15 years, there being seven boys under 10 years of age and 10 of 10 years and upwards; nine are boarders and the remainder day scholars. Of these latter three are of the labouring class. That only three boys and no girls of this class attend the Colonial School at Victoria is a remarkable and, I think, rather a painful fact. As to what may be the real causes of this deficiency I do not feel myself able to speak with confidence. There is evidently a feeling unfavourable to the school existing among some of the people chiefly on the alleged grounds of the irregularity of the master's attendance. With regard to this complaint I will only state the fact that during the three months immediately preceding the examination mentioned above there were given one whole and five half days' holidays; and of these I believe that a part were given on account of the necessary absence of the master on other duties.

In answer to a question relating to the organization of the school, the master replied: 'In consequence of the different ages and abilities of the children I am unable to classify them.' They are therefore taught in detail or grouped miscellaneously. It is perhaps owing to this method that the younger children do not make that progress which could be desired.[17]

2. Report on the Craigflower School, Mr. Clark, Master, up to August 1856.

This school is not well supplied with books and other requisites—a serious defect. I would suggest that an adequate supply should be ordered from England or San Francisco at the earliest opportunity. The books published by the Commissioners of National Education in Ireland are very suitable to a school of this description and are very cheap.[18]

A considerable improvement was remarked by those who had attended the examination of the preceding year. Prizes were bestowed on three children in each class except the lowest, and one on a little girl who had only been eight days absent in 18 months. The examination in Scripture was inadvertently omitted till too late on the day of the public examination, but I had examined the school previously in this subject, in which I did not find that the children had made the same improvement as in some others.

The number of children on the books is 21 of ages varying from four to 16 years, there being 12 under 10 years of age and nine of 10 years and upward. There are 11 girls and 10 boys: three are boarders. Of the day scholars 11 are of the labouring class (five girls and six boys). Of the whole school 14 are from Craigflower, three from Victoria, one from Colwood, two from Burnside and one from View Field.

The school is divided into four classes and the system is that which is usually followed in the national schools in England. The conduct and attention of the children have been always pleasing when I visited the school, and I believe this is generally the case.

In conclusion I would take this opportunity of stating to the council what I conceive to be a great want in this colony and that is a girls' school for the labouring class. It seems greatly to be lamented that those who are likely hereafter to perform so important a part in the community in the capacity of wives and mothers, should be suffered to grow up without education.[19]

1857: Nanaimo's second schoolmaster

James Douglas

In the following letter to Captain Stuart, the chief HBC official in Nanaimo, Governor James Douglas demonstrates his involvement in providing schools on Vancouver Island as he introduces a new teacher, Cornelius Bryant, and sets out the terms of his contract:[20]

Dear Sir:

I beg to introduce to you Mr. Cornelius Bryant who after undergoing an examination before the Reverend Mr. Cridge, and being by him pronounced duly qualified, has been appointed teacher of the Nanaimo School, on the following terms; that is to say, he is to have a fixed salary of £40 per annum, and an allowance of one-quarter a day for ration money; to levy a fee of £1 sterling per annum to be paid by the parents, on every child who attends the school for the purpose of being educated. He is also to have the house occupied by the late teacher, for his residence, and the schoolroom will of course also be placed under his charge. You will install him without delay, and his salary and other emoluments, will commence from the day of his entering upon the office and not before.

I have requested Mr. Bryant to open a Sunday school for the children, which he has cheerfully agreed to do and also to read the church service to the people at large. I trust you will give him every encouragement and support in effecting that laudable and highly necessary object, which will prove an advantage to all and be a means with God's blessing, of maintaining order and decency among the company's servants. You will give Mr. Bryant such instructions in respect to the opening and management of the school, and the distribution of books, slates and et cetera, as you may consider requisite and necessary. I have apprised him that such instructions would emanate from you, and he is therefore prepared to obey them.

I remain Sir, Your obedient servant
James Douglas

The Rush for Gold and the Growth of Colonial Schools

During the first 16 years, the small settlements around Fort Victoria grew slowly and little disturbed the new British enclave on the West coast. As early as 1849, however, American miners began appearing in Victoria's harbour looking for supplies to help them prospect the rivers and creeks of a vast wilderness lying beyond the boundaries of the first Crown Colony. A second Crown Colony at New Westminster was established in 1858 when gold was first discovered along the bars of the Fraser River and, subsequently, along the creeks and riverbeds of the Cariboo.

With the coming of the gold rush, Victoria's harbour was filled with ships from California, and the little town around the fort became a tent city with a population of some 30,000 inhabitants. Although most of the newcomers were itinerant miners, entrepreneurs followed closely in their wake to provide food, clothing, and mining equipment.

In October 1859, the colonial government in Victoria assumed responsibility for schooling on Vancouver Island. The mainland colony at New Westminster opened its first school in 1862 with Presbyterian Reverend Jamieson as schoolmaster. Funding teachers' salaries and the costs of building, maintaining, and heating the schoolhouses was always a contentious issue in the years before Confederation. In the late 1850s, school support became a shared responsibility between the colonial government and fee-paying parents, however it was fast becoming apparent that parents with large families could not afford the cost of sending all their children to school.

1859: Cornelius Bryant's journal

Cornelius Bryant's situation as the teacher in Nanaimo dramatically changed after 1859 in terms of salary and housing when responsibility for his position passed from the HBC to colonial authorities who found it difficult to generate the revenue necessary to support either schools or teachers. Here, Bryant tells of his declining financial fortunes and his loss of company accommodations:

The Cariboo Gold Rush of 1858 brought many newcomers looking for fortunes and adventure to Fort Victoria. With these newcomers came demands for schools that were publicly paid for and accessible to all. **Courtesy B.C. Archives A-3113.**

Had an interview with Mr. Dallas [James Douglas' son-in-law who succeeded him as head of the HBC's western department] this morning who informed me that owing to the transference of the government of the island from the Hudson's Bay Company to the Crown, that from October 31 I must not look to the Company for the payment of my salary as hitherto, but that I must write to His Excellency the Governor Mr. Douglas, asking him by what means I am to receive my salary for the duties of schoolteacher at this place in future. He also gave me to understand that I should have to remove [myself] from the house I now occupy and live in the two rooms at the end of the large house in which my uncle formerly resided. The large room in the other end of the house [is] to be used as a school. Mr. Nicoll wishing to occupy the house which I shall leave, it being so adjacent to the mines and, as the old school house is low and very unfit for the purposes of a school . . . the room to be used for a school will be admirably suited for the purpose, it being lofty and situated in a central and eligible part of the town.[21]

1859: Victoria's Colonial School

Edgar Fawcett

Edgar Fawcett was born in Sydney, Australia, to an English family. His father was a businessman and his mother had worked as a governess in France and Spain where she learned to speak the languages of both countries. In 1849, the family travelled to San Francisco en route to England, however the ship that was to make their fortune in the lumber trade was lost, and Fawcett senior had to seek financial success once more, coming north to Victoria in 1858, where he entered into business until appointed government agent at Nanaimo. In the following passages, Edgar recalls his early days at Victoria's Colonial School when he was about 15 or 16 years of age:

Today 50 years ago I landed with my parents and brothers on the Hudson's Bay Company's wharf, having arrived from San Francisco on the steamer *Northerner*, which docked at Esquimalt, as all large ocean steamers then did. We came from Esquimalt on a small steamer, the *Emma*, or *Emily Harris*. The latter steamer was built, I think, by Thomas Harris, and named after his daughter . . . The scene will ever be impressed on my mind as I saw my future home on the 12th day of February, 1859 . . .

Outside Johnson Street on the north, Blanshard Street on the east, and the north end of James Bay bridge on the south, everything else was country—oak and pine trees, with paths only, otherwise trails made by Indians and cattle.

After we had got settled in our new home the question of sending me to school was discussed, and easily settled, for it was Hobson's choice. The Colonial School, as it was called, was on the site of the present Central School. It was the only one I can think of except Angela College, and maybe a private school. There was a fee of five dollars a year charged, payable quarterly in advance.

After you left Blanchard Street, the way to the school was by a pathway through the woods. The country around View and Fort Streets, up to Cook, was very swampy, and covered mostly by willow and alder trees. In fact there was a small swamp or lake on View Street, where there was good duck shooting in winter. When I went to the Colonial School in 1859, it was taught by a young man named Kennedy, whose father was Dr. Kennedy of the Hudson's Bay Company, and whose brother was in the same service. Some months later he resigned, and his successor was an Irishman named W.H. Burr, whose temper was quick, like my own, and although he tried to make me a good scholar, I am afraid I did not do him or his teaching justice, and I remember two good beatings he gave me far better than the useful knowledge he tried to inculcate.

Our school might aptly be termed a mixed one, for it consisted of boys and girls who sat together. This arrangement just suited me, for I was fond of the girls. There were white boys and black boys, Hebrews and Gentiles, rich and poor, and we all sat close together to economize room. One day a dispute arose between a white boy and a black boy, and ended in a fistic encounter. I was mainly instrumental in bringing it about, and backed my man until the sponge was thrown in by the white boy's friend. Mr. Burr heard of the occurrence through the boys not reporting at the school the next morning, and an investigation by the master revealed my part in the affair.[22]

1860s: "Settlers of colour . . . on Salt Spring Island"

Eric Roberts

Eric Roberts' portrayal of Salt Spring Island's past contained this description of early black settlers from the United States and the part they played in the intellectual and educational life of the Island:

The settlers of colour who sought a haven on Salt Spring were destined to play an important part in the pioneer scene. Contemporary accounts state five of them held university degrees. Of the Jones brothers, John C. Jones held a first-class teacher's degree from the University of Ohio and his brothers, William

> and Elias, had graduated in arts. The departure of William and Elias for the goldfields in the Cariboo was a loss to the island. Two other settlers of colour held degrees from northern universities but their names are not recorded. It appears highly probable one of them was Frederick D. Lester, who proved a most capable teacher and became right hand man to John C. Jones. John C. Jones was in many ways a most remarkable man . . . For ten years, Jones worked unofficially and without a salary . . . It can be accepted that during the first years, he was probably paid in kind . . .
>
> As early as May 1864, the settlers registered their appreciation of the work of Jones and Lester. Every settler in Ganges signed a petition sent to Governor Kennedy to have teachers' salaries paid these men. The petition was not granted and it was not until 1869, when the first board of school trustees was formed by John P. Booth, Abraham Copeland, and Thomas Griffiths that the government awarded a salary of $500 per annum to Jones. Some of the settlers of colour chose subsequently to return to the United States after the Civil War. Others elected to stay on Salt Spring and their descendants are highly respected members of the community today.[23]

1865: Alfred Waddington's inspection of colonial schools

In 1865, the Colonial Legislature passed the first *Free School Act,* providing for the establishment of free and non-sectarian schools for the colony of Vancouver Island. Henceforth, the cost of schooling was to be provided from the sale of land, a provision doomed to failure, as the colonial economy, no longer buoyed by gold fever, was on the verge of bankruptcy.

Alfred Waddington was appointed as the first colonial superintendent of schools. Waddington was born in London in 1801 and received an extensive education in England, France, and Germany before going to work in the family business. He became one of Victoria's biggest property holders in the area bounded by Yates, Johnson, and Wharf Street. He fought for representative government and was elected to the Colonial Assembly in 1861. After a disastrous venture in road building, he was financially ruined.

In 1865, he was one of seven applicants for the post of superintendent of education (future superintendent of public schools, John Jessop, was another). He was given this post by the Colonial Secretary and made responsible for hiring teachers for the Central School, maintaining the building, establishing a school at Nanaimo for the children of miners and, in 1865, convincing the colonial teachers to forego their salaries in order to keep the schools open. Here Waddington reports on his inspection of 1865 and, on so doing, illustrates the barely tolerable state of schools as British Columbia's colonial era was winding to a close:[24]

The first provincial Education Office was located in the Colonial Legislative Buildings, a handful of elaborately decorated structures in the "Raj" style of colonial architecture and known locally as "The Birdcages." They were replaced in the early twentieth century by the present-day Legislative Buildings. **Courtesy B.C. Archives A-00934.**

Saturday June 17, 1865, Mr. Jessop's Central Schoolhouse:
School room 30 ft. x 31, would contain about 100 scholars. Ventilation tolerable. In front are two cup rooms [today cupboards} with a gallery over, the last unfit for teaching purposes. Two district playgrounds furnished with gymnastic apparatus, good but too small; would require the adjoining lot of Mr. Saywards' to the east, or 20 ft. of that to the west belonging to Mr. Timmerman. By moving the partition at the back, a girls' school might be made to contain 50 girls. Expense with painting and whitewashing, about $250. Rent asked by Mr. Jessop $60 per month and by Mr. Timmerman $15.

Wednesday June 21, 1865, visited the school at Cedar Hill:
School held in the church, which is miserably cold; and in winter, when the children come from a distance over bad roads with wet feet, unhealthy. No desks, and the benches have no backs. Books used nearly the same as at the Victoria district school. No maps, no globe, a very small blackboard.

Children 14 in all, were 19 some little while ago; divided into two classes. Mr. Nicholson, teacher, has a second-class Canadian diploma. Salary $500 and the fees $2 per month per scholar, besides $150 from the bishop, which will now be probably withdrawn. Hours of attendance five per day. The general examination for the holidays very good. In reading, rather nasal, arithmetic very good, parsing tolerable, geography and modern history very good.

Friday, June 23, 1865, Craigflower School:
Property consists of five acres donated by the Puget Sound Company. The building cost $4000, was erected in 1854. Requires some repairs to one of the chimneys, the other cannot be swept, the bell tower dangerous. Mr. Russell,

the teacher, has written to the Colonial Secretary on the subject. Ventilation middling. Lobby or cup room [is] small. Desks and seats wretchedly constructed and arranged, must all be altered. Playground a good one, a good well, no gymnastic apparatus. The rooms of the schoolmaster downstairs [are] very inconvenient.

Books used are of every description, not two alike, only two national fourth readers, and one arithmetic [reader]. No blackboard, several large maps and a fine globe. Children divided into two classes, besides the very small ones. The teacher, Mr. Russell, has been there only six weeks. Before him Mr. Claypole was the teacher. Mr. Russell has no diploma. Salary $1000 and the fees. Hours of attendance six per day. Number of scholars 18 boys and 11 girls, in all 29. There were only 14 during the last month of Mr. Claypole's superintendence. No monitors. The Bible read morning and evening. All the children [are] Protestants. Attainments of pupils miserable, especially in parsing, arithmetic and history.

Friday, June 30, 1865, Esquimalt:
School held in the little church there. Desks and seats might be better arranged, but are sufficient for the small number of scholars. Books are very old and dilapidated and of every kind. One good map of the world, and a small blackboard. Slates insufficient. Children in two classes. Mrs. Fisher has been teacher for 21 months, before her a Mr. Partridge. The school was opened January 31, 1863, under the supervision of a local committee composed of Reverend C.F. Woods, George F. Hawkins, and Mr. Wilby, secretary. The admittance is through the secretary. Books and schooling [are] free. The teacher's salary was $50 per month till last November when the remnant of the original subscription gave out; since which it is reduced to the $500 per annum from government, out of which have been taken the books and prizes given by Mrs. Fisher. Hours of attendance nine to 12, and two to four [equalling] five hours. There are 14 boys and six girls, in all 20, the eldest 12 years old. No corporal punishment allowed. Exercises closed with reading the Bible. Attendance very irregular; only 13 children present. [25]

1865: "The blessing of education . . . to the poorest as well as to the richest child"

Amor de Cosmos

A great champion for the idea of free and universal schooling during the colonial era was Alexander Smith who owned and edited *The British Colonist* newspaper under the *nom de plume*, Amor de Cosmos, "lover of the universe." A true exponent of

Victorian liberalism, de Cosmos extolled the virtues of state supported "schooling for all" in the following editorial written six years before British Columbia joined Confederation and seven years before the birth of the public school system:

> For the first time since the colony of Vancouver Island came into existence the blessing of education has been presented to the poorest as well as to the richest child . . . Poverty has at length ceased to be an excuse for idle and ignorant childhood. The opening of the Central School yesterday—the inauguration of the temple of free education—has removed the fearful incubus which has lain so heavily and so long on every parent's heart. Let us hope that what has been commenced so auspiciously, even though it has come at the eleventh hour, will be carried out with success—that sectional jarring will not interfere with the practical usefulness of the institution, but that every person who has a voice in the management of our public education will feel the most sacred responsibility

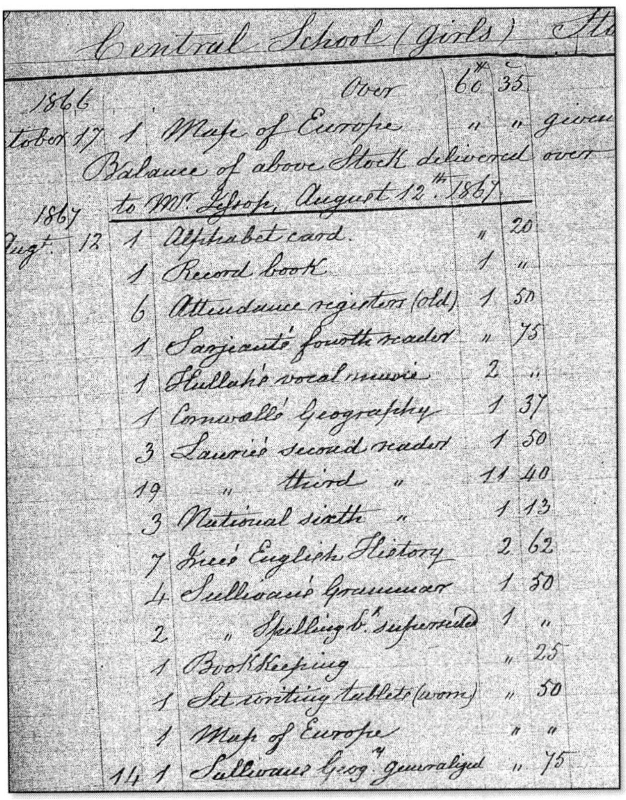
Central School (Girls)
1866 Over 60 35
[Oc]tober 17 1 Map of Europe " " given
Balance of above Stock delivered over to Mr. Jessop, August 12th 1867
1867 Augt. 12 1 Alphabet card. " 20
1 Record book 1 "
6 Attendance registers (old) 1 50
1 Sargeant's fourth reader " 75
1 Hullah's vocal music 2 "
1 Cornwall's Geography 1 37
3 Laurie's second reader 1 50
19 " third " 11 40
3 National sixth " 1 13
7 Ince's English History 2 62
4 Sullivan's Grammar 1 50
2 " Spelling Bk. superseded 1 "
1 Book Keeping " 25
1 Set writing tablets (worn) " 50
1 Map of Europe " "
14 1 Sullivan's Geogy. generalized " 75

List of curricular materials available to teacher in Victoria's Girls' Central School, 1867.

that devolves upon him. In a young community like ours the education of youth is a subject of even more tender solicitude than it is in older countries. We are forming the minds of those who are not only to become responsible for the material progress of the country, but who are to build up, if not indeed lay the foundation of the social as well as political fabric of British rule on this side of the continent. There is a power in the public system of education of creating a national sentiment and inculcating an earnest patriotism almost unknown in the private schools of instruction . . .

We are here on the extreme verge of civilization, with all of nature's obstacles before us. The people who are to carry on the work of building up a prosperous and probably an influential country must not be encumbered with the cogs of sectional feeling of any kind. They must be taught, also, the great practical principles of life, and especially of new country life. It too often happens that education, like many other things, is not appropriate, and that while a child's head is filled with a heap of rubbish never to be used throughout its career, the most necessary rudiments for the country in which it resides and which is to be its future stage, are altogether neglected. Again, we have old country ideas about the various grades of life—the servility of one class to another—sickening enough at all times in the countries from which they draw their sustenance, but transplanted in the repugnant soil of a new land, actually unbearable—we have these ideas sown deeply in the juvenile mind. We want a very different tone to be imparted to our youth.[26]

1867: "Any man who respects himself would not desire to have his children instructed without . . . sacrifice on his own part"

Frederick Seymour

In sharp contrast to Victoria newspaper editor, Amor de Cosmos, Governor Frederick Seymour of the Legislative Council in New Westminster favoured fee-paying rather than "free" schools and a denominational rather than a non-denominational system of schooling. Here, Seymour presents a more restrained view of the state's role in schooling, arguing that the public provision of education interferes with the "natural responsibility" of the family:

On Vancouver Island an attempt has been made to make the education of the youth in the colony a burden on the community. The governor lays before the council statements of the present condition of the relations existing between the government and the public schools of the Island, and leaves the question as to the indebtedness on the one side, or unreasonable expectations on the other to be freely dealt with by the council—one from which the governor stands aloof. He will merely state that in the opinion of his predecessor the system was not successful, and that other objects besides the intellectual advancement of the children of the colony were sometimes allowed entrance into the consideration of the Board of Education.

On the mainland the governor has been compelled to acknowledge that the population is yet too small and scattered for any regular system of education to be established. Where parents have been willing to pay towards the instruction of their children, he has, with the consent of the Legislative Council, assisted them from the public funds. The schools have not been under the direction of the government, and pupils have been led or sent from those that asked assistance from the public to those enjoying the dignity of independence, or back again as the parents might elect.

The governor is of the opinion that the colony is not yet old enough for any regular system of education to be established; nor would he wish, under the present constitution, to press his own views upon the Legislature, though he has no desire to conceal them. He thinks that any man who respects himself would not desire to have his children instructed without some pecuniary sacrifice on his own part. The state may aid the parent, but ought not to relieve him of his own natural responsibility . . .

All that the state can do is to enable children to overcome the almost mechanical difficulties which seem to bar their passage over the threshold of knowledge, and having effected this to leave to parental affection and knowledge of individual character the choice of the arms with which the child shall at a future period fight the battle of life. It is vain for the state to attempt to drive on in an even line the idle and the industrious—the boy of ready aptitudes and him whose brain becomes pained and confused in endeavouring to master the simplest problem. The governor conceives it to be the duty of the governing power to assist in the giving to all elementary instruction, and then to offer inducements to those who are able to come to the front in the intellectual struggle with their fellow men.

The governor is of the opinion that when the time comes for the establishment of a large common school, religious teaching ought not to be allowed to intrude . . . In a colony [likely the British colony of Antigua} with which the governor was recently connected he left the following school system. There was a public school open to all denominations, where the schoolmaster did not presume to open to the children any sacred mysteries. The charge upon the children attending regularly was half a dollar a month. But there were denominational schools, also, to which the government contributed, but in a moderate degree. It was found that these denominational schools, though more expensive to the parents, absorbed the greater number of the children. Such is the system he would desire to see in any concentrated community.[27]

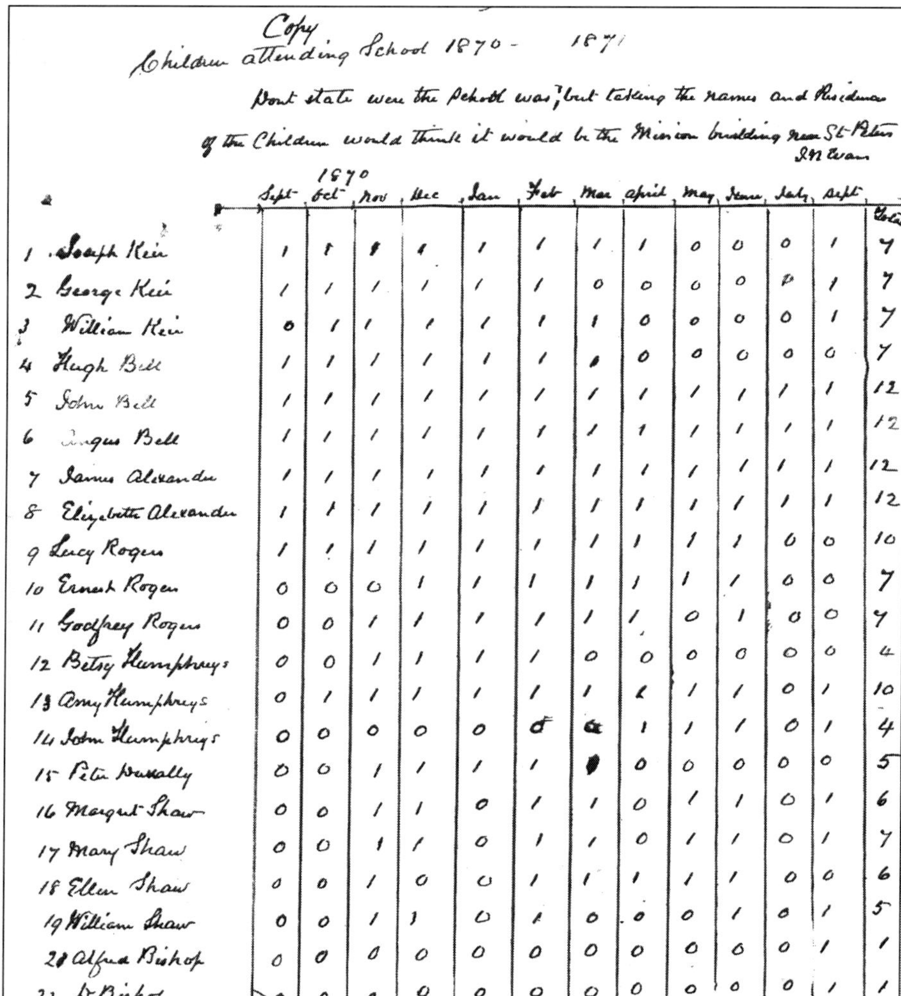

Copy
Children attending School 1870 - 1871
Dont state were the Scholl was; but taking the names and Residence of the Children would think it would be the Mission building near St Peters
J M Evans

	1870 Sept	Oct	Nov	Dec	Jan	Feb	Mar	April	May	June	July	Sept	Total
1 Joseph Kier	1	1	1	1	1	1	1	1	0	0	0	1	7
2 George Kier	1	1	1	1	1	1	0	0	0	0	0	1	7
3 William Kier	0	1	1	1	1	1	1	0	0	0	0	1	7
4 Hugh Bell	1	1	1	1	1	1	1	0	0	0	0	0	7
5 John Bell	1	1	1	1	1	1	1	1	1	1	1	1	12
6 Angus Bell	1	1	1	1	1	1	1	1	1	1	1	1	12
7 James Alexander	1	1	1	1	1	1	1	1	1	1	1	1	12
8 Elizabeth Alexander	1	1	1	1	1	1	1	1	1	1	1	1	12
9 Lucy Rogers	1	1	1	1	1	1	1	1	1	1	0	0	10
10 Ernest Rogers	0	0	0	1	1	1	1	1	1	1	0	0	7
11 Godfrey Rogers	0	0	1	1	1	1	1	1	0	1	0	0	7
12 Betsy Humphreys	0	0	1	1	1	1	0	0	0	0	0	0	4
13 Amy Humphreys	0	1	1	1	1	1	1	1	1	1	0	1	10
14 John Humphreys	0	0	0	0	0	0	[illegible]	1	1	1	0	1	4
15 Peter Dunally	0	0	1	1	1	1	[illegible]	0	0	0	0	0	5
16 Margret Shaw	0	0	1	1	0	1	1	0	1	1	0	1	6
17 Mary Shaw	0	0	1	1	0	1	1	0	1	1	0	1	7
18 Ellen Shaw	0	0	1	0	0	1	1	1	1	1	0	0	6
19 William Shaw	0	0	1	1	0	1	0	0	0	1	0	1	5
20 Alfred Bishop	0	0	0	0	0	0	0	0	0	0	0	1	1
21 D Bishop	0	0	0	0	0	0	0	0	0	0	0	1	1

Cowichan Valley School annual register for the year 1870, two years before public schooling was established in British Columbia. **Courtesy B.C. Archives Add. MSS. 2823.**

Notes

1. James P. Spradley (Ed.), *Guests Never Leave Hungry: The Autobiography of James Sewid, A Kwakiutl Indian* (Montreal: McGill-Queen's University Press, 1969), 16, 21, 22, 23, 26, 27, and 31.
2. Alastair Glegg has pointed out that the population of the school operated by the Sisters of St. Ann in Victoria was diverse and included the daughters of Governor Douglas along with children who were orphans, personal correspondence.
3. In 1858, his father moved the Anderson family into residence in Victoria, where James began his career as a junior clerk in his father's office (now Collector of Customs and Postmaster) and went on to become the first deputy minister of agriculture in 1897, a position he held until ill health forced his retirement in 1908. On 9 April 1930, Anderson was struck by an automobile and killed instantly.
4. James Anderson, Memoirs, BCA Add. MSS. 1912, Chapter 11 Box 8, File 4, 22.
5. The "collects" are distinctive short prayers that constitute an essential part of the three chief services of the Church of England, Holy Communion, Matins (or Morning Prayer), and Evensong (Evening Prayer).
6. Anderson, Memoirs, 17-18.
7. Ibid., 133.
8. Ibid., 151.
9. Dorothy Blakey Smith, *The Reminiscences of Doctor John Sebastian Helmcken* (Vancouver: UBC Press, 1975), 120-121.
10. Ibid., 286.
11. Derek Pethick, *Victoria: The Fort* (Vancouver: Mitchell Press, 1968), 117.
12. D.L. MacLaurin, "The History of Education in the Crown Colonies of Vancouver Island and British Columbia and in the Province of British Columbia," unpublished Ph.D. dissertation, University of Washington, 1934, 15.
13. Ibid., 17.
14. Ibid., 20-21.
15. Alexander Robinson, "The History of Education" in Adam Shortt and Arthur Doughty (Eds.), *Canada and Its Provinces* (Toronto: Edinburgh University Press, 1914), 402-404.
16. Ibid.
17. MacLaurin, "The History of Education," 26-27.
18. These refer to the Irish National Readers used by Egerton Ryerson in Canada West.
19. MacLaurin, "The History of Education," 27-28.
20. Ibid., 31-32.
21. Ibid.
22. Edgar Fawcett, *Some Reminiscences of Old Victoria* (Toronto: William Briggs, 1912), 28-32.
23. Eric Roberts, *Salt Spring Saga* (Ganges, Salt Spring Island, B.C.: Driftwood Press, 1962), 16.
24. Later, Waddington spent a number of years attempting to build a wagon road from the headwaters of Bute Inlet to Fort Alexandria on the Fraser River, an initial step in an ill-fated dream to provide a first link in an overland railway. He died in 1872.
25. Board of Education Correspondence, Alfred Waddington, Superintendent 1865, BCA, GR 1468, Microfilm B04715.
26. *The British Colonist*, "Editorial," 2 August 1865, 2.
27. Cited in Robinson's "History of Education," *Canada and Its Provinces*, 414-416.

Courtesy City of Surrey Archives 192.16.

CHAPTER 2

Schools Under Construction: The Frontier Era, 1872-1899

Sadly, initiatives to promote free schooling failed during the period of colonial rule. Debates about religious influences in schools divided new settlers, as did disagreements about who should pay school costs. Not until British Columbia joined Confederation in 1871 did the political will exist that would allow the new province to bear the costs of public schooling.

With British Columbia's entry into Confederation in 1871, and the new school system's establishment in April the following year, civic interest in education flourished as never before. Public discussions about the purposes of schools and, indeed, about the character and credentials of educators, were reported at great length in Victoria and New Westminster newspapers. In Victoria, for example, between 1872 and 1878, *The Daily British Colonist,* edited by David Higgins, published more than 100 editorials on schooling—besides various educational news items.[1] In a frontier society anxious to prove itself to the country's longer-established regions, fine schools represented the epitome of progress and hope. As Higgins put it, schools were institutions that would make the province's children "better than we are, more gentle, more courteous and more useful in their generation."[2] The new schools offered, again to quote Higgins, "the door to the highest positions . . . to every man's child who may show himself worthy to fill them."[3] Reflecting prevailing Victorian standards, the British Columbia public strongly believed that the province's schools should impart both moral as well as intellectual training. Teachers, accordingly, were expected also to serve as moral custodians of the young.

Overseeing the destiny of the new school system was John Jessop, the first provincial superintendent of education. Jessop was born in England in 1829, came to Canada at the age of 17, and secured his teaching certificate at Egerton Ryerson's Normal School in Toronto. A man of enormous physical energy, he walked from Winnipeg to the West Coast where, after a brief but unprofitable foray into the goldfields, he opened a "common" fee-for-service school in Victoria. Often outspoken on the colonial government's inability to provide adequate funding for public schools, he was sufficiently well-known and politically connected to be appointed superintendent of provincial schools in 1872 and, for most of his six-year tenure, he constituted the entire Education Office.

The greatest challenge facing Jessop—and all the education officers who followed him—was how to manage and supply a new system of schools stretched across a vast and mostly unexplored territory. In many respects, British Columbia's educational development has been largely determined by the province's geography. Only 30 nations in the world occupy a landmass larger than the nearly 950,000 square kilometers that define Canada's Pacific province—and few countries share a climate as forbidding or topography as mountainous and difficult to traverse. From the very beginning, geography would determine that building a new school system would not be easy and that, for a century at least, two worlds of public schools would exist in Canada's westernmost province—one urban and relatively well-to-do and one rural and generally impoverished.

In 1872, Jessop set the stage for more than a century of concern with the state of rural and isolated schools. "The question as to how the educational wants of the interior of this Province are to be supplied," Jessop wrote, "is one that I approach under a deep sense of the responsibility involved in attempting to deal with it." Jessop's dream that the province's common schools would serve as colleges for the people remained a dream deferred at least until the early 1950s. Up to that time, the institution of schooling assumed a common and humble shape familiar to several generations of British Columbians. From the coast to the Rockies, poorly lighted, sparse and often dilapidated one-room schoolhouses, attended by 10 to 12 youngsters, remained the most prominent agencies for learning. From the 1870s to the 1940s, these small and unprepossessing structures swelled in number from little more than a dozen to more than 1,000.

The stories and documents in the following chapter describe the birth of a school system in frontier surroundings and the growing pains it experienced until the end of the nineteenth century. They show the resoluteness of purpose that distinguished early school leaders, how they shaped the fledgling system by will and force of personality and how, in turn, their actions were shaped by the force of the frontier around them. Through official reports, newspaper articles, personal reminiscences and letters, we can see the organizational and social challenges that faced the early school builders, the social stigma attached to schools that were both "public" and "free," the yearning of even a rough frontier society for Victorian respectability, and the scandal that resulted from the province's ill-fated attempt to establish boarding schools for children in the sparsely inhabited Cariboo region. We also learn something about the gradual professionalization of teaching and the restless characters who came west for gold and adventure but who sometimes turned to teaching when their luck and their grubstake ran out. These stories likewise make clear government's iron hand in all matters educational and how the chief architects of the public school system governed schools across a vast territory through the establishment of a school inspectorate whose officers proved quick to note any breach of official policy or school regulation. Through these written records, we can also glimpse into the missionary schools where aboriginal children, legislatively the wards of the Dominion Government thousands of miles away, were educated often in haphazard fashion.

Governing the New Schools

When British Columbia entered Confederation in 1871, it did so, with what was already, according to historian F. Henry Johnson, "the most centralized school system on record."[4] Indeed, the educational world that the first provincial superintendent of schools, John Jessop, inherited from the colonial system had already made decisions about who would control school governance and administration in what was then the dark pedagogical continent of British Columbia. Serving under the direction of the provincial secretary and the "six fit and proper persons" from cabinet who constituted the first Provincial Board of Education, Jessop framed the first *School Act* (1872) which, although modeled in form on Ryerson's earlier Ontario legislation, also reiterated in substance the authority structure of the colonial past.

British Columbia's 1872 *School Act*, as well as subsequent legislation, commonly assumed that only a strong central authority could provide the vision and control necessary to establish a provincial school system in a vast territory with a diverse population and uncertain economic prospects. The next century of school law (1872-1972) was, therefore, written in such a way that the government minister with the educational portfolio was charged with the ultimate policy and decision-making authority in schooling and empowered to intervene in any matter, at any level, for the good of the system. This body of legislation, also made it clear that government officials and their staff in the Education Office would be liberated from the problem of actually delivering school services: this responsibility would accrue to local trustees who were, in the final analysis, "creatures of provincial authority" and ever "subject to the constant scrutiny and, if warranted, intervention" of provincial officers. Thus free, the government's education officers could walk the high ground to organize, manage, supervise, and inspect the operations and practices of a system others maintained.

Acting on the premise that, because of its importance, schooling could only be entrusted to the highest level of government, the province of British Columbia withheld for itself control over the most important aspects of public schooling, namely—the curriculum to be taught; the level to which schools were financed; the training and certification required of teachers; the methods of assessment and standards for student testing; the organizational structures to sustain school governance and management; the establishment of school boards; the design and distribution of curriculum materials; the criteria for opening and closing schools; and overall accountability for the purposes and progress of schools.

Centralization of school authority was roundly welcomed by frontier society. Looking back over the first six years of the new school system in 1878, editor David Higgins proudly recounted in *The Daily British Colonist*:

> Where before there were but half a dozen schools scattered over a wide expanse of territory, with the teachers as fitful as the attendance; where neither order, system, or regularity was observed; where the buildings were mean and dilapidated; where teachers and scholars came and went when and where they liked with a sovereign contempt for the timepiece; and where the education imparted was generally of a crude, backwoods character, we find order and system introduced, with as fine schools and as excellent advantages for imparting instructions as are possessed by any Province in the Dominion.[5]

All in all, such centralization seemed a small price to pay for a governance and administrative structure that offered social order and some crude measure of educational equity amid the welter of social change transforming Canadian life in the final quarter of a century that marked the end of the Victorian Age. Perhaps more than other institutions, schools felt the effects of immigration, urbanization, and industrialization most acutely. Such changes obliged schools to provide services unknown to them a half century before—to furnish vocational, agricultural, and domestic education, instruction in health and hygiene, to socialize non-English-speaking immigrants, to offer night-school classes to adults, and to fulfill an assortment of other economic and social expectations that were emerging as Canada was beginning to shift from a farm to a factory economy in the closing decades of the nineteenth century.

Compared to the provincial government's authority in defining school policy and legislation, the latitude granted historically to locally-elected school trustees to shape public schooling was small.[6] The most important role assigned to trustees was their responsibility to select teachers for their schools, providing, of course, that such teachers had been granted permission to teach by the province. And, although trustees could dismiss teachers, ordinarily they were guided by the assessment of a teacher's competence rendered by a provincial school inspector and, as a rule, proved reluctant to challenge such reports. Trustee influence was far greater, however, over the social behaviour of teachers, especially in small rural communities where teachers would be closely observed to see that they upheld high moral standards. Teachers were also directed as a matter of course by the school board's secretary treasurer, or by other trustees, to find accommodation with certain families in the community, if a teacherage was unavailable. Trustees were also granted jurisdiction in setting the contracts for individuals who would supply water and wood to the school, in supplying "slates" for children to write on, and in deciding who would provide janitorial services (often the teacher), as well as what social uses would be made of the schoolhouse when the day's instruction was over.

Textbooks for Everyone

In the early years, Jessop was insistent on "standardizing" teaching, and one of the best ways to ensure that the same material was being taught throughout the provincial system was to try and ensure that the same textbooks were being purchased and used by all districts and teachers. When a school was established at St. Luke's church in Saanich in 1860, the schoolroom was the nave of the church with the sanctuary curtained off during the week. In some instances, the Bible was the only textbook, and although on the surface of things, this suggests an excess of piety, there was a more practical reason—that this was the only book that the entire class could be expected to bring from home. Thus Jessop, charged with bringing about universal and free schooling, had to provide standardized textbooks to pupils often too poor to buy shoes. His attempts to see to it that every classroom was provided with standard books and globes is well documented in the *Annual Reports of the Public Schools,* where it is recorded which textbooks were to be found in which classrooms throughout the schools of the province. Then as now, there were two schools of thought on the matter, one school that said that the government should provide and pay for everything as "they can well afford it," and another that said that the pupils —or their parents —should assume the cost of textbooks to save the taxpayer the expense which was, after all, for the apparent benefit of the pupil.

At first, the provincial government did buy textbooks for classrooms. By 1873, Jessop had established a textbook depository and ordered $880 worth of textbooks approved by Egerton Ryerson in Toronto. Jessop himself carried parcels of these books to delivery offices in Victoria to send them out to the schools. Around the same time, there was an item included in the statement of annual expenses that covered sums of money remitted to the Education Office from school district trustees towards the cost of books, suggesting that the larger school districts were expected to repay book costs. The rural and assisted schools, however, received textbooks free of charge.

In 1908, David Wilson, the first school inspector, left the inspectorate to become the officer-in-charge of the Free Textbooks Branch. The chore of bulk buying, shipping, and inventory had become too large for the clerks in the Education Office to handle and from that time forward, the Free Textbook Branch supplied standardized texts in increasing variety and complexity to match the needs of an ever-diversifying curriculum.

Textbooks in Victoria's 14 Schools, July 1872[8]

GRAMMAR	ARITHMETIC	HISTORY
10 Lennie 1 Irish National 2 No Books	3 Sangster 2 McMurchy's 2 Thompson 2 Irish National 1 Ontario 1 Colenso's 2 No Books	3 Collier 1 Irish National 1 Ince's 1 English 1 Smith 7 No Books
GEOGRAPHY	**READERS**	**SPELLERS**
5 Easy Lessons 4 Cornell 1 Hugh's 1 Hodgin's 1 Irish National 1 No Books	9 Ontario 4 Irish National 1 Canadian	4 Carpenter 2 Ontario 1 Town's 1 Sullivan 6 No Books

1872: "Free education . . . within the reach of every child"

The Daily British Colonist

Amor de Cosmos had vigorously used his newspaper in Victoria to campaign for free and universal schooling during the 1860s. Not surprisingly, David Higgins, de Cosmos' successor at the paper, likewise proved to be an unflagging advocate for a well-supported public school system. Here Higgins gives John Jessop, British Columbia's first provincial superintendent, a ringing endorsement:

> The deplorable condition of the public schools—perhaps it would be more correct to say the absence of them—long constituted one of British Columbia's chief grievances; and no measure was more distinctly or more unanimously demanded than a system of free non-sectarian education. Listening to the unequivocal voice of the people, it was one of the earliest acts of the new government to introduce a bill for the purpose of supplying this great public want . . . the new School Bill, although making no pretensions to perfection, was admitted on all hands to present a fair basis to work upon; and the country rejoiced at the near prospect of having a free education placed within the reach of every child. That Bill has become law, and a gentleman whose training under the admirable educational system of Ontario, whose long experience in teaching, and whose well-known energy and intimate acquaintance with the province suggested his fitness for the onerous and important position, has been appointed superintendent. It only remains to construct the Board of Education, in order to set the new educational machinery in motion throughout the Province.[7]

1872: "Better for the government to educate those children"

John Jessop

On April 17, 1872, John Jessop was appointed superintendent of provincial education, the first educational official to be appointed after the Crown Colony of British Columbia joined Confederation in 1871. Fired with the zeal of nineteenth-century social liberalism, Jessop made a case here for the support of poor children at the proposed Cache Creek Boarding School. Since this time, Jessop's argument has been restated often by public school advocates. Unfortunately, Jessop's career as superintendent of provincial schools would eventually unravel as a result of events at Cache Creek:

It is expected that parents and guardians will contribute a reasonable sum monthly for their children's board in money, cattle, or farm produce, and keep them comfortably and respectably clothed, and properly supplied with bedding . . . But provision ought to be made for indigent children; and nearly all that would be classed under such a head would be those half-breeds who, deserted by their white fathers, have gone with their Indian mothers to the rancheries. These children, as well as others, will be just what education or the want of it may make them. With it, a majority may grow up respectable members of society, without it many may become inmates of our jails or penitentiaries. Statistics on the subject of education and crime prove that the cost of prosecuting and punishing a criminal is fully three times as great as the expense of giving a child a good public school education. So that, taking a financial view of the question, it will be infinitely better for the government to educate those children, and if need be to board and clothe them, than to run the risk of their growing up nuisances in society. Supposing that there should be 25 or 30 of those children in regular attendance at this boarding school, the $250 or $300 per month that it might cost to maintain them would certainly be money well expended. The question might well here be asked—would not the Indian department, now under the federal government, bear a portion of such expense?[9]

1873: "Boys and girls . . . are getting ahead of the public school curriculum"

John Jessop

Even as he began his position as head of provincial schools, Jessop realized that the province's educational development would be stifled without the establishment of a high school, an institution of learning never available during the province's colonial era. Here, Jessop makes a case for the establishment of high schools in the province's two main centres:

The question of high schools is one that ought not to be left any longer in abeyance: Boys and girls in many parts of the province are getting ahead of the public school curriculum; not that the teachers in our principal schools are unable to give instruction in the higher branches of an English education, and to make the senior pupils of both sexes much more proficient than they now are . . . the time has fully come when two high schools—one in Victoria and the other in New Westminster—should be established. Each might be commenced with one properly qualified master, and the teaching staff afterwards increased as the attendance might warrant.[10]

1874: "Inspecting schools by steamer, canoe, horseback, and foot"

John Jessop

From rented premises on Government Street, Jessop operated the Education Office on a budget of $25,435 for an initial enrollment of 1,028 students in the provincial school system. In 1872, this constituted nearly six per cent of the province's total expenditures. Official reports show that Jessop worked without secretarial help and single-handedly oversaw all educational and administrative matters, including: the election of three-person school boards for every one-room school; the recruitment and appointment of teachers; and ordering, packing and shipping textbooks and maps to all schools. As education superintendent, he was also personally responsible for inspecting every schoolroom in the province across a territory that already stretched from Victoria to the Cariboo region. In his first tour to inspect nine of the new province's schools in 1873, Jessop travelled 1,500 miles (2,400 kilometers) on foot, horseback, buggy, canoe, lake-boat and stagecoach. Here he recounts his even more rigorous travels in 1874 and 1875 to inspect schools strung out across a province where few roads existed and where getting from one small settlement to another was fraught with hardship:

> During the year ending July 31 [1874], I made 64 school visits, entailing 2,580 miles of travel, or an average distance of more than 40 miles for each visit; to this may be added 450 miles of travel in visiting Nicola Valley and Kamloops in September last; and Big Bar, Canoe, and Dog Creeks, and Alkali Lake in June of this year; making a total of 2,930 miles. The great amount of travel necessary, in order to reach all the schools of British Columbia, will be readily understood, when I state that the schools on the Mainland, numbering 12, are, on an average, more than 40 miles apart; while those on Vancouver Island and dependencies, 15 in all, have an average distance from each other of over 10 miles . . . [11]
>
> For purposes of school inspection [1875] and visiting sections of the interior where new districts were contemplated, I travelled 1,200 miles by steamer, 425 by canoe, 500 by stage, 1,255 on horseback, and 184 on foot, making a total of more than 3,600 miles during the year. I have also to report 84 school visits—an increase of 20 over last year.
>
> Since the date of my last report, 516 official letters have been received at the Education Office, and 587 written. During the year, the Board of Education has held 15 meetings for the transaction of business connected with the department, at many of which all members were present.[12]

1874: "Scarcely a foot of breathing room"

John Jessop

Shortage of classroom space remained a problem that dogged administrators and teachers from the schools of frontier period in the 1870s to the exuberant postwar growth of the 1950s and 1960s. Here Jessop makes a plea to the legislators of his day for larger and healthier school facilities following a visit to Victoria's Girls' School:

> The girls are still closely confined in the inconvenient and badly ventilated building on Broughton Street, with scarcely a foot of breathing room outside the schoolhouse, except on the public street. In the heat of summer the close, impure atmosphere in the building . . . cannot be otherwise than deleterious to the health of both pupils and teachers; while in the cold and damp of winter the absolute necessity for so many open windows generates violent colds, which are equally, if not more injurious. Better accommodation must be provided, at an early day, for the constantly increasing number of pupils seeking admission to the girls' department of the public school. The erection of a first-class building, on the school reserve, for public and high school purposes, ought not to be much longer delayed. A special grant from the general revenue of the province, for this purpose, liberally supplemented by the municipal council from the city funds, would enable the trustee board to remedy an evil, before the close of

Late-nineteenth century Revelstoke school. **Courtesy City of Vancouver Archives 667.**

1875, that ought never to have had an existence; and one which affects the health and comfort of one or more members of a great number of families.[13]

1874: "The persistent refusal of . . . families"

John Jessop

In the first half-century of the province's history, schools opened and closed as new communities sprouted or as local economies collapsed. Sometimes, also, early school closures were prompted by parents who resisted sending their children to school in an era before public schooling was universally accepted and before attendance was made mandatory. This lack of parental support obliged superintendent Jessop to close a recently-opened school serving families in the rolling farmlands of North Saanich, some 25 kilometers north of Victoria:

> After a trial of nearly 12 months, the school in this district had to be discontinued on account of so few pupils in attendance. As the trustees have neglected to send in their annual report, I am not able to state exactly the number of school-going children; but there must be between 20 and 25. For the same reason I cannot tell what the average attendance for the year has been; but probably not more than six. On December 3 last, I found seven children at school, all that were on the register, it being examination day. On my next visit, April 14, there were five, one of whom was under school age. The persistent refusal of two heads of families, representing at least seven children of school age, neither of whom are more than two and a half miles from the school house, to send their children to the school, prevents its being re-opened. The responsibility of a closed school rests upon these parties.[14]

Even Then There Was Paperwork

In Jessop's day, there were no typists in the Education Office, and indeed, no typewriter. All Jessop's letters were written by hand—his own hand—and carried to the post office which was not far away on Government Street on his own two feet. When the Education Office moved to the government buildings known as the "Birdcages," as it did within a year or so of its establishment (as far as can be ascertained from casual references found in newspapers of the time), clerical help of some kind was likely made available through the Provincial Secretary's Office. Jessop pointed out early in his tenure that the Education Office increased its paperwork by leaps and bounds every year. In the beginning of his superintendency, it was possible for Jessop to simply close the Education Office door and go away for weeks at a time to inspect the schools of the province, but the mountain of paperwork awaiting his return proved staggering. By the time Richard Clemitson was appointed as deputy superintendent to assist Jessop in 1876, it was necessary for someone to be in the Education Office at least three days a week, seeing to interviews with teachers, correspondence, ordering, shipping and accounting. Jessop noted the burden of paperwork he faced in his 1875 report:

> As more than three years have elapsed since the machinery of our present school system was set in motion, it may not be out of place to notice, briefly, the gradual increase of work connected therewith, as it is indicative of healthy development and substantial progress. Since the date of my last annual report, the item of correspondence amounts to 665 official letters received, and 670 written, an increase in the former of 149, and in the latter of 83, over those of the year ending July 31, 1874. During the 12 months preceding, the number received and written amounted to 380 and 419 respectively. The correspondence, therefore, has increased nearly 100 per cent since presenting my first Report.
>
> Importing textbooks, registers, tablet lessons, maps, terrestrial globes, and supplying the schools with them, form another item requiring considerable care and attention. The teachers in Victoria and New Westminster only partly supply their schools from the Education Office; but all others in the province

Schools were rough and ready across the small settlements that dotted the new province in the late-nineteenth century. Reflecting the exuberant spirit of the age, Barkerville youngsters, brimming with confidence, pose here for a group portrait. **Courtesy B.C. Archives C-09732.**

Rules for Teachers - 1872

(1) Teachers each day will fill lamps, clean chimneys, and clean wicks.

(2) Each teacher will bring a bucket of water and scuttle of coal for the day's session.

(3) Make your pens carefully. You may whittle nibs for the individual tastes of the pupils.

(4) Men teachers may take one evening a week for courting purposes or two evenings a week if they attend church regularly.

(5) After ten hours in school, teachers should spend the remaining time reading the Bible or other good books.

(6) Women teachers who marry or engage in unseemly conduct will be dismissed.

(7) Each teacher who smokes, uses liquor in any form, frequents pool or public halls, or gets shaved in a barber shop, will give good reason to suspect his worth, intentions, integrity, and honesty.

(8) Each teacher shall lay aside from each pay a goodly sum of his earnings for his benefit during declining years so he will not become a burden on society.

(9) The teacher who performs his labours faithfuly and without fail for five years will be given an increase of 25 cents per week providing the Board of Education approves.

Because school trustees were locally elected—and schooling was deemed a local matter— trustees felt entitled to establish their own rules for teachers to follow. The list above is one such list from a rural community in 1872. **Courtesy Valemount Historical Society.**

obtain schoolbooks exclusively from this source. A small stock is usually kept on hand in each of the schools, and disposed of at even less than Eastern retail prices. Not only are the children provided with the necessary text books at an exceedingly low figure . . . but the serious obstacle to school progress of pupils, having to wait days and even weeks for books that may be required, is entirely obviated. In addition to correspondence, and the management of the book depository, there are numerous callers at the Education Office on business; the disbursement of teachers' salaries from month to month; teachers' examinations; the compilation of the school report, and returns of various descriptions. All these beside school visiting throughout the province and annual lecturing in the various districts have, so far, been accomplished without clerical help of any description.[15]

Early High Schools

Although the Education Office in Victoria was responsible for credentialling teachers and paying their salaries, provision of school buildings fell to parents and interested community members, or to municipal governments in urban areas. Victoria Central School, the first brick school in British Columbia, was built in 1875 and replaced the earlier log structure nearby which had served as schoolroom and residence for the teacher and his family.

As school populations increased dramatically, the need for teachers became acute, and students who had successfully completed the elementary grades were accepted into high school classes, primarily to prepare them for teaching careers. The first high school in the west, Victoria High School, was established in 1876. Little more than a decade after the introduction of high school education to the province, British Columbia's four high schools (Victoria, Nanaimo, New Westminster and Vancouver) were supplying more than 100 of the provincial system's 275 teachers and were deemed by government already to have been "of incalculable benefit to the Province."

1876: "The gift of the country"

The Daily British Colonist

Early British Columbians were thrilled with the promise of the fledgling public school system. As the following two editorials show, the press extolled the virtues of public schooling and demanded that the schools be kept "beyond the reach of politicians:"

We admire our school system because it is free—because the state has been brought to recognize and discharge the duty it owes to its young—and because the schools are secular. Free schools in British Columbia have proved a great success. They have overborne prejudice, broken down the barriers that class legislation built up between people and their rulers, and opened the door to the highest positions in the gift of the country to every man's child who may show himself worthy to fill them. The children of the poor are helped with the children of the rich. The fountain of intelligence is free to whoever may come to quaff of its waters. All are welcomed—none need turn away with the thirst for knowledge unslaked.[16]

Built in 1875, Victoria's Central School was the first school to be constructed west of Winnipeg out of "permanent" materials (burnt red brick). Attached to the school was a single storey addition where the province's first high school was convened in 1876 as the first step in a provincial plan to train "homegrown" teachers for elementary schools. When Edward Paul became principal of the recently established high school, he described it as "a set of four dingy rooms sandwiched between the boys' and girls' Central school buildings."
Courtesy Victoria High School Archives.

1876: "Beyond the reach of politicians"

The Daily British Colonist

If our free schools are to be maintained they must be placed on a pinnacle beyond the reach of politicians. So long as this is observed the people will consent to be taxed for the support of the system. But let it be once invaded and the fabric will totter and finally fall for want of a financial prop.[17]

1876: "More . . . English than the English"

Emily Carr

British Columbia's most renowned painter Emily Carr wrote as vividly as she painted. In "The Book of Small," which chronicles scenes from her childhood in Victoria, she shows that her observant eye and sharp sense of the ridiculous was forever at odds with the pretentiousness of the Victorian era. In the following passage, Carr recalls the advent of the public schools in a West Coast society still obsessed with social class, status, and "appearances:"

It took a generation and a half for English settlers in Victoria to accept the Canadian public school which they insisted on calling the 'free school.' They turned their noses up at our public schools as if they had been bad smells, preferring to send their children to old, ultra-genteel-hard-up English ladies' academies. Of these there were quite a few in Victoria; in them learning was confined to good manners. Politeness-education ladies had migrated to Canada, often in the hope of picking up bread and butter and possibly a husband, though they pretended all the while that they had come out on a very special mission—to teach the young of English-born gentlemen how not to become Canadian, to believe that all niceness and goodness came from ancestors and could have nothing to do with the wonderful new land, how not to acquire colonial deportment, which was looked upon as crude, almost wicked. The only teaching qualifications these ladies possessed, and for their services they charged enormously, had been acquired by generations of habit.

So young ladies whose papas had sufficient means learned English manners—how to shut a door, how to bow gracefully, how to address people of their own class and how [to address] a servant, how to write a dignified letter in beautiful script, how to hold their heads up, their stomachs in and how to look down their noses at the right moment. For all this the old ladies were very handsomely remunerated and the girls' brains remained quite empty. Canadian public schools taught book learning but no manners to speak of.

My parents sent their two eldest daughters to a ladies' deportment academy. Their next three children died before they were of school age. We four younger children were sent to the public school. Father said we could 'learn manners at home,' but we could not get education in those days at the private school out west.

Later, Angela College, a Church [of England] school for girls, was built and endowed by Lady Burdett-Coutts. A red brick building, it stood on Church Hill. Education in it was costly. All our friends went to Angela College, but father was by this time so prejudiced against private schools that he sent us to the public school and was very much criticized for doing so. Our manners were watched closely and apprehensively by our friends. It hurt mother but father was proud that all his children, with the exception of me, were good students by Canadian standards. I hated school with the exception of the first two years when, being too young for so long a walk, I went to Mrs. Fraser's school for little girls near our house . . . The dunce stool was very comfortable—much more so than the wooden forms where the good pupils sat; I had ample opportunity of knowing. You could almost say the dunce's stool was specially mine. The thing that I loved best at Mrs. Fraser's school was a big book of *Grimm's Fairy Tales* owned by a girl called Lizzie . . .

By and by other English settlers began to send their children to the public school and the high school too; then that old ladies' type of private school faded out of existence because education required a certain standard set by our public school system if people expected to obtain positions in Canada. Those families who were able to send their sons and daughters to England to be 'finished' did so. They came back more exaggeratedly English than the English themselves, 'patering' and 'matering' their father and mother, saying 'Awfully jolly, don't you know!' and 'No, no rawlly![18]

1877: "Brakes upon the wheels of progress"

"Progress"

Sentiments about public schooling in the 1860s and 1870s were manifest in many ways but most obviously in editorials and letters to the editors of British Columbia's *The Daily British Colonist* and *Mainland Guardian.* In Victoria, the *Colonist* was published every day except Monday and cost twenty-five cents a week, delivered. Mailing expenses were extra for subscribers residing outside the city. Here, one forward-thinking writer under the *nom de plume* of "Progress" questions the practice of schooling boys and girls separately, a practice that remained in Victoria city elementary schools until 1937:

> Is the world to stand still and must man go on considering himself to be the lord of creation, and woman to be a silly, simple creature fitted only to administer in his holiday hours to his wishes? And must women go on quietly accepting her position of dependency upon man, looking to him as her master and guide, a being of higher order than herself?[19] If so, then let my Lord Bishop and you, Mr. Editor, put brakes upon the wheels of progress by continuing to teach boys and girls in separate educational establishments. But if we are to march forward and break down the senseless division walls that exist between male and female in the formation of society, then the system of teaching boys and girls in the same classes is more calculated to accomplish the object than anything I know . . . [20] It seems strange that when the almost impossible-of-change conservatism of the old world should be giving away before the progress of the age, and admitting the superiority of the mixed system that you, sir, should be so laggard in ideas as to wish to hold on to medieval and oriental customs.[21]

A Scandal at Cache Creek

Two scandals—one small and one large—deep in the province's interior at Cache Creek would bring an end to Jessop's six-year career as superintendent of provincial schools. It all began with the construction of a boarding school to serve the children of settlers "up country," deep in the inland empire of the province.

Contrary to the provision of the new *School Act,* which required school trustees to be locally elected, Jessop appointed a three-person board to arrange for the construction of a boarding school to accommodate children of settlers in the interior of the province. He wished it to be built in Kamloops but the trustee board had other ideas and the building was eventually erected near Cache Creek. All went well initially and, on May 12, 1874, Jessop travelled to Cache Creek to arrange for the school's opening.

Eighteen pupils enrolled to begin with and an English couple, Mr. J.T. Jones and his wife, were engaged as teacher and matron for the girls in residence. Soon the school's numbers rose to 36, with parents paying $8 a month toward the youngsters' keep.

Within two years, however, things went horribly awry. Jones and his wife were dismissed after Jessop found that the teacher was moonlighting as a teamster and had used the school as a hostelry for travellers on the Cariboo Road to bolster his meagre teaching salary. Jessop reported the disastrous state of affairs besetting the school in his 1876 Annual Report to the legislature:

> The building which was so well provided with every requisite two years ago is almost destitute of kitchen and dining room furniture. The great amount of breakage of crockery, lamps, lamp chimneys, table forks . . . must have been the result of carelessness on the part of the authorities in charge. The first-class cooking stoves are much damaged and nearly burnt out. One of the doors is completely broken off its hinges and the panels of another are split. Since the completion of the addition to the building last autumn, several panes of glass have been broken. The entire edifice has therefore a dilapidated appearance.[22]

The Provincial Boarding School near Cache Creek in the province's interior was opened in June 1874 but would soon be surrounded with scandal and, eventually, cost the province's first superintendent of schools, John Jessop, his job. Amid other problems, J.T. Jones, the school's principal vanished from the educational scene in 1876 following a failure "to hand in his accounts." **Courtesy B.C. Archives A-03501.**

But matters did not end there. A new principal, Mr. A. Irwin and his wife, again in the capacity of girls' matron, were employed, along with a Victoria schoolteacher, Richard Clemitson, who was charged with acting as Jessop's deputy in overseeing the school.[23] Clemitson's assignment was to supervise the schools east of the Cascades, "to drum up business for the schools," and to "unravel the tangled web into which the affairs of the Cache Creek Boarding School have been allowed to be twisted," as *The Daily Colonist* newspaper put it.[24] What the newspaper was referring to was the allegation that some of the young girls at the school were visiting the boys' dormitory at night. The idea of sexual high jinks both titillated and offended polite Victorian society and unleashed a storm of criticism, much of which was levelled at Jessop.[25] Unfortunately, even with Clemitson's help, Jessop was unable to quell the public and political furor that came to surround the Cache Creek incident and, under tremendous pressure, Jessop was forced to resign in 1878.

The firestorm of blame surrounding events at Cache Creek was likely the province's first major political scandal and encapsulated many of the issues and tensions that would characterize British Columbia politics and education in the century and a half to follow. The Cache Creek scandal illustrates for the first time in provincial history the struggle between the interests of central government and local officials, the competition between public and private agendas in economic life, as well as the contest for power between bureaucrats and ordinary British Columbians, rural and urban constituencies, and those who are and are not supported by the public purse. The following three letters express these historical themes and chronicle various aspects of this first great public scandal in British Columbia history from divergent points of view: the teacher in charge of the school; the deputy education superintendent dispatched to sort things out; and a prominent and ambitious up-country political leader who served on the school's board of trustees. As these letters show, even in the Victorian Age, nothing was simple when politics was involved.

1877: A. Irwin's letter to John Jessop

Cache Creek, B.C.
March 21, 1877

Dear Sir:

About three weeks ago I made the discovery that the girls had, on at least two occasions in the dead of night, left their dormitory, passed down stairs, unfastened the door between the dining room and the passage leading to the boys' dormitory and entered the boys' dormitory; and that they had as often admitted the boys into their dormitory. (I may here explain that the door before alluded to was fastened from the inside of the dining room so as to prevent the boys reaching the girls' room. I never for a moment supposed that the girls would be the aggressors.)

The first offence happened sometime before Christmas; and it was repeated some six weeks ago. I may also explain that the discovery was made through a quarrel arising among the girls, some of the smaller and not guilty ones, through spite, informed Mrs. Irwin on the guilty ones. Otherwise, I am convinced, from the slyness with which these irregularities were carried on and from the untruthfulness of the children when previously questioned that they might have continued for a much greater period undetected.

After making these discoveries I meted out such punishment to the guilty parties as was at my disposal, and purposed bringing the matter before the trustees and having the ringleaders expelled. The trustees were to meet the following Saturday, (it was Thursday I became acquainted with the above facts) so I mentioned the matter to no one. However, the trustees failed to meet. I then told Mr. Clemitson who was as much surprised as I had been. He decided to call a meeting the following Saturday. In the meantime James Uren was taken from the school to assist in collecting his father's cattle, and as soon as possible he made the affair public. Only for this occurrence, I am convinced that it would have been kept from the public ear, until after the trustees had met and investigated the matter. The trustees hearing such reports, met sooner than the time proposed by Mr. Clemitson. They questioned several of the girls and afterwards called upon myself to answer to the charge of neglect in not locking the girls in their dormitory. I replied that it was a precaution I had never been instructed to take, and a precaution that I would not take on my own responsibility on account of the danger from fire, sickness, and that it was opposed to my ideas of inculcating the higher principles of trust and morality—principles which, if inculcated by recourse to lock and key, are not likely to withstand the temptations which are likely to assail them on their leaving school. I was then dismissed from their council, and on the following morning was requested to tender my resignation, which I did, to take effect on the first of April next.

(Signed) A. Irwin[26]

1877: R. Clemitison's letter to John Jessop

The Daily British Colonist

The following letter from deputy education superintendent R.M. Clemitson to superintendent Jessop summarized Clemitson's understanding of events. This correspondence and the account of things it rendered soon found its way into the local newspaper:

Dear Sir:

I intended writing last week, but certain disclosures recently made with respect to the immorality of some of the scholars here, led me to postpone my letter until the trustees should have met and considered the question.

The immoral acts complained of have stretched over a period commencing about Christmas last, and closing some short time before the matter was brought to Mr. Irwin's [the teacher in charge of the boarding school] notice, which occurred during my absence—I think on February 22.

Hoping that the unfortunate business might not become public, Mr. Irwin thought it advisable to defer consulting the trustees till their regular meeting . . . Since that time the trustees have held two special meetings, the first being for the purpose of deciding upon such steps as might be considered necessary to mitigate, if not to obviate, the harm likely to spring from the scandal becoming widely spread.

The majority of the trustees present (Messrs. Sandford, Park, Semlin, and Barnes) decided, Mr. Park opposing, to call upon Mr. and Mrs. Irwin to send in their resignation—a course which, in my opinion, will have a tendency to injure the school rather than satisfy the public mind. At that meeting I gave my view as to the proper course to be pursued—to expel such of the scholars as, after a thorough investigation, should be proved to be the ringleaders, letting it be known that these scholars were expelled in order to protect the interests of the school.

I felt convinced then, and am strengthened in my opinion by the expression of public feeling that I have since heard, that the general sense of the community would endorse such a course: but the trustees took a different view and deemed it imperative on them to suspend Mr. and Mrs. Irwin; charging them with neglect of duty and want of proper supervision.

The specific complaints urged by the trustees may be briefly stated thus: first, neglect of duty in not locking the door of the girls' dormitory every night. Second, want of proper vigilance as evinced by the fact of the long continuance of the immoral practices. Third, breach of duty in failing to report to the trustees at once.

With regard to the first charge I may say that I consider it a very dangerous and imprudent step to keep the door locked. In case of fire breaking out in the dining room at night, the most difficult place to reach . . . would be the very door which should first be opened; and certainly, if I were teacher of the school, I should decidedly refuse to lock the door on my own responsibility. If there is anything blameworthy in leaving the door unlocked, which I do not for a moment admit, then the trustees clearly must be guilty parties, since they never instructed Mr. Irwin to do any thing of the kind; and I am convinced that had any accident occurred through the door's being locked, the trustees would have been the first to censure the teacher.

Taking the second charge, I can only judge Mr. and Mrs. Irwin by myself. In fact, it is plain enough that, as my bedroom was closer to the dormitory than the bedroom occupied by Mr. and Mrs. Irwin and since, on that account, I was in a better position to detect any surreptitious action on the part of the pupils, I am much more culpable than the teacher and matron . . .

With regard to the third charge, I have already spoken to Mr. Irwin's intention of bringing the subject before the trustees at their first meeting. Knowing the members of the board as thoroughly as I do now, and guided by the imprudent and unfair behavior of one of them since the meetings, I feel quite satisfied that their outcry against Mr. Irwin on this score has [been] prompted more by an unworthy feeling of pique than by any sincere conviction that there had been remissness on the teacher's part . . .

I have no intention of saying anything that may seem harsh or overdrawn, but I cannot close my eyes to the effect that the horrible state of social life here must have upon the children brought up under the influence; and there is no doubt in my mind that the trustees should have exercised sufficient self-denial, if it required any self-denial, to have allowed their children to remain at school during the whole of each term, and then the rule could easily have been made general. This continued absence from the hurtful and polluted influences surrounding the home life of many of the children must have had a much stronger tendency to eradicate evil impressions and to build up the higher and nobler life of the scholars than the pernicious system could possibly exert.

Unlike today, when provincial or municipal authorities are responsible for school construction, the province's rural settlers in the nineteenth century and the early-twentieth century were directly responsible for the provision of schools and were expected to construct local schools themselves. Here one work party is preparing to build a school in the Burgoyne Valley on Salt Spring Island, c. 1896. **Courtesy Salt Spring Island Archives.**

Our school is now reduced to 15, a falling off of 11 since my last mention of the attendance . . . With regard to the future management of the school, I am of the opinion that the direct control should be vested in the teacher and deputy superintendent of education; or, in case of a continuance of the trustee system, the board should be reconstructed and the personnel raised by the selecting of men, not only of experience, but of sufficient independence of thought to place them beyond the influence of mere expediency . . .

R.M. Clemitson[27]

1877: C. Semlin's letter to *The Daily British Colonist*

Clemitson's account of events was roundly disputed by Charles Augustus Semlin, a member of the school's trustee board and an important cattle rancher with 1,500 head of cattle and a ranch of some 12,000 acres, at that time one of the largest ranches in the province. Semlin was one of the individuals originally most instrumental in establishing a boarding school at Cache Creek. He was elected a member of the first Provincial Legislature in 1872 but was defeated in two subsequent elections in 1875 and 1878. Semlin was not content to let matters rest with a private communiqué to Jessop. Ever the politician, Semlin sought to put his version of events before the public and did so by writing a letter denouncing Clemitson and accusing Jessop of blaming the trustees for the scandal. The following paragraphs appeared on the editorial page of the province's most influential newspaper:

Will you allow me to trespass upon your space for a time in order to criticize Mr. Clemitson's letter to Mr. Jessop of March 20, 1877, and which is given to the public in your weekly issue of April 18. I have no doubt that Mr. Clemitson feels a certain amount of vexation . . . but this I contend gives him or no just man a right to denounce a whole community as he does, when he speaks of the horrible state of social life here . . . He says that we are not qualified by experience or social standing for the position. It is a well-known fact that social lines are not drawn very tightly up here, and that at our social gatherings all are invited and all are welcome. We have little or none of the kid-glove gentry among us—we are all workers in the hive of human industry. Mr. Clemitson with his nice salary may think he is entitled to some special distinction. Rumour says he receives $1,800 for his onerous labours—looking after Cache Creek School . . .

No wonder he is a believer in his own superiority, and from the top of his $1,800 salary looks down on the trustee board who works for nothing. If the deputy's social standing is as much above the trustees as his pay is greater than theirs, then, indeed, there is a difference. He speaks of the want of experience on the part of the trustees, as though the board was composed of a lot of boys. Now, I think I am right in saying that there is but one man on the board who is not in years an older man than this deputy who prates of experience. Again, he urges that the board has not the judgment necessary for the discharge of its duties. Now, when, in goodness name, did our much-paid and little-worked deputy make this discovery? Where have we excluded the law, in what have we shown such silliness as to merit the report this man sends of us? He has been in possession of our minute book since his arrival here and must be familiar with its contents. If it displays a want of judgment would it not have shown better sense on his part to have pointed that out to the persons in charge than to have written a virulent letter . . . condemning the board in such a wholesale manner.

The proceedings of the board as shown in our minute book were submitted to Mr. Jessop on his visit here and approved of by him. I think Mr. Clemitson came to all his conclusions an evening or so before he wrote to Mr. Jessop, or the first time he differed from the board. But surely this man; though new to power and the responsibilities of office, cannot be new to the fact that very decent men may differ and still be very decent men nevertheless. The majority of the board differed widely from the deputy, and those men would not be an echo for anyone, no matter how great his salary . . .

But can anyone doubt the sources of Mr. Clemitson's spleen against the trustee board? Is it not plainly a case of let me have my own way? And the coolness with which this Salan advises the government to abolish the trustee board and let the deputy and teacher run the institution![28] Now, that is just what they have done all winter, or ever since the arrival of the deputy, the board merely discussing financial matters, the control of the school being in the hands of the deputy and teacher.

Now, after the experience of the past winter I think it would become Mr. Clemitson well to speak very modestly about the continuance of that style of schooling. The school might be run in that manner probably all right if the engaging power could be fortunate enough to secure the services of the right men to fill the positions, but certainly they would want men of more judgment and experience than those who filled the offices last winter. How does the deputy reconcile the fact of the surroundings with the fact that the school has been running for three years with the same surroundings, as far as the neighborhood is concerned, and it was not until surrounded by the deputy superintendent that its greatest misfortune befell it?

C.A. Semlin
Cache Creek, April 28[29]

1883: "Advantageous to amalgamate"

C.C. McKenzie

When Jessop resigned in protest over a reduction in salary—a thinly-veiled stratagem to remove him from his position—Colin Campbell McKenzie was appointed as British Columbia's second superintendent of education. McKenzie came to British Columbia in 1859 and held various teaching posts on Vancouver Island, culminating in 1870 with his principalship of the Boys' School in Victoria. McKenzie was equipped with an M.A. from Cambridge and was first in a long line of gentlemen scholars who directed provincial schools from the 1870s to the end of the 1950s. In his 1883 report to the legislature, McKenzie observes that single-school districts are too small a unit for sensible governance and advises consolidating such districts into larger ones to save government money. The idea of collapsing small districts into larger governance units has remained a persistent theme in the province's school history to this day as provincial governments look to economize on the costs of governing and administering schools:

The question of the number of trustees for a school district was discussed, but though some advocated an increase from three to five trustees it was argued that the former was more workable . . . The opinion was also expressed that in the course of time it would be advantageous to amalgamate adjacent districts, and as an instance the case was given of the three districts in the Saanich Peninsula with nine trustees that could be amalgamated into one district with three trustees.[30]

1884: "The advantages . . . of frequent inspection"

Stephen Pope

Provision for a school inspector, a position distinct from the provincial education superintendent, was first made in the 1879 *School Act*[31] and in the budget estimates of 1882, when $100 per month was allocated for a "temporary inspector of schools."[32] The position was not filled until July 1887, when David Wilson was appointed as an inspector of schools to oversee a system that now boasted 5,300 pupils and 118 teachers.[33] In 1884, superintendent Stephen Pope, the province's third education superintendent, made the following strong case to appoint an inspector of schools:

> The advantages to both teacher and pupils of frequent inspection are manifold, but the schools of the province are so scattered that it is impossible for the superintendent to spend the time necessary in order to visit as frequently as desirable even those schools that are easily accessible. The increased clerical work of this office, consequent upon the enlarged number of schools, precludes the possibility of his giving to them that amount of supervision which he knows to be indispensable to their efficiency. The schools of the city of Victoria, now employing 17 teachers, require more frequent and thorough inspection than it has hitherto been in his power to give to them. The appointment of a practical and thoroughly competent person, who could not only act as inspector of schools, but also assist in the clerical work of the office, would be a great benefit to the interests of education, and in the end prove a wise economy.[34]

1887: "Tall, green, shy, and awkward"

J.B. DeLong

British Columbia's teachers and educational officials in the late-nineteenth century were mostly easterners, in large part people from the Maritime provinces who came west in search of opportunity. One such individual was New Brunswicker J.B. DeLong, one of the first two high school inspectors employed in British Columbia and a figure of legendary stature in provincial education from 1913 to 1946. Here he recounts how he became a teacher, a principal, and later a school inspector within the context of late-nineteenth century family and school life:

I was the only one in the family who cared anything about school. Ours was an elementary school with one teacher and probably 20 pupils. We were not wealthy by any means—we picked wild strawberries, raspberries and blueberries and sold them in the Fredericton market. Socks and butter were also included in the market offerings. We had a few sheep. Mother washed the wool, carded it, spun it and wove it into cloth. Our suits were all homemade. I can still see the big spinning wheel and the enormous loom. I said we were not rich but there was no scarcity of good food. Buckwheat pancakes and pork for breakfast, lots of vegetables and apples and preserves. In the fall we used to kill a young beef, hang the carcass in the barn, let it freeze and cut a piece off when needed. There was always plenty of milk and cream.

During my last year in the Kingsley School we had a university graduate, who because of disciplinary troubles was unable to hold a position in a large school. He was a very odd man but I think I got a great deal from him especially in English and high school arithmetic. Mother decided I should have an opportunity to get an education so we moved to Fredericton when I was 12. I enrolled in the Charlotte Street School and was put in grade seven. The principal was very apologetic but said he had no option as I had not taken French, Latin, algebra, or geometry. The next year grade eight was moved up to the Fredericton High School so I had four years there with a Mr. Foster as principal. Mr. Foster was by far the best teacher of mathematics I have ever seen.

I was very tall, green, shy and awkward. I imagine my clothes were not very stylish. When I was in grade 10, I consented after much coaxing to turn out for rugby. I give rugby the credit for a great change in me. I overcame my shyness to quite an extent and took an interest in school affairs. Miss Etta Phillips and I graduated from high school with an average of 86 per cent and won two book prizes. I worked in Hall's Bookstore while going to high school. I used to open the store and sweep out at 7 a.m. After school I looked after Mr. Hall's horse and barn. I worked out many geometry exercises on the barn door.

My memories of normal school . . . are not very thrilling. The teachers were not outstanding except the principal, who afterwards went to South Africa to organize the school system there after the Boer War. I was captain of the rugby team, editor of the school paper (*The Normal Light*) and valedictorian . . . My first school was Prince William where I had all grades from the receiving class to matriculation. I did most of the work with the matriculation pupils after the elementary pupils had gone home. We seldom left school before 5 o' clock . . .

The next year I taught at Hawkshaw (grades 1 to 8). I was principal of the Harvey Station Superior School in my third year of teaching. I drove to Fredericton one weekend to write two subjects which I needed for entrance to second year of university. While in Fredericton, the chairman of the Fredericton School Board asked me if I would be principal of the Charlotte Street School until Christmas. A Mr. Mills had been hired to take this school but he would not be available until after Christmas. I got someone to take my place at Harvey and moved to Fredericton. My idea was to try to keep up the university work and attend university after Christmas. I played on the university rugby team but was not able because of my schoolwork to do much with the university subjects. After Christmas I took the principalship of St. Mary's Superior School. This school had a very bad reputation. The pupils made things so tough that two principals had been forced out. My first day there I had to handle two boys roughly but had no trouble after that. All the grade eight pupils passed the government examination at the end of the term.

I graduated with first-class honours in economics and philosophy. After graduation I taught in the following schools: Havelock Superior (one year); Milltown High (four years); [and] Hampton Consolidated (two years) . . . I was very proud of the Hampton Consolidated School. There were five divisions. I had all the high school grades. [We taught] home economics and manual training two days a week. We had a boys' basketball team, a girls' basketball team, a school magazine (printed), and a school garden. Debates were held from time to time. Parents were invited. The girls served refreshments. The assembly hall was usually filled. I left the school 50 years ago. I have not seen a school as small as Hampton that carried on so many extra-curricular activities. The school of this modern day and age could learn a great deal from the Hampton School . . .

I taught one and one-half years in British Columbia at King Edward High School in Vancouver. Dr. Robinson, superintendent of education in Victoria, came to my classroom . . . and asked me if I would take the job as inspector of elementary schools and told me he would appoint me inspector of high schools when Mr. MacLaurin was made principal of the Victoria Normal School. My districts when I had the elementary schools included the schools of Vancouver Island, the Gulf Islands, North and West Vancouver, the north side of the Fraser as far as Agassiz.

When I started inspecting high schools I had all the high schools in the province. This included the schools of Victoria and Vancouver. I visited 185 teachers but luckily there were only two schools in the north—Prince Rupert and Prince George. When Mr. Sullivan returned from overseas we divided the high schools. I had the schools in the east half of Vancouver, South Vancouver, Burnaby, New Westminster, the schools on the north side of the Fraser as far as Deroche, the schools in the Okanagan and the Kootenays.

I planned on calling on every teacher twice a year but was unable to do this every year. I had many interesting experiences during the three and one-half years I visited elementary schools. The teacher of the Gambier Island School used to enroll a dog and a cat and marked their attendance in the register each day. These brought the attendance up to 10—the number necessary to keep the school open.[35]

1890s: "A strange man appeared to be following her"

Jan Gould

Journalist Jan Gould is noted for her book, *Women of British Columbia*, and for assorted stories aired on CBC radio. In the following passages, Gould reminds us that the coming of the school inspector at the end of the nineteenth century was occasionally an event long remembered by teachers and students:

A woman teacher had to do a job that met with the approval of local school trustees and her personal life had to be circumspect or they were likely to report her to the school inspector. In early days, mail often took weeks to deliver and transportation was dependent on weather so a school inspector's arrival sometimes came as a complete surprise.

At Spences Bridge in the 1890s, young teacher Miss Hopkins ran over to her neighbor, Jessie Ann Smith, complaining that a strange man appeared to be following her everywhere. What should she do? Mrs. Smith advised her to open the school as usual and promised to send her husband to the school to keep an eye on everything. No sooner had Miss Hopkins started the day's work than she glanced out of the window and saw the stranger marching up the school path. With the help of the larger children in the class, she pushed hard against the door. The stranger pushed from the other side. Harder and harder she and the children pushed until finally they gave up and stepped back. The stranger staggered into the room and fell to the floor. 'I am Mr. Cowperthwaite,' he said slowly as he picked himself up. 'The school inspector.'[36]

1892: "At first Mr. Walker didn't speak Kwakwala"

Harry Assu

Kwagiulth Chief Harry Assu has been described as a "gentle, honourable man whose knowledge of his people reaches across his own experience to . . . childhood memories of elders' stories from the time before European contact." Here he tells of the missionary school experience common to many aboriginal youngsters of his generation:

> The Methodist Mission sent a permanent teacher to live at Cape Mudge [at the south end of Quadra Island}, and in 1892 R.J. Walker arrived with his family. We set aside 2.3 acres for the Mission . . .
>
> We didn't want a single man as a missionary. We had single men come and stay only a year or so and leave . . . We built a house of milled lumber for the Walkers and had it ready when they came. Then Mr. Walker and the men of the village built the school. It was where the nursery school is now. It was only a one-room school, nothing fancy, but it was our chance to learn. Children were taught arithmetic, spelling, and English. Older people in the village came to the

A horse and cart belonging to B.C. Bedding Company at rest in front of Vancouver's Central School, the first important school building to be constructed in the young city c. 1890s.
Courtesy City of Vancouver Archives P807.

school to learn. At first Mr. Walker didn't speak Kwakwala. He spoke English in the school, and we soon got on to it. We could speak our own language in the playground or anywhere else. There was no problem about it like there was up at Alert Bay, where they thought Indians could only learn English if they forgot their own language.

Having a school at Cape Mudge meant the children didn't have to leave home and go away to school at Alert Bay. A few from around here had to go there because of problems in the family. My wife Ida's father died when she was four, and her mother died when she was seven, so she went to that home [boarding] school. Lucky for her; she really liked it.

At first the church services were held in the school. Mr. Walker preached in Chinook. He taught belief in God and Jesus Christ. We had printed hymnbooks in Chinook and Kwakwala. There were picnics and Christmas presents and Sunday school and later on there was hymn singing. The missionaries taught about the holy land and stories from the Bible. We still have a magic lantern and slides in our church that must have been used to show these things. Mr. Walker and his wife worked hard for the church here. They were always helping the people.

The Methodists were against strong drink and gambling. They wanted to keep people from trying to break up marriages, and they tried to stop the prostitution of Indian women in the logging camps around here . . . Our big problem was bootleggers selling liquor to our people. We were always trying to keep them out of the villages. I have heard that my father and Mr. Walker used to patrol the beach off our village at night when they learned that ships from San Francisco were on their way up here selling whiskey. It was in little bottles, and it must have been terrible stuff because it drove people crazy.

By the time I was ready to go to school, Mr. Rendle had taken over from Mr. Walker. He stayed the longest of any teacher at Cape Mudge, from 1904 to 1918. We liked him and I liked school. There were around 20 of us. We behaved in school. We wanted to learn. Oh, that Mr. Rendle was a busy man! He called in on the people in all our villages and the logging camps and was visiting the sick and getting them out to hospital. I used to run his open boat for him, and we were always on the go.[37]

1893: "A casual remark made by a teacher"

William Burns

William Burns was born in England in 1843 and was educated at Queen's University in Kingston, Ontario, before he came west to teach at Victoria High School. He was appointed in 1892 as the province's second school inspector and, in 1901, was made the principal of the Vancouver Provincial Normal School where he remained until he retired in 1920. Here he underscores an important theme in late-Victorian life—the public's expectation that teachers should serve as exemplars of moral living:

> Habits of temperance and morality can always be inculcated by the teachers, not necessarily in formal lessons, but in modes far more effective, namely, by occasional remarks, for which our textbooks furnish ample opportunities to any one desiring to use them, and especially by the example set before the children by one to whom they should look up to as worthy of imitation in every respect. Which of us does not remember in later years a casual remark made by a teacher on some subject, whereas the formal lesson itself has faded from our memory. Surely, then, it becomes our teachers to be careful that every work and action of theirs tends towards urging their pupils to lead a moral life, and to see that neither by example nor by precept they shall ever give one man or woman cause to regret having been under their influence during the impressionable years of childhood.[38]

Notes

1. Susan McRae, "Public Sentiment Towards Education During Jessop's Superintendency, 1872-1878," unpublished paper, University of Victoria, 1992, 5.
2. *The Daily British Colonist*, 25 July 1876, 2.
3. *The Daily British Colonist*, 5 March 1876, 2.
4. F. Henry Johnson, *A History of Public Education in British Columbia* (Vancouver: University of British Columbia Publications Centre, 1964), 88. For a discussion about the success of early public systems, see Thomas Fleming, "Canadian School Policy in Liberal and Post-Liberal Eras: Historical Perspectives on the Changing Social Context of Schooling, 1846 - 1900," in *Journal of Education Policy*, Vol. 6, No. 2, (1991), 183-199.
5. *The Daily British Colonist*, 27 August 1878, 2.
6. From the earliest beginnings of public education, provinces across the country set strict limits on the discretionary authority granted to local boards by carefully specifying trustees' duties. British Columbia's first school legislation in 1872 made it clear that local boards of education would be restricted in what they could do.
7. *The Daily British Colonist*, 18 April 1872, 3.
8. British Columbia, *Annual Report of the Public Schools 1888-1889* (hereafter ARPS), 50-51.
9. ARPS, 1872-1873, 40.
10. ARPS, 1873-1874, 21.
11. Ibid., 10.
12. ARPS, 1874-1875, 25.
13. ARPS, 1875-1876, 25.
14. Ibid., 26.
15. From 1872 to 1892, superintendents seem to have done all this clerical work themselves unless they "borrowed" help from the Provincial Secretary's Office, following a long-standing but "invisible" practice in which one government department rotates staff to another when one office is busier.
16. *The Daily British Colonist*, 5 March 1876, 2.
17. *The Daily British Colonist*, 9 April 1876, 2.
18. Emily Carr, *The Complete Writings of Emily Carr* (Douglas & McIntyre: Vancouver/Toronto, 1993), 160-161.
19. *The Daily British Colonist*, 28 April 1877, 2.
20. Ibid.
21. Ibid.
22. ARPS, 1875-1876, 95-97.
23. Although David Wilson is generally credited as British Columbia's first public school inspector, this distinction, in fact, technically belongs to Clemitson whose work was essentially that of school inspection.
24. *The Daily British Colonist*, 6 October 1876.
25. British Columbia Archives (hereafter BCA), GR 450, Vol. 3, frame 287-299.

26. Correspondence, A. Irwin to John Jessop, 21 March 1877, cited in John Calam, "An Historical Survey of Boarding Schools and Public School Dormitories in Canada," unpublished M.A. thesis, UBC, 1962, 86.
27. *The Daily British Colonist*, "The Cache Creek school scandal! Frightful demoralization," 15 April 1877. The letter was originally dispatched 20 March 1877.
28. Salan refers to a tenth-century duke who advised the emperor of territories that later became the countries of Bulgaria and Hungary.
29. *The Daily British Colonist*, 15 April 1877, 2.
30. British Columbia Department of Education, *One Hundred Years: Education in British Columbia* (Victoria, B.C.: Queen's Printer, 1971), 22.
31. British Columbia, *Sessional Papers*, 1879 c. 30, 8, 2.
32. British Columbia, *Sessional Papers*, 1882, 419.
33. Wilson was born in New Brunswick, and taught school in New Westminster in the 1880s, before being appointed in 1887 to inspect the schools of the Lower Mainland, a territory he covered on horseback.
34. ARPS, 1883-1884, 157.
35. A photocopy of J.B. DeLong's "Memoirs," dated 1946, was given to Thomas Fleming by Bill Lucas in 1983. According to Lucas, this manuscript was given to him by someone in the education department during his time as inspector of schools. Lucas was appointed to this position in 1946, the same year that DeLong retired. See "Memoirs," 4, 5, and 9.
36. Jan Gould, *Women of British Columbia* (Saanichton, B.C.: Hancock House Publishers Ltd., 1975), 108.
37. Harry Assu and Joy Inglis, *Assu of Cape Mudge: Recollections of a Coastal Indian Chief* (Vancouver: University of British Columbia Press, 1989), 86-88, 90, 95-97.
38. ARPS, 1893-1894, 524.

Matriculating class from Vancouver's King George High School on a school excursion, 1916.
Courtesy City of Vancouver Archives CVA 371-794.

CHAPTER 3

Public Schooling's Golden Age: The Institution-Building Era, 1900-1919

The first two decades of the twentieth century represent a golden age in British Columbia education. During these years, all the modern institutional foundations of the provincial school system were built. The Vancouver Provincial Normal School was established in 1901 to provide the province's first formal agency for teacher training and certification. Four years later, in 1905, the British Columbia School Trustees Association was formed. In 1915, a second institution for teacher preparation, the Victoria Provincial Normal School, was established along with the University of British Columbia, the province's first independent degree-granting institution. Four years later, in 1919, the British Columbia Teachers' Federation (BCTF) was founded and, in 1920, the Education Office was granted formal recognition as a "department" of government. These years also witnessed the most ambitious school construction program undertaken to date, ushering in a golden age of schooling. Hundreds of impressive new schools were erected, some designed by the province's most influential architects, to meet dramatic increases in the province's population, especially in and around the city of Vancouver, which emerged during this period as one of Canada's most important centres.

Overseeing much of this development on behalf of the province was one man, Alexander Robinson, provincial superintendent of schools from 1899 to 1919. For much of his long career in educational government, Robinson was a power unto himself.[1] He made virtually every decision for the province's educational institutions, large and small. He decided everything from whether a rural community warranted a school, and whether a school board was in compliance with provincial laws, to selecting the colour of linoleum in normal school classrooms, and whether a flag or a gate in a schoolyard required replacement or mending. Robinson's years at the helm of school government were years of great change: Victorian sentiments about life and schooling gave way to those of the Edwardian Era and, after World War I's end, to even more modern views.

The writings that comprise the following chapter vividly document many of the educational and social challenges that marked this exhuberant era of school development. They illustrate the problems of rural schools, the inefficiencies in their operation, the tricks employed by local communities to keep schools open despite official regulations and, for the first time, the immense inequities that began to distinguish rural from urban schools. This period is also remarkable because we also see the growing influence of government on people's lives at provincial and local levels, the feminization of teaching as an occupation, emerging demands for women's rights to equality, and teachers' growing discontent with the adequacy of their salaries.

As settlement pushed deeper into the province's vast interior during the first two decades of the twentieth century, we are again reminded of the hardship of travel over rough country before the age of automobiles and paved roads, the dedication that children and teachers required to reach out-of-the-way schools, the sacrifices families were prepared to make to see their children educated, and the intrinsic respect immigrant parents demonstrated for an education they would never obtain themselves. Through children's eyes we also glimpse into educational worlds long forgotten where young ladies were called "Miss" by manners-minded teachers, where Latin was deemed essential for serious young scholars, and where dressing for school, like children's games at the time, involved long and complicated rituals. Teaching, we likewise discover, was something of an accidental profession for many, taken up when other plans were thwarted, or for reasons of economic necessity. In time, the ease of access into teaching and egress out of it would greatly reduce its attractions as a career and, sadly, its social and professional status.

1899: "Absurd to expect teachers to take the place of the parent"

The Victoria Daily Colonist

Editors were not hesitant to give families and the public advice about limiting teachers' duties to instruction, or the importance of instilling obedience and discipline in children. Just as the Victorian Age was coming to an end, here is what one editor was thinking:

> There is entirely too much disposition to shift upon the shoulders of the teacher work that ought to be performed by others. It is absurd to expect teachers to take the place of the parent; equally absurd to ask them to perform the work of a policeman, and quite out of the question to expect them to supply religious instruction. The difficulties in the way of the latter are so obvious that most countries are making their schools non-sectarian, if they have not already done so. It is of course right to require of teachers that they shall impress upon their pupils the duty of observing the law, even as children, the obligations of citizenship, but they cannot be expected to be responsible for the conduct of children out of school hours and the school premises. As far as parental duties are concerned, there is not one that can properly be delegated to the schoolteacher.
>
> If the schools take the youth of the country, give them a good ordinary education, instruct them in the fundamental principles on which the state rests and inculcate the duty of obedience, they have fulfilled their part. We lay great stress upon the duty of obedience . . . No fault can be found with the quantity of education imparted in the schools. If this is open to criticism it is rather because there is too much than too little of it. Little exception can be taken to the quality of instruction for it is as a rule thorough. But very great objection can be taken to the influence of the schools upon children from the

standpoint of citizenship. The obligation of obedience is not impressed upon the young mind with sufficient force, and it is needless to say that we do not mean physical force. We may apply this to the case of Victoria and say that much of the youthful vandalism, of which so great complaint is made, may be attributed to the failure of the schools to impress upon young boys their duty to the community in which they live. The very foundation stone of this duty is obedience. And so we may say to the teachers assembled in Victoria today that the cornerstone of their policy towards their pupils should be discipline. Perfect discipline is entirely compatible with freedom, for there is no liberty worth having except liberty under law.[2]

1899: "Not of a character to inspire confidence"

The Victoria Daily Colonist

Since the days of John Jessop, the superintendent of education's position was always a political appointment awarded "at the pleasure of the government." S.D. Pope's dismissal in 1899 necessitated the search for a new superintendent. Vying for the position were two candidates—Alexander Robinson, the Vancouver High principal who was eventually appointed and Hector Stramberg, principal of New Westminster High. In the following editorial, *The Victoria Daily Colonist* mistakenly refers to Robinson as "Robertson "in its criticism of the government's decision:

For much of the first century of public schooling in British Columbia, youngsters such as these children at Beaver Point School, Salt Spring Island (1901), obtained the rudiments of reading and writing in simple country schoolhouses from teachers often scarcely older than themselves. **Courtesy Salt Spring Island Archives.**

Mr. Alexander Robertson [sic], of the Vancouver High School, has been made chief superintendent of education. What Mr. Robertson's qualifications for the office may be, we do not know. He has been an ardent partisan of Mr. Martin and possibly this is sufficient.[3] The record of the Vancouver High School in the matter of university matriculation is not of a character to inspire confidence in Mr. Robertson's educational talents. It is able to show two university against 21 [high school students who graduated into university] for the New Westminster High School, whose principal was also an applicant for the office to which Mr. Robertson has been appointed. Even the [Victoria] *Times* finds itself unable to regard the appointment as satisfactory, and devoted its leading article last evening to an expression of regret that claims of Mr. H.M. Stramberg, of the New Westminster school, were overlooked. Mr. Stramberg is one of the most experienced teachers in the Dominion. He has been associated with educational work in this province for 18 years. He is a gentleman of high attainments and unquestioned ability and would have fulfilled the post with great satisfaction to the public. He has been ignored. Vancouver demanded the place and got it. There is a suspicion, perhaps more than a suspicion, that the attorney general preferred for the office a man who would have less of a mind of his own than Mr. Stramberg.[4]

1899: "A lasting sense of truthfulness in the child"

S.B. Netherby

Many values indicative of the Victorian Age were reflected in school inspector S.B. Netherby's pronouncements on education as illustrated in the following two passages:

The true teacher will endeavor to educate, in the true sense of the word, the pupils over whom he presides; he will draw them by precept and example into the paths of truth, honesty, charity and loyalty; he will instruct them in neatness, and how to become orderly citizens; and this will run concurrently with the development of the mental faculties and the imparting of knowledge. This will be his constant work; and following this, trustees and parents will remember that his value depends upon his influence in molding the character of his pupils.[5]

In the direction of discipline the progress is pleasingly satisfactory to all who are really patriotic. It is plain that we are building a national character that reflects no discredit on our country. In every department of school work accuracy in acquiring and stating facts is demanded; following this course without variableness or shadow of turning, the natural consequence is to create a lasting sense of truthfulness in the child.[6]

1901: "Sudden death of John Jessop"

The Victoria Daily Colonist

John Jessop's passing was noted in the provincial press and his educational attainments were duly celebrated, as was his immense strength of character as one of the members of the famous "overlanders" party of 1858 who walked from Ontario to what is now British Columbia:

The sudden death of Mr. John Jessop, which occurred yesterday, is the cause of general regret in a community that had known and respected him for many years. Mr. Jessop went to his office in the government buildings yesterday as usual, apparently in good health, and attended to his duties till about 12:30, when he left hurriedly to transact some business at the Bank of Commerce. He hastened across James Bay Bridge and was walking rapidly up Government Street, when he suddenly collapsed on the sidewalk. Passers-by rushed to his assistance, but almost before the first kindly hand had touched him his life had sped. It was known to a few intimate friends that the deceased had a weak heart, and possibly his haste to get to the bank before closing time produced the fatal palpitation.

John Jessop was born June 29, 1829, in Norfolk, England. His parents were John and Mary Phillips Jessop. The former died in 1894 and the latter in 1886. Mr. Jessop was educated in private schools and came to America in 1846, settling in Ontario County, Ontario. In 1853 he entered the Normal School, Toronto, where he obtained a second-class certificate, which he taught school on for one and a half years, when he returned to Normal and secured a first-class certificate, after which he taught for three years and a half. He then started on foot to British Columbia via Fort Garry, where he spent two months, and in August 1859, with one companion, reached Fort Ellis; then, with six others, crossed the prairies and mountains via Boundary Pass and Tobacco Plains, and reached Colville on November 5. Proceeding with one companion he crossed the Cascades and reached Victoria on January 1, 1860, eight months from Toronto. He spent some time in Cariboo, where he engaged unsuccessfully in mining on Harvey and Keightly, and had to work out the following winter in New Westminster a debt of $120 . . . He built the old Central School . . . and, in 1861, started the *Daily Press* in Victoria, in partnership with Leonard

McClure. In August 1861, he commenced teaching a non-sectarian school which he continued until 1864, when the Vancouver Island free-school system was introduced with Mr. Jessop as principal of the Victoria schools. He helped to frame the first school act of British Columbia. During 1872-1878, he was superintendent of schools for the province, and, resigned in the fall of 1878, joined the *Colonist* staff, of which he was a member for two years.

He was appointed provincial immigration agent in March 1883, which position he held up to his sudden demise. Mr. Jessop was in politics a conservative, and in religion a Methodist. He was a member of the Masonic order. Deceased was married in Victoria on March 31, 1868, to Miss Margaret Fausett, daughter of William Fausett, M.D. of Dublin, Ireland, who died in 1897.

Mr. Jessop was a devoted and valued member of the Methodist Church, to which he rendered faithful service for many years. He served as trustee in connection with the Pandora Street Church for 39 years, and for many years as secretary of the joint board. In early days he was superintendent of Sunday schools, and during all his life was a generous subscriber to the church. He was several times a member of the annual conference, and in 1894 was representative to the general conference in London. His only surviving relative in Victoria is a niece, Miss Scott.

The funeral will take place tomorrow afternoon at 2:45 o'clock, from the Metropolitan Methodist Church, Pandora Street.[7]

1901: "The board will have to take the advice of the ladies"

The Victoria Daily Colonist

Among the new social forces unleashed at turn of the twentieth century were more strident demands on the part of women for social, political, and economic equality. Amid suffragette marches for women's emancipation in New York, London, and other world centres, women in Canada's newest province were also demanding recognition of their rights. British Columbia's most important and outspoken women's advocate was the progressive-minded educator, Agnes Deans Cameron. Miss Agnes Deans Cameron was entirely the product of the British Columbia school system in the latter part of the nineteenth century. She graduated from Victoria High School's inaugural class in 1876, taught initially in a private school, and then in public schools in Comox and Vancouver. Cameron returned to Victoria in 1890 to become the first female high school teacher in the province and, soon after, principal of South Park School. Miss Cameron garnered

Miss Agnes Deans Cameron. Courtesy B.C. Archives AO-1143.

widespread provincial attention in her day as an advocate of great causes including the liberalization of immigration policy, human rights, women's suffrage, and equality. In many respects, Cameron was typical of a well-educated, strong-minded and self-sufficient group of socially-involved women who were beginning to make themselves heard in the late Victorian Age.

As the following newspaper account reveals, Cameron was insistent on equity in all things, including teachers' salaries:

> 'The lady teachers heartily approve of any move to give the gentlemen of the city teaching staff an increase of salary,' said Miss Agnes Deans Cameron, principal of South Park School, yesterday, when approached for an opinion as to the attitude of the ladies toward the proposal to increase the salaries of male assistant teachers as decided upon by the trustee board at its meeting this week.
>
> 'What the ladies do not approve of, though,' continued the lady principal, 'is the setting up of precedent for any other basis of remuneration for teachers than that of services rendered. In other words, the lady teachers are one in the opinion that it is a vicious principle to establish any basis of payment of salary as that of sex. With the move to have the standard rate of wage increased the ladies are in full sympathy, but if that is done in the way that seems to be the intention, it will be a most unfair discrimination and one that has never yet been recognized, though in many minor ways it has long been tacitly attempted to discriminate in favor of the men who teach in the city schools.

> From Miss Cameron it was gathered that the ladies had been getting their heads together to decide what action was necessary to protect themselves from the discrimination they see about to be established. They think that not only will it be grossly unfair to them, seeing that many of them have not only devoted themselves to the profession for years but spent long periods of training and preparation specially fitting themselves for the work, and that they are not in it only for a day. They intend to remain, while many of the young men look upon teaching as merely a stepping-stone to some other profession more attractive and remunerative. The ladies also urge that the establishing of a different standard of wages for the men from that paid to women, will result ultimately in driving men out of the profession altogether just as it has done elsewhere . . .
>
> Miss Cameron said there was a move of some kind to be made by the ladies but they had not yet had a meeting to consider what form it would take. They wish to work together with the gentlemen and hope that the latter will be ready to recognize the justice of the claims of the ladies for equal rights as far as salaries are concerned . . . As having the longest service record in the city schools, Miss Cameron is in a position to form a fair opinion on the effect of the move the board has announced as its intention tentatively to make, and she unhesitatingly says it will be retrogressive and demoralizing.[8]

1901 and after: "The fear of God into every one of us"

The Lake News

Three decades after the school inspectorate had closed, a journalist recalled the effects inspector A.C. Stewart had on Okanagan Valley schools. Stewart served as an inspector from 1901-1909 and from 1920 to 1931:

> There was one terrible day which was just as though a huge black cloud had come across the whole valley, and that was the day the school inspector came . . . He put the fear of God into every one of us, he put the fear of God into the teacher.
>
> The inspector, A.C. Stewart, caused one of the older girls to cry and even once caused a teacher to leave the school to be found later, crying, by one of her pupils, convinced that the inspector's poor report of her school would damage her reputation as a teacher.

For reasons best known to himself, the inspector was always attired in black—black bowler hat, black three-piece suit, dark necktie, black shoes, and black umbrella in case of rain, and this funereal appearance did not create an impression of good will nor of cheer. And, although in childhood he may have mastered the art of smiling, somewhere along the way he had forgotten the secret.[9]

1901: "Suspensions of Miss Agnes Deans Cameron and Miss Mary Williams"

The Victoria Daily Colonist

Miss Agnes Deans Cameron was almost never out of the news for one thing or another. On this occasion, along with her colleague Miss Mary Williams, principal of the Girls' School in Victoria, she defied the superintendent of city schools, Frank Eaton, over practices used in promoting pupils:

Rumors of serious friction between the city superintendent and some of the principals of the public schools were current in the city yesterday. Inquiry confirmed the reports of trouble, which culminated yesterday morning in the suspension of Miss Agnes Deans Cameron of the South Park School.

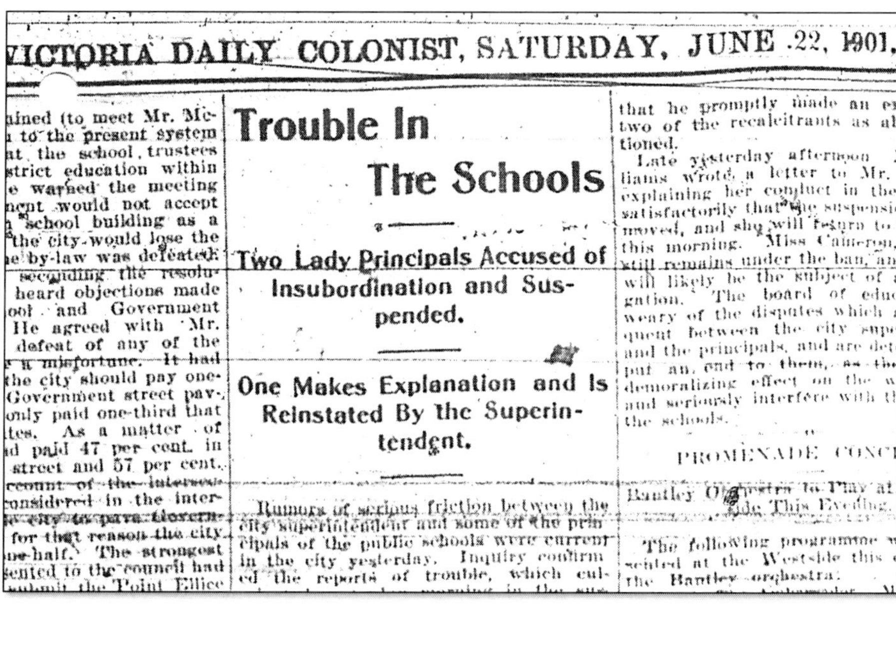

VICTORIA DAILY COLONIST, SATURDAY, JUNE 22, 1901.

Trouble In The Schools

Two Lady Principals Accused of Insubordination and Suspended.

One Makes Explanation and Is Reinstated By the Superintendent.

Rumors of serious friction between the city superintendent and some of the principals of the public schools were current in the city yesterday. Inquiry confirm ed the reports of trouble, which cul-

The difficulty arose from a conflict of authority between the superintendent and the principals, regarding the observance of the new regulations governing promotion examinations. The new rule is that oral examinations shall be substituted for written ones in all the subjects except two . . . This, it is alleged, did not meet the views of certain principals, and they resolved to ignore the instructions of Mr. Eaton and continue to use written tests as under the old system. The principals are accused of having so far forgotten their duty of obedience as to hold a meeting and decide to openly defy the superintendent, but they strenuously deny this, declaring that the meeting was held for a wholly different purpose.

The matter was brought to the attention of the trustees, and they referred it to Mr. Robinson, superintendent of education, who regarded it as so serious that he promptly made an example of two of the recalcitrants as above mentioned.

Late yesterday afternoon Miss Williams wrote a letter to Mr. Robinson explaining her conduct in the affair so satisfactorily that the suspension was removed, and she will return to her duties this morning. Miss Cameron, however, will remain under the ban, and her case will likely be the subject of an investigation. The board of education is weary of the disputes which are so frequent between the city superintendent and the principals and are determined to put an end to them as they have a demoralizing effect on the whole staff, and seriously interfere with the work of the schools.[10]

Teachers learning rural science in Victoria, 1914. **Courtesy B.C. Archives D-07298.**

1902: "When I passed into Miss Cameron's classroom"

Ada McGeer

The first woman to teach high school in the province, Miss Cameron was well known for her strong educational views and her insistence on high academic standards. Here, a former student recalls her experience in one of Miss Cameron's classes and some details of the principal's life:

After several primary years at private schools, where I learned nothing, my parents decided to send me to South Park Public School which was near our home. This was in 1902, when I was 12 years old. School then became a delight rather than a drudgery, particularly when I passed into Miss Cameron's classroom.

The school is in a lovely part of Victoria, near the northern end of Beacon Hill Park. We lived at the southern end. Every morning on my way to school, I would see Miss Cameron returning from her daily walk through the park. She always wore a tailored suit, becoming to her slim mannish figure. When the bell rang, we lined up in the schoolyard and marched into the assembly room to say the Lord's Prayer, sing the national anthem, and listen to any pithy comments concerning the school and ourselves, which Miss Cameron saw fit to make. I well remember the day I was the embarrassed subject.

A well-known Shakespearian company had come to Victoria to perform *The Merchant of Venice*. As a publicity ploy, one of the newspapers offered a prize for the best essay on the play, written by a pupil. I sent my contribution in without consulting anyone, not even checking the spelling of the characters' names. As I won the prize, the newspaper printed my essay, incorrect spelling and all. The next morning at assembly Miss Cameron read it to the whole school, making scathing remarks on my carelessness and the dishonour I had brought the school. After 70 odd years, I still remember my humiliation. Hers, too, apparently for she had already selected me to pass first into the high school!

Miss Cameron taught all the subjects for high school entrance, except drawing. The teacher for this subject was a poor disciplinarian and so her lessons were periods of high jinks for the class. When our drawing books were submitted as part of our final entrance exams, the examiner failed many of the class, contending that we had drawn most of the freehand lines with a ruler. I got a bare pass mark that pulled my average down considerably.

A bitter controversy arose between Miss Cameron, the examiner and eventually the school board, which ended in the whole class being summonsed to appear in court. We all enjoyed showing our drawing books before the fatherly judge, who settled the matter satisfactorily for both sides. I remember another altercation carried on for some time between Miss Cameron and the city council over the proposed extension of Birdcage Walk, now Government Street.

At that time the street ran from Belleville, past the legislative buildings, as far as Michigan, where it stopped smack in front of the Cameron house. Mrs. Cameron, in her 80s did not wish to leave her home. From her front windows she could look down Birdcage Walk as far as the James Bay Bridge. She could see the homes of her two married sons and those of other pioneers, like herself. She could chat over the fence with her neighbors such as the Carr girls, including Emily 'with her outlandish ideas and painting kit.' Her indomitable daughter delayed the action of the city with every device she could think of and succeeded, until her mother settled the matter by dying in 1906 at the age of 84.

There were other contentious matters in Miss Cameron's life at this time, which finally ended her career as a schoolteacher. This proved to be a blessing, for she then devoted her life to writing, lecturing and travel, which brought her world fame. But there are many of her pupils who remember her for her criticism of

The first Vancouver High School c. 1893. **Courtesy City of Vancouver Archives LGN 480.**

outmoded ideas and her untiring work for school reform. It is the fortunate child, who, in the course of school days, encounters a teacher that kindles a spark for learning. Agnes Deans Cameron did this for many of her pupils. Thankfully I was one of them.[11]

1903: "Pouring out money so lavishly"

Alexander Robinson

A massive increase in the province's population during the first decade of the twentieth century led to an ambitious school building program and placed enormous burdens on provincial coffers. In the following comments, provincial superintendent Robinson complains about rapidly rising expenditures and recommends that the capital and operating costs of schools be more fairly shared between provincial authorities and taxpayers in the new and prosperous British Columbia:

> The total cost of education will soon absorb a larger proportion of the provincial revenue than any other single service in the estimates. As a matter of fact, it is now exceeded by one item only . . . the interest on the public debt. It is quite impossible to cut down the cost of supporting our rural schools, especially

Schools were frequently the most impressive architectural constructions in the golden age of schooling from the late-nineteenth century to the end of the 1920s, as this photograph of the East End School c. 1890 illustrates. **Courtesy City of Vancouver Archives SGN 47.**

those in the isolated parts of the province . . . It becomes imperative, therefore, that a change be made at once in the policy heretofore followed of pouring out money so lavishly to populous and comparatively wealthy centres such as Vancouver, Victoria, Nanaimo, and New Westminster.[12]

1905: "Safer in the hands of a central administration"

The Vancouver Province

The control historically granted to school trustees by provincial officials over most aspects of schooling was generally small. Government authorities set standards for school construction, teaching supplies and furnishings, even though, in some cases, trustees were themselves obliged to build and furnish early schools. Constraints were placed on trustees for several reasons. Trustees were generally not perceived by the public as men and women of learning and their authority, such as it was, was diminished by the perception that they were incapable of providing the stewardship that the institution of schooling warranted. The formidable challenges of nation building, province building, and the crusade for social progress seemed to be tasks far beyond the understanding of small-thinking village politicians. Moreover, those who served in local school government, it was argued, could simply not represent the larger public

Mount Pleasant School, Vancouver, c. 1893 looked very much like a cathedral.
Courtesy City of Vancouver Archives, SGN 45.

interest. The editor of the *Vancouver Province* newspaper forcefully made this point when he commented in 1905 on the inaugural meeting of British Columbia School Trustees Association (BCSTA):

> We doubt, however, whether on the whole anything of value has been accomplished by the meeting except to awaken the trustees themselves to the facts that the requirements of one locality are not those of another and to make it manifest that the interests of the province at large are safer in the hands of a central administration than when placed in those of the municipal boards . . . The public will be at a loss to understand the desire displayed by certain members of our local board to secure for the trustees the handling of money. It seems to us that it is much better that the school board should direct its attention rather to securing value for expenditures than the control of funds.[13]

1900-1920: New Educational Cathedrals

Turn-of-the-century programs to construct new schools were unprecedented in their ambition—not just in respect of the large numbers of schools slated for construction but, also, in the attention increasingly directed to the quality of the schools themselves and to the space and equipment requirements connected to the new educational and social functions of schools. Toward such ends, provincial and local authorities employed prestigious architectural firms to oversee school construction. W. Ridgeway Wilson, Thomas Hooper, Hooper's student C. Elwood Watkins, and J.C. Keith consistently won open competitions for school design in Victoria and on Vancouver Island.[14] Watkins' presence was particularly prominent in Victoria where he designed and oversaw construction of six major city schools and one smaller school between 1909 and 1921.

The most important of the new schools were the high schools, some of which were imposing structures and comparatively palatial in quality when set beside other institutions at this time. Particularly significant for their size and architecture were two Vancouver high schools, King Edward and Britannia, established in 1908 to replace the old Vancouver High School. In nearby municipalities, South Vancouver High was established in 1912 and, a year later, Point Grey (later renamed Magee). Other schools followed—King George in 1914, Cecil Rhodes High School of Commerce 1917 (later Fairview High School of Commerce), Kitsilano High in 1918, Prince of Wales in 1919, and Fairview Junior High in 1922, to name but a few.

New school buildings were also accompanied by changes in curriculum developed by the provincial Education Office in Victoria. As enrollment increased, and the province developed its economic and industrial importance, so did pressure increase to make school subjects more vocationally relevant, and less focused on the academic and classical studies favoured by the educated elite of the nineteenth century. As the twentieth century began, the curriculum was stretched beyond academic subjects to include courses in woodworking and metal working for boys, needlework and cooking for girls, co-educational typing and bookkeeping classes and, in response to a Dominion Government initiative aimed at encouraging young people back to the farms, an agricultural program in the form of school gardening.

1903: "As efficient and attractive as possible"

A.C. Stewart

Proposals to consolidate small school districts in the interest of efficiency reach back to the late-nineteenth century. However, beginning in the early years of the twentieth century, intermittent calls were expressed about the need to amalgamate rural districts, demands that would be taken up more seriously by Putman and Weir in their school survey of 1925 and by H.B. King and the education department in the 1930s. Here, school inspector A.C. Stewart offers his views on the "inefficiency" of small schools and the need for consolidation:

Vancouver's growing prosperity and size was amply reflected in the construction of King Edward High School. **Courtesy City of Vancouver Archives CVA-99-996.**

> The inefficiency of the small isolated rural schools to meet the requirements of modern education has led, in 18 states of the American union, to the movement known as the centralization or consolidation of rural schools; and an experiment along this line is now being inaugurated in each of the eastern provinces of Canada . . . It is all-important in this country, and especially in this province, that the rural school should be made as efficient and attractive as possible.[15]

All Decisions, Small or Large

The province's chief school officer, the superintendent of education, "sat next to God," or so it was said in the Victorian educational universe. From stately offices on Victoria's Government Street, provincial superintendents controlled the entire educational system by "remote control" through the postal service and a small corps of school inspectors. All decisions, small or large, fell under their purview, even into the mid-decades of the twentieth century. Between 1872 and 1919, only four individuals held this high educational office.[39]

Although nominally supervised by ministers, the government's senior civil servants were given a remarkably free hand during the first century of public schooling in determining governance and administrative policies for schools. Archival records, as well as Putman and Weir's report of 1925, amply illustrate this.[40] What this meant was that the educational civil service enjoyed wide latitude from political

King Edward High School c. 1912 with pupils on north playing field.
Courtesy City of Vancouver Archives CVA 7-228.

"interference," certainly by today's standards. Indeed, prior to the appointment of UBC professor, George Weir, as education minister in 1933, no cabinet officer likely held a coherent view about education, or understood the role that education could play as part of a government's larger social agenda. In the absence of strong political control, educational policies came to be made rationally and out of public sight in the quiet of departmental offices by senior education officers, typically middle-aged grey-haired men who were, by their own admission, "mild progressives and small 'l' social liberals."[41] Once made, these decisions were rarely challenged, at least openly, by public or professional constituencies, or were subject to much in the way of second-guessing by school professionals. Special interest group influence, or public pressure, commonplace in government today, was largely unfelt by members of the education department before the 1970s.

Alexander Robinson

Between 1899 and 1919, Alexander Robinson served as British Columbia's fourth education superintendent, and presided over the greatest era of educational growth to that time in the province's young history. "Ministers of Education came and went," school inspector Alex Lord later said of Alexander Robinson's influence, but "Robinson was the Department of Education. There was never any doubt about that." During his tenure, Robinson served eight premiers—and acted also as civil service commissioner for three years. Following his dismissal from government, Robinson spent a brief and unhappy time as principal of Victoria High School (1919-1921). He finished his career as an English and classics teacher at Oak Bay High in Victoria.

Born in New Brunswick, Alexander Robinson was a brilliant scholar, a gold medalist at both the Fredericton Normal School and Dalhousie University, and was renowned for his love of the classics, particularly Latin. Robinson moved to Vancouver in the early 1890s to become principal of Vancouver's first high school.

In 1899, Robinson was appointed British Columbia's fourth superintendent of provincial schools, a position he held for 20 turbulent years, outlasting 16 Ministers of Education (four in 1903 alone). During his tenure, the number of schools in British Columbia grew from more than 300, including seven high schools, to 900 with an enrollment of approximately 90,000 and a staff of 3,000 teachers. Robinson established the first Provincial Normal School in Vancouver in 1900, from which generations of young men and women left to teach in hundreds of rural schools scattered around the province. Prior to the First World War, Robinson laid much of the groundwork for the establishment of the province's first university (UBC) which opened its doors in 1915.

Alexander Robinson **Courtesy B.C. Archives HP-51916.**

Despite a reputation as an obstinate, intolerant pedant of "definite views" and "uncertain temper," Robinson was greatly admired by the provincial education community for his high educational standards, hard work, and his efforts to modernize the school curriculum by including technical courses for boys and girls.

1906: "Tsar of a scholastic empire"

The Vancouver World

As the following editorial indicates, not everyone was in favour of the immense power and influence over teachers and trustees that superintendent Robinson wielded in the Education Office. Here the editor rails against the provisions of a new school act that would allegedly allow the province's chief school officer to reach into every classroom:

> Alexander Robinson, B.A., superintendent of education, is henceforth to be known . . . as the tsar of a scholastic empire . . . Included in the new education act which went into effect in January is a clause giving the superintendent the power of dismissing any teacher in the province . . . Framed for the purpose of enabling the department to deal with the cases of unfit teachers who impose themselves upon rural boards and wander from school to school, the new regulation is an instrument which may be used most oppressively and the very existence of which will simply stifle criticism of the department by those

IN REPLY TO
No. Vesuvius North

EDUCATION OFFICE,
VICTORIA, Sept. 16th, 1901

THE GOVERNMENT OF THE PROVINCE OF BRITISH COLUMBIA

Miss M. J. Mouat,
North Vesuvius School,
S.S.Island, B/C.

Madam,

In compliance with the request contained in your letter of the 14th inst. the Department hereby grants the 25th day of September as a holiday to allow the children of your school to attend the S.S.Island Agricultural Fair.

I have the honour to be,
Madam,
Your obedient servant,

Alexander Robinson

Superintendent of Education.

Superintendent Robinson's long reach into the province's schools was legendary. He controlled almost everything in the provincial educational universe. Here he grants permission to Miss Margaret Mouat to close the North Vesuvius School to allow children to attend an agricultural fair, an educational event of no small importance in a province still far more rural than urban.

best fitted to criticize it, the teachers of the country . . . Needless to say the regulation renders quite powerless the trustees, the representative of that local public opinion which often protects and supports the teacher when there is a collision with the central authority. No matter how highly the board may value the services of a principal or an assistant, he or she must now be discharged should the autocrat of James Bay so proclaim.[16]

1907: "And . . . Chinese school after that"

Gordon (Won) Cumyow

Gordon (Won) Cumyow was a son of Won Alexander Cumyow, the first person of Chinese descent to be born in Canada. Like his father who was a court interpreter in

New Westminster and, later, in Vancouver, Gordon Cumyow also became a court interpreter and was the first notary public of Chinese descent in Canada. Here he recalls his father's great reverence for learning and describes some of the challenges facing Chinese immigrants on the West Coast during the first decade of the twentieth century:

> My father was a self-made man, you know. He went to school whenever he had a chance, and as a matter of fact, he went and studied law too . . . My father talked Chinook. His father, having opened a store in Port Douglas [at the northern end of Harrison Lake in the Lillooet region], a lot of Indians patronized him. So that's how my dad learned to speak Chinook. As a matter of fact, back when the Indians couldn't talk English, they talked Chinook, my dad used to interpret for them in police court. It must have been strange to see a Chinese talk Chinook . . .
>
> My father sent us to school when we were six, and then made us go to Chinese school after that. That was killing, spending five or six hours in school and then, at half past four, I'd have to come down to Chinatown and go to Chinese school until half past seven, then go home and do my homework. We lived up in Grandview; my father didn't want us to get mixed up with certain elements in Chinatown. In those days, it was more or less of a bad influence down here, when the gaming houses were wide open and the police were raiding them, and opium was being smoked. My dad wanted to keep us away from that.

Chinese children in Victoria walking to school at the turn of the twentieth century.
Courtesy B.C. Archives F-06763.

> At one time, servant girls were brought over from China as daughters, they got around immigration that way. They used to treat the servant girls very good, except in Victoria where they did abuse them. That's why the Methodist church started that girls' school, to give the Chinese servant girls refuge, [girls] who'd been abused by their owners. It could be either one, the man would abuse her sexually or his wife would lick the daylights out of her. [The Methodists] taught them English and they taught them Chinese, gave them an education. And of course, they converted them to Christianity. The Methodists did a wonderful job in Victoria there, just cut slavery right out practically, knocked the bottom out.[17]

1910: "Some children had been 'imported'"

Harold Campbell

Like countless other British Columbia teachers, Harold Campbell began his first teaching assignment at $63 a month in a one-room rural school in an "up-Island" community, Campbell River. Campbell River, like many small coastal communities in B.C., struggled to establish a permanent school. In 1910, the first students to receive formal instruction were taught in an older part of the resort hotel known as "The Willows." "I would sit in the bar on Saturday nights—I didn't take a drink in those days—and watch the loggers," Campbell later recalled. Here Campbell, who later served as the province's deputy minister of education (1953-1958), described his time at his first school in Campbell River:

The growth of North Vancouver was reflected in the construction of the schoolhouse at Lynn Valley c. 1910. **Courtesy City of Vancouver Archives A-677-856.**

I was the first schoolteacher in Campbell River. That was in 1910. There was nothing there in the Campbell River village except two hotels, the old one and the new one, the Thulin house and the general store, that was a Thulin enterprise as well. The Thulins had made this room available in the old hotel for the school. They had 'imported' two or three families to get the school open.

The only way of getting to Campbell River was by Union steamship. I got in around 1:00 in the morning, so I went up to the hotel and sat in the lounge until 7:00 or 8:00 o'clock.

I'd had no teacher training. I was just out of high school. I knew Dr. Robinson, the superintendent of education, because his son and daughter attended high school with me and I used to be at their home frequently. So I went over with some papers of my father's (my father was a school principal) and Dr. Robinson said, 'What are you going to do, Harold'? I said that I'd applied for a job with the government civil service in Ottawa. 'Oh,' he said, 'You won't get it. Your father's too good a Liberal.' So he said, 'I need a teacher for the Campbell River school. You haven't had any training but there were good teachers before there ever was teacher training.' He said, 'You come from a teaching family, your knowledge is very fresh, so I'd like you to take this school.'

As I recall it, the inspector of schools had visited the district in the spring of 1910, and had counted 10 children who were supposed to be available before a school could be authorized. As was the custom, I suspect that some children had been 'imported' for the occasion from Lund and waypoints. In those days such schools were called 'assisted schools' which means that the government paid the teacher and provided maps and text books, while the district had to provide the school, wood and water, and other necessary supplies. A ratepayers' meeting was supposed to be called, three trustees elected and a sum of money voted to meet the expenses of the school. The government was supposed to be notified of the amount of this sum and it was included in the provincial tax for the district and sent to the secretary of the school board, who was one of the trustees. In most cases, however, the pioneers disliked taxes so they took up a collection, or had dances in the school, or gave a day's work, or provided a load of wood. In the case of Campbell River, I suspect that Mr. Thulin, the only significant taxpayer, provided everything for the first school.[18]

A Typical Teacher

Miss Margaret Mouat was entirely a product of the provincial school system and her tragically short life and death were typical of the late Victorian Age. Pictured here at about age 15, with one of her brothers, the handkerchief in her hand signified the tuberculosis that would shortly thereafter take her life. Overcrowded and poorly-ventilated schoolrooms in rural areas contributed greatly to the spread of infectious diseases among children in the early decades of provincial schooling. It was also thought that the tight corsets dictated by fashion during the Victorian Age constricted women's lungs.

The daughter of a well-known store owner, Miss Mouat completed seven grades in a one-room school at Vesuvius on Salt Spring Island, passed her high school entrance exams (for which she received a magnificent diploma), and boarded off-Island in Nanaimo where she completed two years of high school. Her high school studies entitled her to a temporary teaching certificate. She later completed a year at the Provincial Normal School in Vancouver and returned to the Island to teach at the same school she attended as a youngster.

Courtesy Ivan and Sue Mouat.

1911: "Dressing for school in winter"

Clare McAllister

Clare McAllister attended UBC in the 1920s and has contributed reminiscences to UBC's archives on her time as a student. Here she recalls her days as a child and the lengthy protocols associated with dressing for school in rural British Columbia:

Dressing for school in winter involved a child in quite a bit of winding [wrapping]. I am thinking back to a time around 1911, when I would have started school in British Columbia's West Kootenay.

For me, as a small child, heavy, black cotton, ribbed drawers buttoned at each hip were the cold weather winter garment. There were heavy ribbed, black cotton stockings to put on, over. First the drawers' long legs had to be wrapped carefully, tight round each ankle, the stockings then cautiously pulled over the underwear, hopefully leaving the pant legs still neatly and tightly round. A long white vest had been slept in all night, affording additional warmth under a heavy flannelette nightgown. For daytime wear a 'waist' was put on over the 'shirt' (which was what we mostly called an under-vest). The waist was a sort of bodice, double layers of heavy cotton, additionally strengthened with tapes sewn over its surface. It was perhaps a hangover from days when young girls would have to be prepared for later wearing of a corset?

The new cosmopolitanism on the West Coast in the early-twentieth century was reflected in fashionably-dressed teachers on school outings. Here a teachers' group can be seen picnicking on Denman Island. **Courtesy B.C. Archives A-07081.**

Its purpose, beyond warmth giving, was to serve as a point of attachment for garters. Some called those suspenders, but, in our house, suspenders were what help up men's pants. Each garter had a metal nipper to hold one elastic strand to the waist; this bifurcated below, to hold two elastic strands, each terminating in a metal nipper, two to a stocking top. The next wrapping task was to get the stockings over each underwear knee without too much bunchiness, and held by garter nippers, with just enough slack to permit movement. One petticoat of cotton covered this assemblage . . .

The moment of being finally dressed (at least for indoor purposes) culminated, along with the rattling of the coffee grinder on the kitchen wall. The day's chosen dress, perhaps of scratchy, good wool, blue serge, dropped over the under-things. A dress might often be covered by a pinafore—a kind of sleeveless sack of cotton print. In the days before cleaning establishments, when mothers wished to avoid having to sponge spots off serge, pinafores were a useful labour saver—that is, if one did not think of washing and ironing and starching the pinafores!

What were the boys wearing? The boys, obscure spectators of feminine flutter. The old picnic photos show at mothers' skirts small boys in long cotton Buster Brown stockings, above their well-polished boots. Some wore sailor suits with short, and some with long pants. Later there were Knickerbocker pants for

Port Alberni youngsters in front of their school in the early-twentieth century.
Courtesy City of Vancouver Archives S-9222.

boys, buckled below the knees, with three-quarter hose over the cuff ends. For summer wear, even town boys might resort to that most comfortable of garments, the loose blue overall, with shirt well tucked within. Summer-hot boys wore farmers' straw hats. Winter found them wearing caps. Immigrant English small boys wore grey flannel pants, striped belts and round grey felt hats. The dashing young males, those affluent enough to proceed on to high school, were indeed gloriously arrayed. Most conspicuous were their bright silk socks—red, purple, Paddy-green.[19]

1913: "I wondered if I'd come out safely"

J.B. DeLong

To ensure that teachers throughout the province followed the prescribed curriculum, and that their teaching methods were effective, the provincial government relied on a corps of school inspectors to enforce departmental standards. One of the earliest and most famous of these men was J.B. DeLong, who visited thousands of classrooms during his long career as an elementary and high school inspector (1913-1946). In the following passages, he describes various episodes that made his days in schools memorable:

When I was inspector of elementary schools I started out one day to visit the school at Salmon River. The steamer landed me at the mouth of the river where the tide was low. I learned that small boats from farther up the river could not navigate the river at low tide. Accordingly I had to walk about five miles to reach the school. I made the trip in a pouring rain and met the teacher and some of the children coming home from school. I got them to go back to the school and stayed about an hour with them. I spent the night at the house where the teacher boarded. She rustled some underwear and outer garments for me while my soaked clothes were drying. The clothing must have belonged to a man a foot shorter than I so I must have been quite a spectacle.

When I inspected the schools on the north shore of the Fraser, I made my headquarters at Haney or Mission. Automobiles were very scarce in those days so I had to get a team of horses from a livery station. In order to reach a school at 9 o'clock I often had to leave at 7.

My first special [assignment] was to a district up the coast. The people had asked for a school. I went up to see if they had a sufficient number of children. I was told we had reached the place. A rowboat was put in the water and I was rowed to shore. I thought it strange they did not have a wharf if they thought they had enough children for a school. I saw a group of shacks about one-half mile away. I clambered over the rocks but found the shacks deserted. I climbed a tree and located a house across the water two or three miles away. I decided the only thing I could do was to get into the rowboat where I had landed and row across to this house. The rowboat was the kind one had to row standing up. I started out but decided the task was impossible. I then noticed a trail leading up the mountain. I climbed the mountain and followed the trail about a mile into the woods and came to a bunch of bunkhouses. The last shack was the cookhouse. The coffee pot was warm so I decided there were some people around.

After about an hour's wait two men appeared. One of them told me this was Dempsey's Logging Camp that the camp was shut down for the season and that they were left to look after the place. I had lunch with them. Each of them ate half-a-dozen eggs and thought there was something the matter with me since I ate only three. I was told I was two miles away from the place I was looking for. One of them rowed me down there after lunch. I learned afterwards the steamers called at the wharf only at high tide. The man who brought me to my destination would not accept any money for his trouble. He told me his companion refused to talk, that he went all day and every day without saying a word. He said I am going to kill the son of a gun if he does not start talking soon.

Smith Inlet is many miles up the coast.[20] The people asked to have a school opened there and I went up to check on the number of children. The steamer deposited me at the mouth of the Inlet. I was met there and was taken by rowboat quite a distance. Then I had to walk about a mile through the woods. I found quite a settlement of one-room shacks. There was one two-room house occupied by a Scandinavian with his wife and a daughter about 12. I had to stay with them a week until the steamer returned. I slept with the man in a homemade bed. The wife and daughter must have slept on the floor in the other room. My host went out every morning trying to get a deer for me but was unsuccessful.

I had to stay a week at Ucluelet. The water was so rough the owner of a motorboat I had engaged to take me to Alberni refused to make the trip. I was forced to wait for the steamer.

It was my practice to stay a week at Lund when I was inspecting the Island schools in the northern part of the Gulf of Georgia. I hired a motorboat, visited a school in the morning, ate lunch on the boat and inspected another school in the afternoon. An isolated settlement in this locality sent in a petition for a school. I arrived there at midnight and got the people out of bed to learn how many children there were of school age. I have gone through the Green Point Rapids and Seymour Narrows in a motorboat and wondered if I would come out safely. I am the only inspector who, up to that time, had visited the Cape Scott School [at the tip of Vancouver Island].

I left Port Hardy in a motorboat which took me to Shushartie Bay. There I changed to a larger boat for the rest of the trip to Cape Scott. I remember it was a beautiful day (June 1). The Pacific Ocean looked perfectly calm but the breakers on the shallow shore were as high as houses. I had no desire to go back the same way so I dismissed the owner of the boat and walked back to Shushartie Bay (10 miles). There was an excellent stand of timber and very fertile soil at Cape Scott. Perhaps there will be very thriving communities there some day.

One day I had lunch with a family on one of the islands. The father had had a very successful business in Victoria. He gave up his business and moved his large family up to this island. We ate in an outside building with a dirt floor and no door. The chickens hovered around picking up crumbs and pieces of bread thrown to them. They all seemed quite happy. It is hard to understand how they could be satisfied with a life so different from what they had been used to in Victoria.[21]

In almost all parts of the province, geographical barriers and extreme distances made transportation to and from school a major hurdle. If youngsters lived within three miles of school there were expected to walk. In towns and cities, a bicycle shortened the time, if not the distance, for those fortunate enough to have them. In rural areas, an old and reliable horse helped with the journey and, around many schools, a fenced field or a lean-to shelter could be found for the care and comfort of the animals. For the children in Summerland, there was a horse-drawn school bus as this 1909 photograph shows. **Courtesy B.C. Archives D-07919.**

1914: "Latin scholars by the yard"

Bernard Gillie

Bernard Gillie was born in Victoria in 1907 and was educated at Strawberry Vale in Saanich outside Victoria and at Oak Bay High School in the eastern part of the city before attending the Provincial Normal School in Victoria. After a teaching stint in northern British Columbia, he taught outside Kelowna before returning to Victoria where he was principal at S.J. Willis Junior High. For many years he was an influential member of the BCTF and an ardent supporter of university education for teachers. In 1962, he was appointed superintendent of education for the Northwest Territories, a post he filled with distinction until he retired in 1972. Here he recounts details of his family life, his early days at school, and the individuals who taught him:

> I'm a member of a pioneer family. My people have been in Victoria for 135 years. My great grandfather came here in 1858 and we've been in and around this province ever since. The year 1872 was the year my mother was born here. I was born here in Victoria. I went to school out in Strawberry Vale in a little one-room school in 1914. The little one-room school—a red schoolhouse—is still there and still in use, not as a school but as a kindergarten or pre-school. My mother and father owned a farm out there in Strawberry Vale . . . My father was a cattle rancher in the Nicola Valley until he lost his eyesight . . . My most memorable tasks, and they were tasks which I really did enjoy when I look back on it now, were reading the newspapers and books and magazines that came to him.
>
> I went to Strawberry Vale School until I wrote the then-infamous high school entrance examinations in what would be the equivalent of grade 8 today. It wasn't called grade 8 in those days. It was called 'entrance.' You were in the 'entrance' class. That was the end of public school. I wrote the government exams in 11 subjects (how did they manage to dream up 11 subjects?) in what was then the Tolmie School. It was exceptional in that day for a student to go beyond the 'entrance' level. A relatively small percentage, very few youngsters, went on to high school.
>
> My parents were not wealthy by any means. My father was Scottish and, although he had a very limited education himself, he had a great respect and understanding, as so many Scottish people do, a 'reverence for education.' He and my mother were both thoroughly convinced that, through education, and if you wanted to, you could 'get anywhere in this world.'

In that day, there were no high schools in Saanich . . . Parents could send their children to Victoria High School, where my brother and sister had gone, or you could go to Oak Bay High School, or Esquimalt. The school board—the Saanich School Board, would pay your total costs if you went to Victoria High, but if you went to Oak Bay or Esquimalt—the fees were a little higher. Your parents had to pay the difference.

I used to remember the exact figures. It seems to me that it was $120 a year at Victoria High and I think the figure at Oak Bay was $175. I can remember very vividly that that meant a tremendous sacrifice on the part of my parents because my father was running the farm as a blind man with mother helping him.

Of course we had no car . . . In that day there was the old interurban railroad ran out there and we were close to where it was, and I came in and took a streetcar out to Oak Bay to visit the home of the principal of Oak Bay High School. He wanted to interview me to see if I was acceptable. I had a pretty good academic record. So he accepted me . . . I participated in most of the athletics at the high school. I played soccer. I even played cricket . . . There were five classrooms and the principal was H.P. Hope, who later inaugurated a private school which is now Brentwood College at Cowichan. He was a graduate of Cambridge and a very fine classical scholar . . . Anyway, Oak Bay was a well-known aristocratic area, largely British, and I remember being very shy just because I was not used to that kind of social environment.

Interestingly enough, one of the members of the faculty of Oak Bay High School at that time was Dr. Alexander Robinson, formerly provincial superintendent of schools, and principal of Victoria High School at one time also. He took over and he taught me two years of Latin. 'Sandy' Robinson was a 'character' in the best sense of the word. Tall in appearance with a great mane of white hair. He, obviously, had been a very handsome man. Slim. Carried himself well. Wore glasses of the kind that hooked over your nose and had an attachment on his vest. He simply loved Latin. In my earlier years I used to wonder, how could anybody love Latin? I didn't know anything about it. After two years with Dr. Robinson, I came to have a great interest in it really. He could stand up and recite Cicero and all the other Latin scholars by the yard, and he would, when he was teaching. He was a great one when he was teaching for pacing up and down. I remember this was one of the things in normal school they told us not to do, I remember, but he did it, and did it with such flair, with such a flourish, that your attention just never failed. Severe looking. Severe manner. Had very piercing brown eyes. I remember him in many ways. There were only four of us boys who took Latin.

My fondest recollection of Dr. Robinson was when it came to an Easter examination and I wasn't good in Latin. I got so I liked it in many ways, but I wasn't good at it, and I was very afraid, very nervous of this exam. I walked in the morning of this exam, sat down at the desk, and Dr. Robinson was there and he put the examination paper down and I started to read it through and, as I read it through, I was quite sure there was nothing on the exam that I could do. My mind went blank. I just couldn't think of sitting there any longer, and I got up and walked out. And of course, it was an extremely dumb thing to do, but it's the sort of thing you do on the spur of the moment. Dr. Robinson walked out with me, and I remember him putting his arm around my shoulders and saying, 'What's the matter, Gillie? Don't you feel well?' And I said, 'Yes. But I can't do the exam.' He said, 'Why not? And I said, 'There's nothing on that exam that I can look at.' He said, 'Don't be foolish. Just sit and look at it.' And I said, 'No. No. I can't. I'll fail.' He said, 'Let me talk to Mr. Downs, the principal.'

He went in and talked to Gordon Downs and he came back and Mr. Downs came with him. The two of them! Kindness and understanding. If they had said a harsh word, I'm sure I'd have walked out and never gone back. But they were understanding and sympathetic and helpful. And of course, I'd been out of the exam room now for half an hour and so I remember Mr. Downs saying, 'Gillie!' (We were always addressed by our surnames), 'Won't you go back? Give it a try!' And I said, 'Yes, sir, I will.' And I went back and sat down and wrote and did the best I could. I got a passing mark. That little incident, I guess was one of the most important turning points or decision points in my life. Had I not gone back, I wouldn't have gone any further in education, I'm sure.[22]

1914: "The teacher has no control"

J.B. DeLong

Here inspector DeLong describes more of his adventures in visiting schools around the time of the Great War:

One day in Creston, I had to leave a few minutes before school closed to catch the train but my rubbers had been hidden. The teacher finally found them and I proceeded to the railway station. The train was late and school was dismissed before it arrived. Two little girls from the school came up to me and told me that no one in their room had hidden the rubbers. I told them it did not make any difference. They said 'Oh! Yes it does because if you thought we did it you would think the teacher has no control over us and he has.'

One year when I visited Slocan City the chairman of the school board met me and told me the Anglican church had had no minister for some time so they asked the teacher to conduct the service. The chairman told me the first Sunday he preached an excellent sermon but the next Sunday he was so drunk he knocked the pulpit over. I understand he contracted quite a few debts. At the end of the school year the southern exit [of the city] was guarded by the people to whom he owed money but he fooled them by leaving by the northern exit.

The Nelson school board dismissed their high school principal because of poor work and lack of discipline. Friends of the principal started an agitation, called a public meeting and wrote many letters to the Education Office. The trustees were greatly worried and asked me what to do. I asked them if they thought they had done the right thing. They said they were sure they had. I told them not to worry that I would take the responsibility. I figured very prominently in *The Nelson News* for weeks. A new principal was appointed on my recommendation. Both principals appeared at the opening of school next term. The board finally got rid of the former principal by paying him $500. The superintendent of education summoned me to Victoria to state my side of the case. I told him I had told the trustees I would accept the responsibility. 'A very foolish statement to make' was his comment. I could not debate the matter with him but I knew I had done the right thing.

The principal of one high school punished a boy for copying during an examination. The father of the boy took the principal for a drive, manhandled him severely and told him the Klu Klux Klan would beat the life out of him if he remained in the school. The principal immediately resigned, came to my office in Vancouver and told me the story. I have only his word for the truth of the story. The man who made the threats was afterward a Member of the Legislative Assembly [MLA] and a minister in the provincial government.

Only once during my many years of inspection was I interfered with by a politician. A girl in her first year of teaching was unable to keep discipline. I advised her to resign and take a school away from home. Just after my visit she told her tale of woe to the MLA for her district. He asked me to call at his store and told me the girl could not be fired as her father was leader of the Italian community in his riding and they were the people who elected him. Needless to say the girl was dismissed.[23]

The teacher at Van Anda told me he had married his brother's widow. He said he had to support her so he thought he might as well marry her. The primary teacher there had two little girls (sisters) who used very bad language. She tried

> to cure them of the habit and thought she was getting along quite well. One day one of the girls walked to school with her and said 'Teacher I don't swear any more but my sister still swears like hell.'
>
> North of Burns Lake was a small community with a lumber mill called Pendleton Bay situated on Babine Lake. There was a two-room school there with sufficient pupils to justify two teachers. In early October the school population suddenly dropped to such an extent that keeping two teachers was ridiculous. On investigation I found 90 per cent of the school enrollment were [children of] native Indians and early in October the parents left for the winter to go trapping and, of course, took the children with them. I managed to find employment for one of the teachers and everything went along smoothly until early in May when the Indians returned from the trap lines and sent their children back to school. So I was faced with finding another teacher for two months.[24]

1914: "Reduced to tears"

Bernard Gillie

At the time of his appointment in 1911, W.H.M. May was one of eight school inspectors who patrolled the province ensuring that the province's school legislation and regulations were followed to the letter of the law. The classroom visits of such men were often feared by young schoolteachers who knew that a poor report on their performance might cost them their jobs. Here, Bernard Gillie returns to his own childhood days at Strawberry Vale on Victoria's outskirts to describe in unflattering terms school inspector May's icy approach to classroom supervision:

> I remember one inspector very well. He was famous all across the province, inspector W.H.M. May. Feared by everybody. We had some good teachers at Strawberry Vale, believe it or not. I can always remember him coming, and we all knew when he arrived, because you could see him coming into the school. The teachers were frightened to death, reduced to tears. And yet when I got to know him a little, and I did get to know him and his family in later years, he had some charming daughters that I thought were very nice, but he was a most repelling-looking man. Tall. Gaunt to the point of looking like a ghost. Almost like a walking cadaver. Unsmiling. Very pale faced. Steely blue eyes and rarely said a word. He would walk in with a kind of cat-like tread and everybody just froze. We just sat there in terror. And the teacher stood at the front of the room, equally in terror. He would look at us, and then he'd ask questions or write things on the board and ask you to analyze a sentence or whatever it might happen to be. Never a comment. Never a smile. Never a word of commendation. Rarely

ever spoke to the teacher. If I were to write a list of all the things that an inspector or supervisor should not do, he was the living example of it. Afterwards I got to know him a little bit and his family, a very shy, quiet, self-effacing man who could be in a room and you'd hardly know he was there.[25]

1915: "That teacher's rating would suffer"

Frances Decker, Margaret Fougberg, and Mary Ronayne

In *Pemberton: The History of a Settlement,* Frances Decker, Margaret Fougberg, and Mary Ronayne tell this story of rural schools and the non-pedagogical responsibilities teachers were expected to fulfill:

> When it was needed, usually the teacher lit the fire. In winter months, if classes were to start on time, with ink thawed, and children at their desks, the fire would be lit well before school opening; if not, pupils would stand for an hour or more, books in hand, close to the stove. One inspector, as superintendents were then known, arrived one morning very early at Pemberton Meadows School, even before the teacher. No kindling had been cut to start the fire and, even worse, the axe handle was broken. That teacher's rating would suffer.[26]

1916 and after: "All my schooling was in Victoria"

Dorothea Stafford

Dorothea Stafford, née Smith, was born in Victoria in 1908 and attended the city's elementary and secondary schools.[27] In the following passages, she recalls her days of childhood and adolescence in the schools of Victoria. Her description is remarkable in its completeness and because it provides a rare first-hand glimpse into a child's life in school almost a century ago:

> All my schooling was in Victoria. I first attended Burnside School. In those years, the present 'grades' were known by different names. Beginners entered 'first primer,' then 'second primer,' [before proceeding to] 'first,' 'second,' and 'third' readers. There probably was an extra year but I do not recall it. By the time I had finished the public school system 'grades' were replacing the other names. 'High school' was for three years [arranged according to] preliminary, junior and senior grades.

There were no kindergartens in the public school system. Many children started school with some knowledge of reading. Burnside School did not offer all the classes and I went on to North Ward School for my senior year. Before the end of the year our family moved to the Fairfield district . . . I went to South Park School on Douglas Street. I spent an extra year there because Mr. Allison Campbell, the principal, thought that I was too small and young to go to high school. I hadn't reached my 12th birthday but I was ranking in the upper half of the class. I repeated the year and finished second in a total of 72 pupils in two classes. I did enter high school just before my 13th birthday!

I remember Burnside School very well. It seemed so big in those days. The classes for the younger children were on the first floor with the older children occupying the second floor . . . Classes were called into the building by the ringing of a hand bell. Each class lined up in a designated place near the entrance closest to its classroom. Each teacher supervised the lineup of his or her class. The pupils marched in two lines up the steps and to the cloakroom adjacent to their respective rooms. Writing was taught very methodically. We did not print. With chalk, the teacher drew letters on our desks. Then she distributed a handful of split peas to each of us which we used to outline the letter. We were also probably one of the last classes to use slates and slate pencils! We brought rags from home to clean our slates and desktops. I can remember our first exercise books which we did not use until we had shown that we 'knew our letters.' Phonics was very much a part of learning to read. The teacher printed lists of words on the blackboard. Emphasis was placed on sounding out the syllables of new words after we had learned the basic one-syllable words by rote.

I cannot remember a library in the school but as I loved to read, I found that the Sunday school at Centennial Methodist Church had a library with a wide range of children's books. It provided adventure stories for boys and girls. I read the *Hardy Boys* series, *The Bobbsey Twins, Ben Hur* (fine print and only one picture) and others. The real treasures were the *Boy's and Girl's Own Annuals* from England with their variety of stories and pictures. I think I read these books before I was 10 years old.

One of my first teachers was Miss Kathleen Coates. She read books to us as a reward for finishing assigned work. We looked forward to hearing 'the next chapter' or the start of a new book. Unfortunately I cannot remember the names of these books but we looked forward to the reading sessions, particularly on Fridays. J.M. Barrie's *Peter and Wendy* and *Peter Pan* were given to me by Miss Coates as a spelling prize. Long before I went to high school I discovered that the public library on Yates Street was a source of books to read for pleasure as well as to give information.

Rules for Vancouver's Female Teachers - 1915

(1) You may not travel beyond the city limits unless you have permission of the chairman of the board.

(2) You may not dress in bright colours.

(3) You must wear at least two petticoats.

(4) You are not to keep company with men.

(5) You must be home between the hours of 8:00 p.m. and 7:00 a.m. unless attending a school function.

(6) Your dress must not be shorter than two inches above the ankle.

(7) You may not ride in a carriage or automobile with any man, unless he is your father or your brother. (No kissing cousin).

(8) You must sweep the floor at least once daily; scrub the floor at least once a week with hot soapy water; clean the blackboards at least once a day; and start the fire at 7 a.m. so the room will be warm by 8 a.m.[27]

I cannot recall too much about learning arithmetic except for the multiplication tables. We said these in unison and out loud in a sing-song manner. It must have been a good method as I learned them thoroughly . . .

Recess was the best time of the day for us. We went home at noon for lunch as most children lived within easy walking distance. We looked forward to recess when we were able to get out and play games. Some of these games are probably still found on school playgrounds. I am sure that each year when early Spring comes around, and the grounds are still muddy, little boys will be playing marbles and little girls will be playing jacks or skipping rope to little rhymes.

'Tag' was always a popular game. Its many variations included 'poison tag.' In this game the person tagged had to place a hand over the place where he was tagged before chasing another person. 'Hide-and-Seek,' 'Farmer in the Dell,' and 'Blind Man's Bluff' were the games played mostly by younger children. 'Statues' was a game where the leader swung his playmates around by one hand. When he let go the playmate had to remain perfectly still in whatever position he found himself. The new leader was the person who stopped in the most unusual, awkward position.

Group games were often played in a fashion similar to the dances of the late-nineteenth century. Two lines of children faced each other. In couples, one after another, hand in hand, each couple would skip to the top of the line and back again singing a little tune. Music was not taught as a subject but we were taught

Grade 1 pupils at Beacon Hill School, Victoria, 1914-1915. **Courtesy Dorothea Stafford.**

many songs. There may have been a piano somewhere in the school but there were no other instruments. As it was wartime, many of the songs we learned were patriotic ones. We knew, 'Rule Britannia,' 'The Maple Leaf Forever,' 'Hearts of Oak,' and most verses of 'O Canada' and 'God Save the King.' On the lighter side we sang 'Tipperary,' 'My Little Grey Home in the West,' and 'Drink to me Only With Thine Eyes.'

Our principal, Mr. T.W. (Tommy) Hall joined the army and went overseas . . . He was one of the most dynamic teachers I have ever met. He was very energetic. One day he came into the classroom where our teacher was telling us about Boadicea. Mr. Hall took over the lesson. He stepped to the front of the class, sat on the teacher's desk which immediately became a chariot as he told us the story of Boadicea in an interesting way. The blackboard pointer became a whip and as he urged the imaginary horses to go faster he swung the pointer high over his head. There was an abrupt end to the story as the pointer smashed the single light bulb hanging on its cord from the ceiling over the teacher's desk.

I know we were taught some history and geography from stories and maps. I remember that we had to identify rivers and bays in their proper places on a map of Canada. I vaguely remember a subject called 'civics,' which was probably a very basic study of government. It wasn't a favorite subject and it didn't seem to take much class time. Perhaps nine and 10 year-old children were thinking of more interesting things and teachers hadn't found a way to handle such heavy material with them.

I believe I was in one of the first classes in domestic science in a B.C. school at North Ward. We were taught sewing at the beginning of the year when we made the caps and aprons we were to use later in the year in cooking class. We learned to make buttonholes by making large ones in the caps through which a black ribbon was threaded. We looked like little English parlor maids! I still have my cap. We were also taught how to make a neat darn in a sock that we brought from home.

Tommy Hall was probably the best loved and respected teacher I had in the public schools I attended.[28] When he returned from overseas he went back to Victoria schools as a principal at George Jay School and later as an inspector of schools with the department of education. I saw him twice after my school days. Once was at the Willows' Race Track and Exhibition Grounds where he seemed to be in charge of a track and field meet for Victoria schools. The second time I saw him was a chance meeting at a bus stop on Richmond Road. He was retired and recovering from throat surgery. As we chatted I realized what a good memory he had. He recalled that as a very small girl I carried a handkerchief wadded in one hand. He asked me if I still did and my answer was 'yes.' I never saw him again.

Mr. Allison Campbell was the principal of South Park School and four teachers who taught grades 7 and 8 rotated instruction of the four classes. I was at South Park School for less than two years but they were happy ones. I remember that our classroom was very large, there were over 30 pupils and the teacher's desk was on a raised platform at the front of the room . . . I must have been getting more adventurous in those years as my friend Belinda and I 'played hooky' and in one afternoon we explored the Parliament Buildings. We even climbed up between the layers of the main dome and stood below the statue of Captain Vancouver!

I remember that lady teachers were unmarried but I never could tell whether they were young or old. Some were prettier than others and they all had long hair worn the way my mother wore hers. They were dressed in long dark skirts. They wore white shirtwaists [blouses] with high necks and long sleeves. A few wore pretty brooches or a watch on a fob pinned to the blouse. If a teacher married she stopped teaching.

Men teachers wore dark-coloured business suits, white shirts with stiff collars and cuffs and dark ties. It wasn't until I was in high school that I noticed both men and women teachers had become more casually dressed.

Willing to hazard all for King and country, here are two Vancouver high school officer cadets in full uniform c. 1913. **Courtesy City of Vancouver Archives CVA 99-24.**

In 'public' school little girls wore dresses or middy blouses or sweaters with dark skirts. We did not have the quantity or variety of clothing that the children of today enjoy. I can remember that I never had more than two or three dresses at any one time and one of these was kept for Sunday wear. They were all homemade by my mother. With these we wore petticoats. Our stockings were cotton rib knit, black for school and white for Sunday. Our shoes were black leather, low laced boots or black patent strap slippers (Mary Janes) for Sunday wear. Many of us wore hair ribbons. I wore them until I was 16.

Boys wore short pants or knickerbockers that fastened below the knee. Some boys wore pullover sweaters. Others wore jackets and white shirts with ties. They too wore sturdy black leather boots sometimes with metal toecaps to lengthen the life of the shoes.

I went on the attend Victoria High School on a three-year program. During that time I was aware of older students in classrooms on the top floor. They were the senior matriculation students (1915-1920) who would go on to college or university. In the years 1919 and 1920 there was a class of war veterans and it was strange to see some of them in uniform . . .

Victoria had only one high school [Victoria High]. Pupils walked to it, rode bicycles, rode the streetcars or the jitney and, in the case of Saanich students, they had a choice of riding the Interurban (a railway that operated between Victoria and Sidney) or boarding in town with friends or relatives.

High school courses offered very few options. Some students took business courses but most were enrolled in the arts program with basic courses in English, mathematics (algebra and geometry), history and geography and physical education. We had to take two of three optional courses: French, Latin or science (chemistry and physics). I chose French and science.

Drama was well taught by Mr. Ira Dilworth as an after-school activity. Victoria High School was well known for its annual Shakespearean plays put on by the seniors. In my senior year it was Julius Caesar and I had the role of Calpurnia. Auditions were held early in the spring and roles assigned. To those of us who liked drama it was a chance to take part in one of the big events of the school year. There was no problem of making costumes as they were all rented from a theatrical outfitter in Victoria. We felt and looked like professionals! The plays were held in the auditorium which seated almost 1,000 people.

Morning assembly was a brief period before going to the classrooms . . . We also had special assemblies to hear distinguished speakers who were in Victoria on tours. We were privileged to hear Bliss Carmen, the poet; Rabindraneth Tagore, the Indian philosopher; and others including the Anglican bishop who admonished us not to make 'addled eggs' of our lives.

The activities in the gymnasium were different than those of today's physical education classes. There was very little emphasis on team sports although we were taught how to play basketball. The exercises were an extension of the type we had in the first years of our schooling. For the girls it was rhythmic dance, exercises with wands and Indian clubs.

Although there may have been showers near the gym, we never used them after class. We had changed from our navy blue pleated skirts into navy blue bloomers. These voluminous garments had elastic to hold the legs firmly below the knee. On days when we knew we had gym class we wore white middy blouses with navy collars. Gym class was the only time we ever wore running shoes. There was always a scramble after gym class to change clothes and get to classrooms on time.

Although there was no uniform dress code for the school we did conform to acceptable dress standards; dark skirts, white blouses, and sweaters of various colours for the girls and dark trousers, sweaters, jackets and shirts for the boys.

In those days teachers called their pupils by surnames not first names. For example the girls were called Miss Smith or Miss Jones and the boys were called by surnames only. It would seem strange today for a 13 or 14-year old girl to be called 'Miss' by a teacher.

I managed to get through high school with a minimum of detentions for work not done and only one request to 'report to the principal.' One morning my friend and I were in a hurry to avoid being late. We knew it was forbidden but we rode our bicycles on the sidewalk in front of the school. That happened to be the morning the principal was looking out over the school grounds from his office window. We were summoned to his office and told that 'girls from good families' didn't do things like that![29]

1917: "Thinking I had gone to heaven"

William Plenderleith

Like many of the province's teachers before 1920, William Plenderleith was a newcomer to Canada and to British Columbia. He was born in Edinburgh and spent part of his childhood in Wales and Ireland. Here he looks back on the strange set of circumstances that led to his career as a teacher:[30]

I was a professional baseball pitcher at the Foundation Shipyard [in Victoria] when it was started in 1917. They had a baseball team. I was put on the payroll as a corker at the huge salary—which was the highest salary paid to any tradesman in the shipyard—of $7.70 a day. Well, I didn't know a corking mallet from anything.

In 1917, the French representative here, Bouchard, had a contract for 22 wooden ships to be built in Victoria and it was all on a cost plus basis, so he didn't care what they cost. The first ship which was being built was the War Yukon; it was pretty nearly half-finished when I was appointed there and our job was to go to the shipyard, to be there by 8:00 and hang up our little brass tags, and at 8:30 there would be a little bus come along and take us to the Royal Athletic Park to practice ball and then it would bring us back again at 11:30 to check in again. In the meantime we were to keep out of sight for half an hour so they put us into the oakum room which was a stinky place with tar.

Victoria High School girls' field hockey team celebrates its accomplishments.
Courtesy Victoria High School Archives.

The second day out I got tired of being in the oakum room so I thought I'd go and see what they were doing on the ships. I went up onto the top, the captain's cabin on the War Yukon, and I was looking down below—the coal hatch was right underneath the pilot house—I was standing on the pilot house roof looking down below and all of a sudden I found myself in mid-air. I didn't know what was happening, I had read that morning about someone falling out of a two-storey window and because he was a good athlete he landed properly and just walked away. Well I was a good athlete at that time. I was nothing but muscle, 190 lbs., six feet tall and I thought I'll land properly. So after a couple of somersaults I traveled about 64 feet, landed, broke both wrists, cut myself across the face, smashed my knee completely, jammed my hipbone into my ribs and passed out of course.

The next thing I remember was being up in the air and thinking I had gone to heaven. They had loaded the stretcher onto a sling and then had the crane drop down and I was being lifted up. In the first aid office they asked me where they could get in touch with my next of kin. I gave them my father's address. Then I remember going in the hospital. They wired my leg up and put a silver kneecap in. At the end of three months I was walking around again and the compensation board came along and wanted to know what I wanted to do. They said I wouldn't be playing any baseball again but there seemed to be good openings for teachers.

They said, well we'll give you $20 a month expenses and put you through arts and then through normal school. And so I took two years of high school and one year at Victoria Normal and got my first-class certificate. That was just fine

Vancouver typing class under the direction of W.K. Beech illustrated the growing interest in commercial preparation for high school students in the early twentieth century.
Courtesy B.C. Archives D-07554.

with me. In the meantime, after I graduated and got my certificate I marched down and saw [provincial superintendent of schools] Dr. Willis and said: 'now listen Dr. Willis, I am going to be a teacher and I don't want to be a teacher all my life and I don't want to be a principal all my life either. I want to get into the department and become an inspector.' I knew Dr. Willis . . . that's why I went down there. He said 'If you take a job in Victoria as a teacher, which you can get, in two or three years you might be a principal if somebody dies. But, if you go outside and take an un-graded school and work your way up through getting good inspector's reports and having good results in your teaching, then we will be looking at your record for an inspector.'

So I said okay and I went down and saw Mr. Watson who was the teachers' registrar at that time.[31] All vacancies came into Watson and he doled them out to the various people, told them who to apply to and what places were vacant. I said I would like a school in the outskirts and I want to have a few entrance pupils so that I can indicate that I am a good teacher. He said all right and put me in at Unsa Valley [situated west of Wisteria between Ootsa Lake and Southbank]. Watson didn't have a photograph [of the school] but he said it was a one-room log school, has so many pupils and is situated six miles south of Southbank. It was an isolated district, just opening up and most of the people were trying to cut and develop farms out of a fairly heavily wooded area. Most of these people . . . spent their time in winter cutting down the trees, the Jack Pine, chewing them into ties and then taking them down and dumping them in François Lake to be taken to the railroad where they sold for two bits a piece.

Well, I went up to Unsa Valley and the secretary up there was Jim Pedley and he was supposed to meet me at Burns Lake and take me in with my baggage. Well, a fellow named Charlie Drennan who was going to teach in Southbank, which is six miles from Unsa, and I went up together. The train got in about midnight. We didn't have any money to go the hotel so we looked around for a place. There was a church there [and] the door was open so we went into the church. There was a room with a bunch of surplices and things in it, we put the surplices down on the floor and lay down and spent the night there.[32]

Everything went fine. I had two entrance pupils and they both passed. When H.C. Fraser who was the inspector of schools in Prince Rupert came in at the end to see me he said 'You are doing a fine job and you shouldn't stay in a one-room school any longer. I will talk to somebody in the south and see if we can get you a better job.'

Fraser was an old preacher. He had been a preacher with an M.A., a good scholar and very immaculate, with nails cut and clipped and polished. He had a little talk to Inspector Hall in the Okanagan and when I was down at summer school I got a wire from Hall asking me if he could see me in Vancouver.

The first year I went to improve my certificate I took 12 units and got away with it. I went at seven in the morning to UBC, went right through the lunch hour without any lunch, and then right to six at night. When the winter students found out, they kicked up a fuss of course. So the next year it was reduced so that you could only take nine units, and the year after that it was reduced so you could only take six, but you could take two winter courses. I got through and got my bachelor of pedagogy and a B.A. in five years.

It ended up that I was president of the summer session in my last year there. I saw T.R. Hall. Oh, he was a very smart man, too. All those inspectors were picked for being bright. I mean, there wasn't a dumbbell among the whole lot of them. I was eventually president of the inspectors' association and I bet there wasn't one that you would consider, in any way, inferior. I also knew Albert Sullivan because he used to come to the Victoria High School to inspect. He had been overseas and I can still remember him reading the 'Declaration de Mons' when the Canadian troops went in and freed the town of Mons. He had it all written down. He was a very good man. And I knew J.B. DeLong [the other high school inspector] but only as an acquaintance.[33]

1918: "The one avenue open to a girl"

George Hindle

George Hindle was a principal in Kaslo during the early years of the twentieth century before heading east to complete a doctor of pedagogy degree at the University of Toronto. He was the first person in the province to write a full-length study about the state of schooling in the province, *The Educational System of British Columbia* (1918). In the following passage, he speaks about feminization of teaching in the early-twentieth century and wonders what young women will do for a living when the profession becomes "so crowded:"

In many of the interior towns that have experienced business depression for a decade, teaching provides practically the one avenue open to a girl and the anxiety of parents to provide this means of earning a living accounts . . . for the large number of high and superior schools that one finds scattered over the province. What girls are to do when the profession becomes so crowded that this avenue is practically closed will be a serious problem for parents to solve.

There was a time when women of marriageable age readily found suitable mates in British Columbia. That day is past. Our cities are as full as eastern cities of charming and attractive young women, but eligible men of marriageable age are at as great a premium here as elsewhere. Another illustration of the saying that the west transforms itself into the east while you wait.[34]

1918: "Settlers in out of the way places"

Samuel Spetch

On December 30, 1918, Samuel Spetch sent a letter of petition to Premier John Oliver for provincial assistance in educating his three children—Elizabeth, Muriel, and William—who were the sole school-age children in his district. School law at the time insisted that 10 children between the ages of six and 16 be resident in a district before a school could be established.[35] Spetch's letter awakened the government's sense of responsibility for the education of youngsters in remote areas and led to the establishment of the elementary correspondence branch a year later.[36] The case that Spetch made in his letter to the premier included the following passages:

In much of rural British Columbia, horses provided transportation for young riders, albeit usually for fewer youngsters than mounted here in the Okanagan Mission in the early twentieth century. **Courtesy Kelowna Museum Archives 3342.**

We live in an outlandish place known as Pemberton Portage, there are not sufficient children to call for a school, none but ours at school age. Would it be possible to form a correspondence school for such cases as ours with headquarters in Victoria or Vancouver where the lessons could be mailed from the many children who are as unfortunate as ours as regards to public school? The lessons to be returned by mail corrected.

Possibly the Dominion Government would consider favourably the franking of such correspondence. Even if the Dominion authorities would not grant that favour I feel sure the system once inaugurated would meet a much felt want and would prove to the settlers in out of the way places in B.C. (of which there are many) that your government is not unmindful of its obligations to its rising generation and I think you would secure the gratitude of a good many parents.[37]

1918: "A genius for . . . routine work"

George Hindle

Criticisms of the government's educational bureaucracy are certainly not new. Hindle's comments below, however, are likely the first criticisms ever to be registered in British Columbia about the amount of paperwork teachers were obliged to complete to satisfy the incessant demands for information on the part of early educational bureaucrats in Victoria:

The strong point of the Education Department of British Columbia is a genius for classification and routine work. At the end of every month, as well as at the end of every year, teachers are required to make out certain statistical returns on printed forms supplied by the Department. These must be made or the government grant is withheld from the school. They are all carefully tabulated by the office force at the Education Department and published in neatly arranged tabular form in the Annual Report.[38]

The school law of the province is comprised in 147 sections, covering but 30 pages of the school manual. The act is, therefore, characterized by extreme brevity and is remarkable for its omissions.[39]

Monthly Register for Early British Columbia Schools

1. Prescribed school days
2. Days school was in session
3. Total daily attendance
4. Total actual attendance
5. Average daily attendance
6. Average actual attendance
7. Pupils actually attending during month
8. Boys actually attending during month
9. Girls actually attending during month
10. Greatest number of pupils present at any session (a.m. or p.m.)
11. Lowest number of pupils present at any session (a.m. or p.m.)
12. Highest register number to date
13. Monthly reports sent to parents
14. Expulsion of pupils
15. Suspension of pupils
16. Truancy of pupils
17. Corporal punishment of pupils
18. Tardiness of pupils
19. Tardiness of teacher
20. Days absence of teacher
21. Visit to school by trustees
22. Visit to school by Superintendent of Education
23. Visit to the school by other persons
24. Have the rules and regulations been observed

The Education Office administered schools scattered across British Columbia by using a simple management information system based on teachers' registers. Once the above information was recorded for one class, it could be aggregated at the school, district, and inspectorate level before assembling a statistical portrait of the province's schools as a whole. It was, at once, immensely simple and immensely revealing about the state of schools from one-room institutions to the system as a whole.

1919: "The nearest I ever came to a nervous breakdown"

J.B. DeLong

With the establishment of Victoria High School in 1876, the first institution of "higher learning" west of Winnipeg, the Education Office set out a series of "entrance" and "exit" examinations for high school students to be undertaken, respectively, by students at the completion of the first eight grades and upon completion of junior matriculation. The high school "exit" exams, commonly referred to as "departmentals" throughout the system were dreaded by students universally and were viewed as a severe burden by senior staff within educational government who had insufficient resources and systems to mark and keep track of students' performance. Here, J.B. DeLong describes his experience during the June and July "testing season" of 1919 and its effects on his health:[40]

George Deane had the job of looking after the departmental examinations.[41] I was told to work with him so that I could take over the job next year. I was with Deane just a half day when the government asked Deane to look after the wounded soldiers who were returning from the First World War, so I was on my own. Dr. Robinson was very worried. He said to me 'If you make a mistake God help you and God help me.' For quite a few years I checked over all papers to see that nothing was included outside the course of study. I proofread all papers, counted the number for each examination centre, tied them and sent them out to all centres. Afterwards, this work was done by the registrar with three or four girls assisting. I was in charge of the marking of papers, tabulating results and mailing out certificates. Several hundred people were needed for this work. Professors from the university usually acted as chairmen of the subject committees. I remember with pleasure my association with these men from UBC. They often performed very menial tasks, entering marks, mailing returns (without complaint). In later years, mailing was done by a staff of young people. The majority of the markers were high school teachers.

For several years the examination work was done in the Parliament Buildings. Each year I was given a young chap as helper. This was very trying work but I really enjoyed it; in fact every year I looked ahead to the Victoria work. My enjoyment was largely due to the fine body of men and women who appeared from year to year. There was never the slightest evidence of friction. For some years the university had charge of the junior and senior matriculation examinations, but it was then decided the education department would take on the work. There was no card-index system in use; consequently after four years the registrar had great difficulty in finding marks when requests came in. One year after the examination work was over I offered to make out a card-index system. I was promised the help of two young ladies but they were unwilling to take on extra work. I could have obtained their services by making an issue of it but I felt that as they would be working under protest, I could not depend on them to do the work accurately. The result was I did it all. I had finished the job and was on my way to the Education Office for my last appearance when I collapsed on the street in front of the house occupied by Inspector Daniels. He took me into his house, called a doctor and put me on the Vancouver boat. That was the nearest I ever came to a nervous breakdown.[42]

1919: "Even fair progress cannot be expected"

British Columbia Department of Education

Long before government ever commissioned a major survey or study of provincial schools, it was evident to officials inside the educational bureaucracy and the school inspectorate that enormous disparities existed in the quality of graded and ungraded rural schools and in the opportunities for educational development that rural and urban youngsters received. Here, an inspector's annual report puts such matters squarely:

> One is struck by the vast difference in the efficiency of our city and rural schools. The city schools are well organized under capable principals, assisted by a strong staff of experienced teachers. The results are most gratifying. This may also be said of some of the graded rural schools . . .
>
> The results in the entrance examination from the city and graded rural schools are very satisfactory, but those from the majority of the rural schools were somewhat disappointing. This is due in large measure to the frequent change of teachers. In this inspectorate, when schools resumed on September 2, about 90 per cent of the teachers in these ungraded schools were new to these appointments. Under such conditions even fair progress cannot be expected.[43]

1919: "The buttocks of a peasant"

Harry Dee

Following his resignation as provincial superintendent of education, Alexander Robinson spent one ill-fated year as principal of Victoria High School. At an historical reunion a half-century later, Victoria High teacher, Harry Dee, told this humorous story about Robinson walking with a student, Ira Dilworth, who would himself become principal of Victoria High. At once, Dee's story illustrates the closely-knit character of the provincial educational community at the time, the notion of social selection through education, as well as the importance of a good physical appearance to Robinson, a man recognized throughout the province for his own striking looks and elegant bearing:

> I always remember Ira Dilworth's story about Alexander Robinson.[44] Robinson used to parade the halls just at ten-to-one when all the students were coming in and pouring down. I suppose to help preserve a semblance of order. And Ira was very often called in to walk alongside of him and as they walked along one day, a certain boy, whose name I shall not give, waddled in front of them, going down the corridor quickly as anything, wobble, wobble, wobble, wobble, wobble, and Robinson turned to Dilworth and he said, 'My dear Dilworth . . . the buttocks of a peasant.'[45]

Notes

1. For a discussion of Robinson's remarkable career, see Thomas Fleming, "Letters from Headquarters: Alexander Robinson and the British Columbia Education Office, 1899-1919," in *The Journal of Educational Administration and Foundations,* Vol. 10, No. 2 (1999), 7-31.
2. *The Victoria Daily Colonist*, 5 April 1899, 4.
3. Joseph "Fighting Joe" Martin was leader of the provincial Liberal Party and provincial premier for 106 days in 1900, the shortest reign of any provincial premier to this time.
4. *The Victoria Daily Colonist*, "A Political Appointment," 7 April 1899, 4.
5. ARPS 1892-1893, 59.
6. ARPS 1900-1901, 251.
7. *The Victoria Daily Colonist,* "Sudden death of John Jessop, an old respected Victorian," 31 March 1901.
8. *The Victoria Daily Colonist*, "What Lady Teachers Say: Do Not Approve Discrimination as to Sex in Fixing Salaries," Saturday, 20 April 1901, 3.
9. *The Lake News*, "That school inspector," 7 January 1987.
10. *The Victoria Daily Colonist,* "Trouble In The Schools: Two Lady Principals Accused of Insubordination and Suspended," Saturday, 22 June 1901.
11. *The Victoria Daily Colonist,* "Victoria Memories," 14 October 1919, 10.
12. ARPS 1902-1903, C68.
13. James B. London, "The Dynamics of a Non-Professional Organization: A History of the British Columbia School Trustees Association, 1905-1980" (Ann Arbor: University Microfilms International, 1985), 58.
14. John Fleming, "W.T. Whiteway's Design for the Duncan Public School of 1913," *West Coast Review,* Vol. XV/4, (Spring 1981), 46. Watson's commissions included: the 12-room "severe but attractive" George Jay Elementary (1909); Victoria High School (1911); Burnside Elementary (1913); the 12-room Monterey Elementary (1914); the eight-room brick and stone Quadra School (1914); the eight-room brick Willows School (1919); and the four-room Quadra Primary (1921).
15. ARPS 1903-1904, C32.
16. *The Vancouver World*, "A James Bay Autocrat," 17 March 1906.
17. Daphne Marlatt and Carole Itter, *Opening Doors: Vancouver's East End, Sound Heritage,* Vol. 8, No. 1 and 2, Aural History Program, Ministry of Provincial Secretary and Government Services, Provincial Archives, Victoria, British Columbia, 1979, 15-19.
18. Harold Campbell, "School days: a collection of memories," *Musings,* Vol. XIII, No. 3, October 1994, 1-3.
19. Clare McAllistair, "Getting Dressed," *B.C. Historical News*, 8:1 (November 1974), 23-26.
20. Smith Inlet is slightly south of Margaret Bay and north of 51 degrees latitude on the coast of British Columbia.
21. J.B. DeLong, "Memoirs."
22. Interviews with Bernard Gillie, Victoria, Thursday 3 November 1988 and Wednesday 16 November 1988.

23. To meet provincial standards for an "assisted school," school districts were required to demonstrate that they had an enrollment of 10 pupils. Otherwise, by law, they would be required to close. In practice, however, things were different. See Thomas Fleming, "'Our Boys in the Field:' School Inspectors, Superintendents, and the Changing Character of School Leadership in British Columbia," in Nancy M. Sheehan, J.D. Wilson, and David C. Jones (Eds.), *Schools in the West: Essays in Canadian Educational History* (Calgary, Alberta: Detselig, 1986), 289.
24. J.B. DeLong, "Memoirs," 5, 6, 7, and 9.
25. Interview with Bernard Gillie.
26. Frances Decker, Margaret Fougberg, and Mary Ronayne, *Pemberton: The History of a Settlement* (Pemberton: Pemberton Pioneer Women, 1977), 153.
27. Dorothea met and married Harold Stafford who became a principal and, later, an inspector of schools. A keen photographer and social observer, Dorothea accompanied Harold on many of his school inspections and photographed many rural schools in the late 1930s and early 1940s.
28. T.R. "Tommy" Hall was a provincial inspector of schools from 1922 until 1929 when he became an instructor at the Vancouver Provincial Normal School. Prior to his appointment as a school inspector, Hall had earned a B.A. degree at Dalhousie and had served as principal of the high school at Kamloops. He completed his career as an instructor at the Vancouver Provincial Normal School.
29. Dorothea M. Stafford's manuscript "A History of Burnside School," was written in December 1988 and the 20-page manuscript was mailed to Thomas Fleming on 6 July 1989.
30. After a remarkable career as a principal in the Okanagan Valley and at Ocean Falls, Plenderleith joined the education department as a school inspector in 1934 and gained public prominence for consolidating school districts in the Peace River district in 1935.
31. J.L. Watson was the teachers' registrar in the education department from 1920 until his death in 1944. One of his most important duties was to assist local school boards in finding teachers who were willing to work in rural and isolated schools.
32. Surplices are loose fitting vestments usually worn over a cassock by clergy or choristers.
33. Interview with William Plenderleith, Saanich, B.C., 15 December 1988.
34. George Hindle, *The Educational System of British Columbia* (Trail, B.C.: Trail Publishing, 1918), 21 and 141.
35. Donald Leslie MacLaurin, "The History of Education in the Crown Colonies of Vancouver Island and British Columbia and in the Province of British Columbia" (Seattle: University of Washington, 1936), 152-153.
36. Although Spetch's request was not immediately met, the Education Office replied in May 1919 that the province would provide the authorized program of studies by mail with free tuition and textbooks upon receipt of information about his children's age, gender, and previous schooling.
37. Correspondence from Samuel Walter Spetch, Pemberton Portage, Owl Creek Post Office, to the Honourable John Oliver, Premier of British Columbia, Victoria, 30 December 1918, Transcript in the hand of Samuel Walter Spetch, BCA, GR 396, box 1, file 1.
38. Hindle, *The Educational System of British Columbia*, 141.
39. Ibid., 23.

40. For a comprehensive discussion of the provincial government's testing programs, see: Thomas Fleming and Helen Raptis, "Government's Paper Empire: Historical Perspectives on Measuring Student Achievement in British Columbia Schools, 1872-1999," *Journal of Educational Administration and History,* Vol. 37, No. 2, September 2005, 173-302; and Alastair Glegg and Thomas Fleming, "Teaching to the Test or Testing to Teach: Educational Assessment in British Columbia, 1872-2002," *Historical Studies in Education,* Vol. 16, No. 1, 117-137.

41. George H. Deane served as an inspector of schools from 1908 until 1913 when he was appointed as assistant superintendent of education under Alexander Robinson.

42. DeLong, "Memoirs," 8 and 9.

43. ARPS 1918-1919, A34.

44. Ira Dilworth also became principal of Victoria High and, later, director of the western region for the CBC.

45. Duncan Lorimer, "Memories: Victoria High School (taped conversations), 3 February 1972, 39.

Youngsters at the Pemberton School in the 1930s. **Courtesy B.C. Archives C-01053.**

CHAPTER 4

Schools in Good Times, Depression, and War: The Era of Deferred Equality, 1920-1945

Two events in particular determined the course of the province's educational development from the end of the Great War to the end of World War II. The first was publication of J.H. Putman and G.W. Weir's survey of provincial schools in 1925, a report that introduced progressive ideas about schooling, known widely as the "new education," to the province's teachers and to the administrators who governed the system.[1] No one embraced these new ideas more fervently than Major H.B. King, technical assistant to the minister and later (1939-1945) chief inspector of schools.[2] Under King's direction, principals and teachers administered thousands of I.Q. and standardized achievement tests, and otherwise attempted to break the grip of longstanding classical and formal instruction through new approaches such as the project method of learning, socialized recitation, and silent reading.[3]

The second event shaping schooling in the years between the wars was the economic collapse known as the Great Depression. A decade of wrenching economic hardship brought into sharp contrast the inequities that had long existed between rural and urban schools and deferred any dreams British Columbians had about equalizing opportunities for youngsters throughout the province. Such inequity could only be addressed when the Depression—and the War that followed it—were over. Meanwhile, in many parts of rural British Columbia, where harsh living conditions had long been the norm, hard times grew even harder. Nowhere could the terrible effects of this economic deprivation be seen more clearly than in the hundreds of small roadside schools that served rural British Columbia.

The writings that comprise Chapter 4 of this volume offer a rich variety of personal experiences in schools that had not changed all that much since the nineteenth century. In the following narratives, we see from various perspectives the diversity of provincial life in the interwar era—what it was like to attend an aboriginal day school in a coastal community, how aboriginal boys obtained traditional knowledge by observation and working with their hands, the problems aboriginal children faced when schooled in a new language and a new culture, and the rites of passage that marked the transition from boyhood to manhood in their own culture. We also see how older settlers dealt with new immigrants, how newcomers tried to learn English as a second language, the immense faith of many immigrant peoples in the promise of education, and the experiences of young teachers in overcrowded urban schools.

These stories likewise reveal the diverse circumstances that brought individuals into teaching, how many of the young men and women left the provincial normal schools of the day and the comforts of the city to take jobs in small rural schools where the challenges of everyday life were often far different than anything they had ever encountered. Some triumphed despite the adversity of their new surroundings or, in some instances, a school inspector's negative report on their teaching effectiveness. Some despaired of their newfound isolation and left at the first opportunity. Not everyone could overcome the loneliness and hardship that such postings usually entailed. For some, homesickness, along with the narrow-mindedness and prejudice that occasionally marked life in small settlements, proved too much. But many survived long odds to make a career for themselves in remote schools and communities, heartened by the friendships and the simple joys they found. Letters from home, the gift of a box of chocolates, or an ear willing to listen often made all the difference between staying and leaving.

The stories in this chapter also illustrate the relatively small size of school and provincial communities during this era, a time when everybody seemed to know everybody else, or at least someone else who knew them. The web of social relationships was strong, certainly among members of the educational community. For decades, young teachers stayed closely connected to the high school teachers who had once taught them and, later, to the instructors they met at the normal school and even to the much feared school inspectors who supervised them. Children also remembered their teachers vividly and could recount years later the various ways special teachers influenced their lives. Communities, too, seemed generally less fractious than in modern times. Pulling together in moments of difficulty was the expected thing to do. With little fanfare, schools in times of crisis were converted into temporary hospitals during epidemics of Spanish influenza and infantile paralysis and educators were reassigned other chores. Little mention was made of the fact that some communities were quarantined for several months during such outbreaks or that people were restricted from travel of any kind. These stories remind us that life in British Columbia was simpler then, as were the aspirations and expectations that people held for their lives.

1920: "That's how I got my little education"

James Sewid

James Sewid's formal schooling was episodic and consisted of little more than three years at a segregated Indian school with a poorly-trained teacher. Through his own efforts, he became a respected Kwakiutl leader and was selected by the National Film Board of Canada in 1955 to appear in a film on the achievements of Canadian Indians. These excerpts from his autobiography sketch out his early days at school:

> I was born during the cold winter of 1913 . . . Robby Bell is just a little older than me but he's the very youngest of my uncles. When we were about six or seven Robby was sent to school by my grandparents. I don't know what the law was about a child going to school in those days, but poor Robby was just more or less dumped into the Anglican residential school at Alert Bay. I wanted to go and asked them if I could but they said, 'No, no, you can't go. We don't want

the other kids to tease you and all that. We don't want you to go there because that place is no good. They're going to teach you things that aren't good for you.' But Robby had to go to that residential school where he would live for most of the year.

Another reason I didn't like not being allowed to go to school with Robby was that I knew it was important to have an education and learn to read and write and speak English. My other grandmother, Old Lucy, wanted me to go to school, and so later on I had to go to Alert Bay and stay with her in order to get any schooling . . .

When I was about seven years old I left my mother and went to Alert Bay to stay with my grandmother, Old Lucy, and go to school. That's how I got my little education because I stayed with her off and on until I was about ten years old . . . I stayed with her during that time and she encouraged me to go to school and stay with school as long as I could. She could see that education was necessary. But I found it awfully hard as a young boy with nobody . . . to support me. We used to just look after ourselves, Lucy and I. Our relief at that time was only two dollars and fifty cents a month . . .

On Saturday when I wasn't in school I used to go down to the big sawmill that was in Alert Bay and get old pieces of wood to sell. There was an Indian teacher in the day school where I went, and I would go and borrow a wheelbarrow from him and take this wood around to different people in the village and sell it to make a little money.

We were living right near the Anglican church and the minister there and his wife, Mr. and Mrs. Corker, were very kind to us . . . Every now then they used to give us a loaf of bread or sometimes some cookies. Sometimes Mr. and Mrs. Corker would give me some clothes that were too small for their children and I used to be the happiest boy in Alert Bay when I wore those new clothes.

The Indian teacher at the day school, George Luther, was a great friend of mine. He liked me somehow . . . He just thought the world of me and I used to go and help him make the fire in the big drum stove that we had in the school. Going to school was new to me and I found it awfully hard. I really enjoyed school and that was the main reason I came to Alert Bay. I wanted to go to school pretty badly, and there was no school on Village Island, and that is why I started thinking about going to live with my grandmother.

I never used to buy anything to play with and nobody had to buy anything for me because I made my own toys. My grandmother had a little handsaw and an axe that I used as a hammer. Every time she found a wooden box she would tear it up and save all the nails in a box for me. She would give me these tools and the box of nails and tell me, 'Now you bring it back when you are finished with it.' I would take them out on the beach beside my house and start building things and when I came home I would put everything away. I used to make little toy boats and pull them along the beach. One time when the pile driver first came into Alert Bay I made a nice little pile driver that was just like it.

I made all those things by myself by just copying whatever I saw. After my second year in school I spent most of the summer with my stepfather Dave. He was a fine man and a real gentleman. He was very, very kind to me and he'd do anything for me . . . He was my great friend and we were together a lot travelling and fishing and logging. He didn't know how to read and write but he was a great engineer who knew everything about diesel, gas and steam engines. He knew how to take anything apart and put it back together again. I used to go with him when he was driving those big steam donkeys. I used to ask him, 'Can I drive it?' He used to put me on the seat as a little boy and I would pull those big levers. For part of the summer I fished with him on his small gill net boat. He was a very quiet man and not like those fellows who just talk and talk. I can't remember him ever punishing me or even saying a lot to me. If I went to him and asked him a question he would just answer and that was all. But I would watch him working on the engines and fixing things and take little lessons from him that way.

The next year when I was about 12 they started a little school at Village Island and I went there a little when I was staying in that village. Miss O'Brien was a missionary and came there to be the district nurse. She had a little house down at the beach on a float and the teacher would stay with her. I used to go down to her house and visit them every night and look at all the magazines and books they had there. I really liked to look at books. They were nice old ladies and would hold church there at Village Island and I used to go every Sunday morning and evening . . . I always stayed in school because I liked school. I remember we used to have a drill where we would raise our arms up and down in time with music from a little gramophone that our teacher played.

That same year when I was 12 I started running an engine on a seine boat by myself for the first time. My grandfather was in his last year as skipper before he retired and I ran the engine for him. It was only a 20 horsepower engine but it was so big I could hardly turn it over. I used to use a big bar to get it started and he used to come and help me. That was on the seine boat called the 'Sunrise' and even though I was only 12 and our crew was pretty weak we were catching fish the same as the other boats. I worked like a man and tried to be one.

I used to stay down in the engine room and watch how the engine worked because I was so interested in engines. I never thought I would be a skipper even though sometimes I would ask my grandfather if I could take the wheel. If we were going through a nice big channel he would let me take the wheel and sit beside me telling me where to go and how to go through that channel.[4]

1920: "Inspecting us, not the teacher"

Christopher Wright

Chris Wright began his administrative career as principal of Armstrong Junior and Senior High. He was appointed as a district superintendent of schools in 1959 by the education department. Before he retired, he was serving in Salmon Arm. Here he writes about his first days at school:

Alan Fraser Matthews may have been the first inspector of schools of whom I was aware. In the fall of 1920, I attended the newly-opened Westsyde School a few miles north of Kamloops. It was a disorderly school with well over 30 pupils in the eight grades. One afternoon an unusual hush descended on the classroom. A small dark man took charge and, I believe, we were told that he was Mr. Matthews.

A.F. Matthews, a Nova Scotian, had come to Kamloops about 1910 as teacher of Latin and mathematics. In due course he became principal of Kamloops High School. In 1920 he was appointed inspector of schools for an area that not only included the North and South Thompson Valleys, but also extended south beyond Merritt, then west to Lillooet, and somewhere north of Ashcroft. Schools were much smaller then, but far more numerous. Nevertheless, Mr. Matthews visited every elementary school twice each year. In spring and autumn he travelled by car to outlying schools; the more accessible ones were reached by train during the winter.

For the few years after Westsyde my education was erratic: six months here, four months there, interspersed with 'home schooling' and the first B.C. correspondence courses. In autumn 1925, I entered grade 8 at the Stuart Wood School in Kamloops. There I met Mr. Matthews again, and felt the pressure of the arithmetic and spelling tests he administered. We pupils were sure that he was inspecting us, not the teacher. Mr. Matthews' daughter was in that class and not doing well. After Christmas, he took a position in Victoria with the Department of Education. The grade 8 class was sure it was so that his daughter,

> Dorothy, could attend a school which recommended pupils, not subjecting them to the dreaded [high school] entrance exams which we in Kamloops all faced. We appreciated the replacement inspector, Harold Campbell, who encouraged us to tell him what we were working on.[5]

1920s and after: "The only school nurse in Vancouver"

Concerns over the health of children in schools may be traced as far back as the early reports of the first provincial school superintendent, John Jessop, in the early 1870s. However, it was not until the explosive growth of Vancouver in the early decades of the twentieth century that school board and other civic officials began to take the matter of children's health seriously as school populations rose dramatically in size and as the fear of epidemics increased. Here, two teachers from Strathcona School—Miss Gertrude Doyle (1923-1958) and Jennie Schooley (1926-69)—recall the importance of Miss McLellan, the school nurse, and her work among newcomers and working-class families in Vancouver's "east end:"

Beginning in 1910, the provincial Education Office provided medical and dental inspections in a handful of cities in an effort to halt the spread of infectious diseases. This became particularly important after 1918 when the powerful Spanish influenza pandemic wiped out entire families. **Courtesy B.C. Archives I-60780.**

Gertrude Doyle: Miss McLellan was the only school nurse in Vancouver for many, many years . . . And later on, when she went in any of the stores around town, she'd meet the head of the store and she'd say to him, 'Well, I remember the days when I used to look down your throat.' All the businessmen of Vancouver went through her hands, one way or another.

Jennie Schooley: If a child was away from school, she'd go down Hogan's Alley, any place in town, the toughest parts of town. And everyone knew her . . . She was safe any place, and she'd go any place.[6]

Gertude Doyle: And those dark, dark nights after school—her hours were till 5 o'clock, which was pitch-black, and one time she was down just outside Woodward's, and she felt somebody feeling around to the belt of her coat. So she looked around and here was a poor drunk, and he said, 'Don't worry, nurse, I'm just straightening up your belt a little bit.' She loved the neighbourhood. She could go down into their homes, you see. We didn't have truant officers or anything, the nurse and the teachers looked after things like that. She'd go into their homes and, in the Italian homes, they always offered a drink of something, and she wasn't having any. But that didn't matter to them. She never insulted them: she just didn't take it, that's all.

Jennie Schooley: And another thing about her, she knew all the children's problems. If we had a child in our class who had a problem, she'd come to us quietly and tell us. After she left the district, there was one little guy I had, and that poor little guy never once brought his pen, pencil, ruler and eraser—those four things, and I'd bawl him out. In grade 8, he ended up in my badminton club, and he couldn't buy a racquet. Another boy, who was a pain in the neck but a likeable kid, bought him a racquet and I said, 'Oh, that was good of you to buy him that racquet.' And he said, 'Oh, Miss Schooley, his mother's no good. She's the very worst of those on Cordova Street.' Now if Miss McLellan had been there, I would have been told about him. She had a monetary fund that the teachers contributed to—we just gave her this money. And children who needed something that she didn't have in stock, well she'd buy it and give it to them. We also took clothing, and other things. And Miss McLellan would give them these, and the children never knew it came from the teachers.

Jennie Schooley: They had a bathtub down in the senior building, and children who were really unclean, were sent down there to wash. But what could you expect—many of the kiddies lived in these apartment buildings in just a cold-water flat. Some of them didn't even have cold water, they had a sink and a toilet down at the end of the hall on each floor.

Gertrude Doyle: That's all they had, and when you went into their buildings and saw how they were living, you couldn't make a fuss about them coming to school dirty.

Jennie Schooley: But others were absolutely immaculate, clean as could be. Their things might be well worn, but they were absolutely immaculate.

Gertrude Doyle: Yeah, we had problems, and one time it got too bad with one boy, and Mr. Brown was our principal then, and he took that boy, after lots of warning, and said, 'Now, if you come again in this mess, I'm going to take you down to the basement, and I'm going to bath you.' So he thought that would be enough, but the boy came dirty again, and he took him down and he turned the hose on him, with cold water, and everybody in the building could hear this kid screeching at the top of his voice, 'You're killing me, you're killing me.' And he never came back dirty.[7]

1920s: "Nothing like a union"

Doug Wallis

Victoria High School teacher Doug Wallis recalled two stories about principal A.G. Smith, nicknamed "Caesar Augustus" by students for his imperious ways. He was also renowned for his Scots accent as the first of the stories illustrates and, as the second story shows, for his outspokenness on professional matters:

Prior to the mid-1920s, Ontario and British influences were strongly felt in British Columbia educational circles. The high school in Nanaimo, portrayed here in 1922, changed its name to the Nanaimo Collegiate Institute in keeping with Ontario fashions in naming academic institutions. **Courtesy British Columbia Association of School Superintendents Active Retired Members.**

In those days the auditorium had less use than it does in the present day. I only recall, outside of the odd concert, that whenever we were called in there it was to get a dressing down from the principal [A.G. Smith] over some particular point. For instance, 'It has been brought to my nautice that certain girls are walking across the lawn and making a path there. Now this practice must cease.' Boys used to go around talking in his voice all the time . . . And they were saying: 'It has been brought to my nautice.' He always liked to start out like that . . . 'Certain boys have been frequenting the Metropolis Pool Room.' This was another practice that had to cease . . .

I was the first membership secretary of the Greater Victoria Teachers' Association. It was my job to round people up who weren't volunteering to join, and I went out to see him and I had quite a talk with him and he said, 'Ah, Douglas, now listen, I'll have nothing to do with it. The BCTF is nothing but an appendage of the Greater Victoria Teachers' Association' . . . That was about the time when teachers were volunteering to take part in the new . . . curriculum revision and so on. They were doing it free of charge actually except the fare paid over to Vancouver, and he objected strongly to this. He felt that it was nothing like a union should be. As he said, 'it's becoming an appendage of the department of education.'[8]

1921: "The cruel overcrowding of our children"

Arthur Anstey

John Jessop spoke about the problem of overcrowding in the Victoria Girls' School in the early 1870s. In what would be just one of many cries of alarm about this matter in the twentieth century, school inspector Arthur Anstey raised the issue once again for many parents, teachers, and children in the province's swelling urban schools when he made this comment in his report on the school year 1920-1921:

There is one dark and disturbing feature of our work that we cannot escape. I refer here again to the cruel overcrowding of our children in the public schools. The old woman who lived with her numerous progeny in a shoe had large, spacious, and luxurious quarters compared to those in which thousands of benighted children spent their hours of school.[9]

The downside of Vancouver's rapid growth in the early-twentieth century was swelling pupil ranks and, all too often, overcrowded schools. Classes topped 40 commonly in both Vancouver high schools and grade schools and, occasionally, turn-of-the-century public schools had as many as 100 youngsters in the care of one teacher. **Courtesy City of Vancouver Archives Sch N4.**

1922: "He would have been prime minister"

Carlyle Clay

Carlyle "Mike" Clay began his teaching career at Dome Creek and Rutland. He was appointed principal at Armstrong Public School in 1936. He became principal of Vancouver Junior and Senior High School in 1945 and, in 1946, was appointed as an inspector of schools. This excerpt is taken from an interview with Clay during which he told the following story about his colleague, Phillip Sheffield, when he was a principal in Kimberley, B.C.:

> Premier John Oliver was a farmer in Ladner. When he was up in Cranbrook the principal of the high school there, Phillip Sheffield, thought it would be nice to have a premier speak to his class, as you didn't very often get a chance to have a premier speak to a class. So he arranged for John Oliver to speak to the class but John Oliver had only [completed] grade 4 in school. Oliver was emphasizing this quite a bit throughout his address to the youngsters.

Thanking the premier for his address, the principal said that he felt very honoured. One thing he noticed was that the premier mentioned the fact that he only went to grade 4 in school. The principal said, 'I couldn't help but think how unfortunate it was that Premier Oliver didn't have the same opportunity that you boys and girls have going through high school. 'If he had had your opportunity,' the principal said, 'he wouldn't have been premier of the province of British Columbia. He would have been prime minister of Canada, if not Great Britain.'

When Oliver returned to Victoria, he called on Dr. McLean, the Minister of Education. 'That young fellow you've got up in Kimberley,' Oliver said: 'He's a bright young fellow. He should be an inspector.' McLean said: 'Mr. Oliver, there are no vacancies at the present time.' Oliver said: 'There is. You put him in. He's too good to lose.' The next inspector appointed was the principal, Phillip Sheffield.[10]

1923: Best-educated farmers get the biggest returns

The B.C. Teacher

As the following article illustrates, the economic value of secondary and post-secondary education was recognized long before the "human capital" school of economics in the 1960s. Here *The B.C. Teacher* features a short article excerpted from California's *Sunset Magazine* on the value of learning to farmers:

If times are going to be tough for farmers there will be fewer farmers by-and-by. Of course, it's the poorest, most inefficient farmers who will get the axe first; the efficient ones, those who know what to grow and who have the largest output per acre, will survive.

When this weeding-out process is completed, it will be found that the bulk of the efficient farmers had more than the ordinary rural education. By virtue of their schooling they will survive the ordeal. The cash value of an education is startlingly demonstrated by investigations made in the Middle West and East among large numbers of farmers.

Assuming the average working life of a farmer to be 40 years, one investigation showed that the amount the agricultural college farmer would receive during this time was $41,000 more than the earnings of the common-school farmers, while a high school education added $5,000 to his labour income.

Confirmation of these figures was supplied by the Kansas Agricultural College, which ascertained the educational status and the labor income of 1,237 farmers to be as follows:[11]

EDUCATION OF FARMERS	ANNUAL EARNINGS
Common School	$422
High School	$544
College Short Course	$859
Agricultural College	$1,452

1923-1924: "Why I became a teacher"

Dorothea Stafford

Like many young women of her generation, Dorothea Stafford (née Smith) chose teaching as a career because it was, at this time, one of only a few professions open to young women who sought financial independence. Following a stint teaching in northern British Columbia in the 1920s, she married an up-and-coming school principal and, later, school inspector, Harold Stafford. Here she describes her entry into the profession:

Prosperity and professionalism: A Victoria schoolteachers' social in the 1920s.
Courtesy Greater Victoria School District Archives.

From Victoria High School I went on to attend Victoria College for one year and Victoria Normal School the next year. To obtain a second-class teaching certificate, a young person went directly from high school to normal school. To obtain a first-class teaching certificate it was necessary to have one or more years of university. The benefit was in the annual salary scale for teachers that provided up to $100 a year more for having taken university courses. Beginning salaries ranged from less than $600 a year for second-class to $640 a year for a first-class teaching certificate. Board and room for teachers in country schools was as low as $20 a month. Tuition fees at Victoria Normal School were $40 for the year (1924). I lived at home so I did not have the expense of board and room that was incurred by out-of-town students. I earned spending money by working for half a day on Saturdays and in summer holidays. My pay envelope held $1.09 each day. For a full day at Woolworth's '15 cents-store' I earned $1.39 or $1.69. It paid my week's streetcar fares!

Many teachers taught for a few years to save enough money to return to university to get certification to teach in high schools. I taught for three and a half years before I married another teacher.

I have often wondered why I chose teaching as a career. I do not have the answer. Probably it was because there were so few vocations open to women. I didn't want to be a nurse. I didn't want to work in a store or an office. My youngest sister told me a few years ago that as a teenager I tried to teach her.

I know now that I made a good choice . . . There was a deep satisfaction in watching students make discoveries and learn to make decisions. I may have had a small part in that experience and that may be the answer to 'why I became a teacher.'[12]

1923-1930: East Vancouver's "square mile of crime"

Here, two other Strathcona teachers—Miss E.G. Farrington (1926-1969) and Miss E.M. Morris (1930-1939) join Misses Gertrude Doyle and J.G. Schooley to discuss the challenges they perceived teaching in Vancouver's multicultural "east end" during the 1920s and 1930s:

Gertrude Doyle: My first impressions of Strathcona School? I hated it! As a matter of fact, when I went there as a substitute and it came to the end of the year, I thought, 'I hope to goodness I don't get appointed to Strathcona.' And I did! I stayed on because of the number of nationalities, the kinds of people, and the teachers . . . And I had chances to go to Europe, or to transfer to anyplace around the city, but I wouldn't go.

Eileen Farrington: It was the same for me. I wouldn't have left Strathcona on a bet. They couldn't have paid me to leave it, after I got to know the children and became involved with them. I really loved them all.

Elva Morris: Isn't that funny? I wanted to go to Strathcona. I was hoping that was where I could go, because I thought the teachers were all so friendly. Now, it just depended who you met, didn't it? And I never changed my mind, they were a great bunch.

Jennie Schooley: They were. They were a swell bunch there. Well, I substituted first, and when the word came that I was to go there—I'd substituted in grade 8, and the boys were all bigger than I was and I was frightened when I thought of going there, but after I got there, I loved it. Some of the boys were over age for one thing. They had come from a foreign country and were late in starting to school, but all the time we were there, many of the grade 8 boys were bigger than we were. You know, many of the European boys were full grown. And as teachers, we were all in our 20s, when we started there.

Gertrude Doyle: When I had to go and look up a kid, I had to go to Hogan's Alley and of course, I went at noontime. I went down there . . . and it was only about eight feet wide, I guess, and every window as I went along had an eye peering out—it was the spookiest feeling I ever had. We got down to the house, and I found the little boy, and there was nothing in the home at all, just the four walls. Another time I had to go up to a Chinese place. There were about three floors, and I had to go to the top floor. Nobody understood English and we went into the office and went up there, and as we went by, every door opened a little bit, and a head appeared out that door. But I found the kid.

Jennie Schooley: But we were safe at any time of the day or night. Everybody knew us, 'Teacher, teacher.' And yet, that was the centre of the 'square mile of crime,' that's what they called it, that was the general talk in town. But we could walk down any street, and we walked down that Hastings Street from Main westward, it was always, as long as I can remember, very tough, and we could walk down there. We were never molested in any way, and never a word was said out of place, to any of us.

Gertrude Doyle: I thought it was my schoolteacher look that saved me.

Elva Morris: There were policemen on the beat in the neighbourhood, because I can remember once I said, 'You have to do right,' and this boy said, 'No, you don't if you give the policeman—whatever his name was—a chicken, it's okay to open your store on Sunday.'[13]

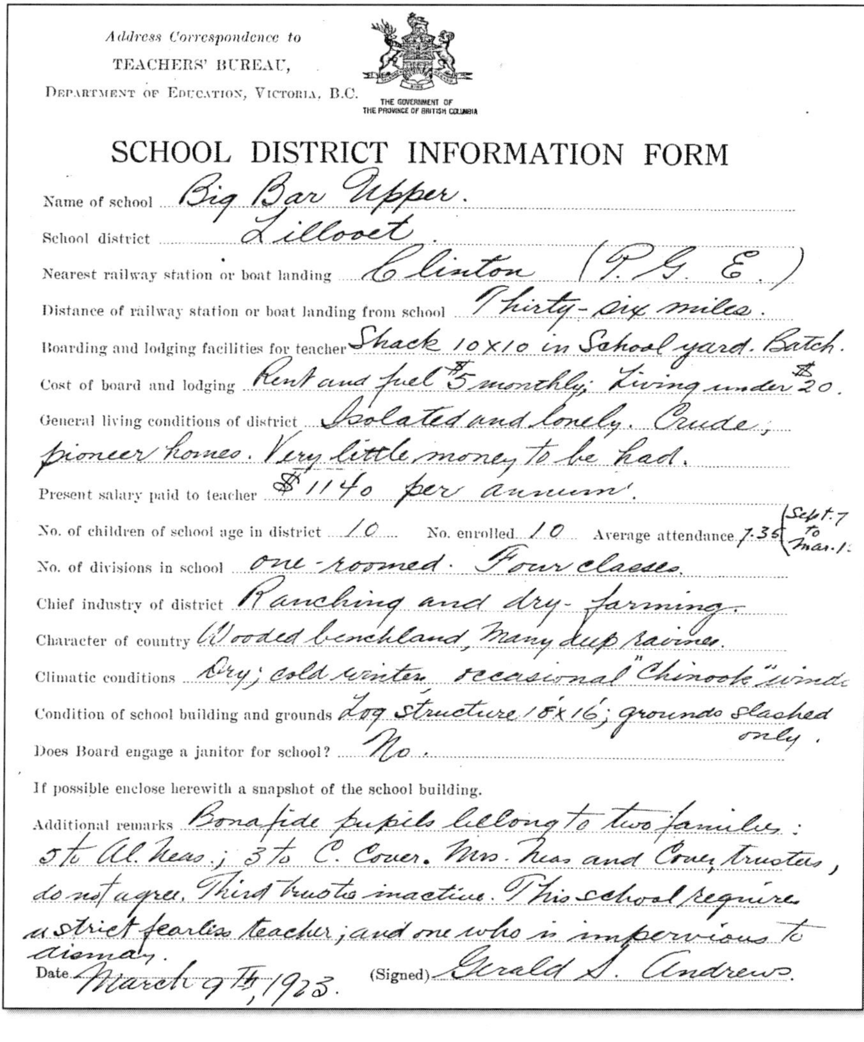

Address Correspondence to
TEACHERS' BUREAU,
DEPARTMENT OF EDUCATION, VICTORIA, B.C.

THE GOVERNMENT OF THE PROVINCE OF BRITISH COLUMBIA

SCHOOL DISTRICT INFORMATION FORM

Name of school: Big Bar Upper.

School district: Lillooet.

Nearest railway station or boat landing: Clinton (P.G.E.)

Distance of railway station or boat landing from school: Thirty-six miles.

Boarding and lodging facilities for teacher: Shack 10x10 in School yard. Batch.

Cost of board and lodging: Rent and fuel $5 monthly; Living under $20.

General living conditions of district: Isolated and lonely. Crude, pioneer homes. Very little money to be had.

Present salary paid to teacher: $1140 per annum.

No. of children of school age in district: 10 No. enrolled: 10 Average attendance: 7.35 (Sept. 7 to Mar. 1)

No. of divisions in school: one-roomed. Four classes.

Chief industry of district: Ranching and dry-farming.

Character of country: Wooded benchland, Many deep ravines.

Climatic conditions: Dry; cold winter, occasional "Chinook" winds

Condition of school building and grounds: Log structure 18x16; grounds slashed only.

Does Board engage a janitor for school? No.

If possible enclose herewith a snapshot of the school building.

Additional remarks: Bonafide pupils belong to two families: 5 to Al. Neas; 3 to C. Cover. Mrs. Neas and Cover, trustees, do not agree. Third trustee inactive. This school requires a strict fearless teacher; and one who is impervious to dismay.

Date: March 9th, 1923. (Signed) Gerald S. Andrews.

Before his posting at Kelly Lake in the Rocky Mountain Trench the following September, Gerry Andrews taught for a year at Big Bar Upper School, near the railway station at Clinton. In his 1923 report to J.L. Watson in the Teachers' Bureau in Victoria, Andrews advises that his successor will need to be "a strict fearless teacher and one who is impervious to dismay" if he or she is to rise above local disagreements. Such were the qualifications for survival, if not success, in many rural schools of the time. **Courtesy B.C. Archives GR461.**

1924: "Report on Kelly Lake"

G.H. Gower, Inspector of Schools

As a school inspector, G.H. Gower was expected to visit each school in his district once or twice a year, depending on weather conditions. In the most isolated settlements, where travel was difficult, inspectors were rarely able to visit rural schools except during late spring or early autumn. Here is a typical report by Gower on the Kelly Lake School (located south of Pouce Coupé and west of Beaverlodge in the Rocky Mountain Trench) and its teacher, Gerry Andrews, who taught a class of Métis children. Gower's brief comments obviously reflect the language and the prejudices of the day:

> The children in this district are all 'breeds.' When the school opened last October, for the first time, hardly a child had any knowledge of the English language. Under Mr. Andrews the children are acquiring knowledge of the language and are progressing favourably along other lines. Mr. Andrews is well adapted to work of this type. He has an abundance of patience and shows skill in the teaching and management of non-English speaking pupils. His work in this district is very commendable.[14]

1925: "The courage to go back and go on"

Bernard Gillie

The following story tells how Bernard Gillie ventured from Victoria to his first posting in Hutton Mills (about 60 kilometers east of Prince George). After a somewhat rocky start in the classroom, thanks to the harsh appraisal of inspector G.H. Gower, Gillie would go on to become one of British Columbia's most prominent educators:

> My first year was up in the north country, way up north at Hutton Mills, and it was, of course, right on the railway.[15] In those days there were no roads up there. You got to your school by rail. That was the only way to move around, and we were connected, not by telephone, but usually by telegraph on the railroad. When I lived there, I boarded and had my meals with a man whose name was Brogan, who was the telegraph repairman for the railroad, and so by keeping in touch with him, we knew the whereabouts and activities of any suspicious individuals who might be regarded as likely inspectors, or 'snoopers' as we sometimes called them, from the Department of Education. So we always knew who was coming . . . [and] when the inspector was going to arrive. You'd get a message that he was on the way.

My first inspector was a man by the name of Gower. I must confess I never liked him. He gave me a horrible report, which I probably deserved. I don't remember. I had a dreadful day. I was having a terrible time in this school. I was a beginner. I'd been to normal school but I hardly even knew where to begin. I had about 28 or 29 youngsters in a one-room school in a lumber town. A beginner's class, quite a large beginner's class of eight or nine just starting. One of the things, you see, I had learned in normal school was that I had to make a lesson plan. If you were going to teach sensibly, you had to have lesson plans for all of your lessons. It didn't take me too long to figure out that if I had to have a lesson plan for seven or eight classes for every lesson for a day, it would take you a good week to do it, and that obviously, there wasn't a week available to do it in, so I very quickly abandoned that form of entertainment.

But he came in the fall when I was still trying to get myself sort of unravelled and I did, or tried to do, what every beginning teacher did then, and I guess does now. I kept thinking 'Now what did my teachers do? What kind of things did they have their kids do? And it dawned on me that they just did it by the seat of their pants most of the time. That's what I tended to do, like everybody else. Virtually every teacher I ever knew over the years, tended to revert to what they had seen their own teachers do. They went back to the only model they knew really well. Most of us, I should say, had the good sense to model ourselves on pretty capable people. All the things they had taught me at normal school went in one ear and out the other. By this stage, I had realized that most of the things I had learned were not very practical.

Most of the schools had a board of three people. There were more than 750 school districts in British Columbia at that time and in rural areas, one-board, one-school. That was the way it was at Hutton where I was, and it happened that the chair of the board was the wife of the manager of the mill, the big lumber mill where I was, and she was a well-educated and cultured person, fortunately for me. And I remember going to her after seeing this report, utterly crestfallen, just totally chagrined. I went to her and said: 'I've come Mrs. Howarth to offer you my resignation.' It was the only thing I could think to do, you know. 'I'm a failure. That's it. I've had the course. I've got to get out of this racket now.'

What I would have done, if she had said, 'Okay. I'll accept it.' I don't know, because I didn't even have the money to find my way home. I'd have had to go to work in the lumber mill, I guess, in order to get home. But anyway, she didn't. She was a very perceptive, very kind, understanding woman. She said, 'Here, Mr. Gillie. Don't be upset.' She said: 'You're a beginner. I know you've had your difficulties like everybody else under the circumstances. Much of

PROVINCE OF BRITISH COLUMBIA

SURVEY

OF THE

SCHOOL SYSTEM

BY

J. H. PUTMAN

Senior Inspector of Schools, Ottawa, Ontario

AND

G. M. WEIR

Professor of Education, The University of British Columbia
Vancouver, B.C.

VICTORIA, B.C.:
Printed by CHARLES F. BANFIELD, Printer to the King's Most Excellent Majesty.
1925.

No twentieth-century study of provincial schooling proved to be as influential as Putman and Weir's 1925 survey of British Columbia schools. The survey formally introduced progressive ideas about education from the United States to Canada's westernmost province and made progressivism the official dogma of the province's education department. From this time on, schooling in British Columbia would become far more American than British, both in thought and practice.

what you've done has been very successful and the children like you very much, and the parents really like you. You go on. You just carry on. Don't worry about Mr. Gower's report.' So that gave me the courage to go back and go on.[16]

1925: "Education is life, not a mere preparation for life"

J.H. Putman and G.M. Weir

In the early summer of 1924, school commissioners J.H. Putman and G.M. Weir were instructed by the minister and superintendent of education to undertake a comprehensive examination of provincial schools and to report their findings. Putman, the senior inspector of schools for Ottawa, and Weir, the first professor of education to be appointed in British Columbia three years earlier at UBC, produced their 556-page report on May 30, 1925. Publication of Putman and Weir's report, *Survey of the School System*, proved a watershed event in the history of provincial education.[17] It marked the formal introduction of American progressive ideas about schooling to British Columbia and, also, the first large-scale application of intelligence tests in Canadian schools. More than this, it provided a blueprint for educational developments that would be rigorously followed by the provincial education department for the next 35 years. Simply put, before Putman and Weir the character of curriculum and instruction in British Columbia was essentially British in origin and formal or classical in nature. After Putman and Weir, the chief influences on the province's curriculum and methods of instruction were increasingly American and progressive in character:

> The tendency is to transform the school into a mere knowledge factory, where drill upon lifeless subject matter is made an end in itself. In such a routine of mechanized procedure, quite the antithesis of the modern project activities discussed elsewhere . . . the formal disciplinarian finds a congenial environment for his soul-dwarfing, Gradgrind methods of instruction . . . If the child is to be enabled to 'see life steadily and see it whole,' nothing less will suffice. Physical education, scientific temperance instruction, biblical instruction, and sex education, as well as the usual activities of the classroom, should all be considered in the light of this supreme objective from which they cannot be logically divorced. The personality of the teacher, the many subtle and indefinable influences of daily social contacts in the classroom and on the playground, are also powerful, though less tangible means of moulding character.

The child should be taught, as a child, in terms of the life about him, in which he is an active and interested participant, and not merely as an adult for a mere future life. Education should take account of present as well as of deferred values. The greatest exponent of modern sociological theory underlying rational school practice is probably Professor John Dewey, whose viewpoint, discussed elsewhere in this Report, should be constantly kept in the foreground. Education is life, not a mere preparation for life consisting of the memorization of facts and principles and the mastery of a formal curriculum. Furthermore, life is real throughout and no artificial distinctions between the so-called preparation period of childhood and the alleged realization period of adult life should be set up. Many academic schools with their traditional curricular and formal methods of instruction have consistently ignored the admonitions of such educational philosophers as Rousseau, Dewey, and others, with the result that failure is written across the record of their activities. Such modern types of school organization as the platoon school and junior high school have come to the rescue in their attempt to put a little more life in education as well as more education in life.[18]

Fish Creek School, Peace River in the 1930s. **Courtesy Bill Plenderleith.**

1925: "J.L. Watson, the prince of administration"

Bernard Gillie

James L. Watson joined the government's education department in 1920 as registrar and secretary to the Provincial Board of Examiners. In these capacities, he was responsible for placing teachers in schools throughout the province and for making all arrangements necessary to conduct the annual examinations for matriculation and high school admission. His ability to recall the names and qualifications of teachers, as well as the location and condition of hundreds of small schools, was legendary in and outside the education department for many years.[19] Here Gillie, like many other teachers who were helped by Watson, remembers Watson's great generosity and kindness:

> When I finished my year at the normal school, and I got a standing that was called an honours standing at that time, then I came to look for a job. This was 1925. I remember this very well because I had no money. My parents were tremendously good to me but they said: 'You're on your own. We can't help you now.' I wanted to go on to university, but they said: 'You'll have to do that yourself.' So I wrote 56 applications for positions that were theoretically available in the province and went to see Mr. J.L. Watson, the registrar in the Department of Education. He was the prince of the administration of education of that day, and I guess I've never seen his equal from that day to this. He was well known by everybody. And I went into his office, I remember, and I said who I was and he said, 'Oh yes, Mr. Gillie. You were an honour student from Victoria, weren't you?' He'd never seen me. I could have wandered in off the street. He knew everybody and never forgot. Absolutely phenomenal.
>
> 'Well,' I said: 'Mr. Watson, I've written 56 applications, and I haven't even had a reply. Not a nibble.' And this was now getting on towards the end of July or early August. And he said, 'Well, there's a job going up at Hutton Mills. Do you know Hutton Mills?' I said, 'Sorry.' He said: 'Well, it's up on the Grand Trunk between Prince George and McBride, it's a lumber town. That's a pretty good job. Would you like a job there?' I said: 'I'll take a job anywhere.' 'Well,' he said: 'You send them an application. I think you'll find they'll accept you.' I said: 'Thank you very much. I'll do that.' And I went home and wrote the application and I got a reply back from Mrs. Howarth saying that they would accept me.
>
> Next summer, I came back to Victoria, and, of course, home. I went in. I was again looking for a job and I went in to see Mr. Watson. I went into his office. I walked in the door. He said: 'Good morning, Mr. Gillie. How are things in Hutton?' He said: 'Your report from Mr. Gower wasn't all that good, was it?' It was just a friendly form of conversation. A friendlier, more helpful, understanding man, I've never dealt with in education anywhere. I used to go and see him from then on, from time to time, for various things. I just used to go and see him, 'cause I liked him.[20]

1926: "A sense of humour is sometimes useful"

William Burns

One of the most important early figures in the history of provincial schooling was William Burns. From 1892 until 1901 he served as the province's second inspector of schools. In 1901, he was made principal of the Vancouver Provincial Normal School, an institution that trained thousands of British Columbia teachers until 1956 when the College of Education opened at UBC. Decades after his career as an inspector was over, he recalled his days inspecting schools and some of the experiences he had:

> Our teachers of today are so accustomed to visits from an inspector, and so well acquainted with their mutual duties, that it would seem difficult to imagine that only a few years ago the inspector was looked upon with suspicion as an intruder upon the teacher's rights and privileges; yet such was my experience during my early visits to some of our outlying school districts.
>
> After visiting a school and making some suggestions after school hours to the teacher for improvements in her work, she said: 'Well, I have taught here for some years and have never previously had an inspector's visit. I should like to know what you have got to do here at all?" I told the lady that I was a sort of scholastic father-confessor to give her any advice and assistance she might wish, but at the same time to suggest any improvements which seemed necessary.
>
> At another school which I reached after a 25-mile drive that morning, I requested the teacher to call up a class for reading. This he absolutely declined to do, saying that the class had taken their reading lesson in the morning and could not have another that day. It was after some little argument that this teacher was persuaded to allow the inspector to do as he desired for the remainder of his visit to the school. The chairman of the board, however, informed me afterwards that the board had received a complaint from their teacher in regard to my interference . . .
>
> Another teacher I found had gained a reputation for knowledge in a novel way. I had visited that school on a Friday and was much dissatisfied with the work done. Stopping over there until the Monday, I was sitting on the verandah of the inn when the village postmaster brought me a letter from the superintendent of education. 'I suppose you are the school inspector?' said this official, and I answered in the affirmative. 'Have you a teacher's certificate?' was the next question. I confessed to being the holder of one. 'What is yours?' 'A first-class,'

was my reply. 'Oh, well, you are not as good as our teacher, he has a third-class.' I found afterwards that the teacher had given this information to offset my unwelcome criticisms—merely an inversion of the numerical values.

Sometimes, however, I found that the pupils held a small opinion of the inspector's knowledge. I remember especially on one occasion when visiting a school that after some reading and spelling had been gone over, I requested the teacher to take a class in their geography lesson. It happened to be on the rivers of Africa, and after it was finished I asked some questions about British Columbia, and found as often the case, that little was known of this province. During the evening I called on the chairman of the board, who said he was expecting to see me. In conversation he told me that one of his boys had said: 'Father, we had a fellow in school today who pretended to know a lot, but he had to ask me a lot of questions about things. He looked out of the window and said he wondered what was the name of that river and of those mountains over there; so I told him that was just the creek, and them's the hills; they ain't got no other name as I knows of.' Surely a sense of humour is sometimes useful, even to a school inspector![21]

1926: "You can't do here what God Almighty didn't do."

Carlyle Clay

Like so many teachers in late-nineteenth and early-twentieth century British Columbia, Carlyle "Mike" Clay hailed from the Maritimes and, like many male teachers of his generation, his entry into teaching in the 1920s was prompted by the prospect of a steady job in otherwise uncertain economic times. Here is his own account of his entry into the teaching profession:

I was born in Nova Scotia. We came across and lived in the prairies, the Okanagan, and the coast. We travelled with the Canadian Pacific to Calgary, Calgary to Edmonton by Canadian Pacific, and Edmonton to Vermillion by Canadian National. Later, we went from Vermillion to Saskatoon by Canadian National and from Saskatoon to Summerland by Canadian Pacific—the rest of it was pretty well Canadian Pacific. My family came out West in 1905. We came to B.C. in 1915. We were on the prairies from 1905 to 1915. I was 16. I was born in 1898. My father was an accountant, my uncle on the other side was a lawyer; and on my father's side, there was a minister, a dentist and a doctor. So I came from an educated home. There were two boys and a girl in my family.

I guess I would have been classed as a bit of a radical. Because I can remember in grade 7 in Saskatoon, the principal there was going to strap a girl. Three or four of us thought it was a real terrible thing to strap a girl and we went to his house after school one evening and told him that if he strapped the girl we'd beat him up. I was expelled from school five times, but I think that helped me a lot.

I attended the Vancouver Normal School in 1925 and 1926. I had only a second-class certificate, so I taught elementary classes. Then I went back and did my senior matriculation on Saturdays and weekends and took summer school in directed reading courses to get my degree at UBC. I took my senior matriculation at the B.C. School of Pharmacy and Science where a lot of the fellows and women did as well. It was a coaching school, really.

Before I came out, I was digging sewers on 10th Avenue in Vancouver and we had to go down eight to 10 feet and then we tunnelled four feet each way and that was what I was doing. I was covered with mud when I came up from down there. I came up to get a pipe and I saw one of my normal school teachers coming up the road and I didn't want to see him in the condition I was in. However, he spotted me before I could get away and he came over and said: 'Have you got a job yet?' I said: 'No, I haven't.' 'Would you go up to the Cariboo?' I said: 'Sure!' I would have gone anywhere because jobs were scarce. So he gave me the address of the inspector up there who was in town just then, a Mr. Gower. He was also the official trustee. His headquarters were in Prince George and the school was halfway between Prince George and McBride, a one-room school with 32 pupils, grades 1 to 10. I got the large amount of $100 a month for teaching and $5 for janitorial work.

Homesteaders throughout the province put up simple buildings for themselves using local materials. **Courtesy Bill Plenderleith.**

Like homesteads of the day, schools were also simple in construction. Students and teacher at Noralee School, Burns Lake (left), c. 1940 and Mapes School, Vanderhoof, c. 1940 (right). **Courtesy Dorothea Stafford.**

The corral to the left of the school could be used for children's or teachers' horses.

Mr. Gower was quite a character. He was a tall, thin man, and he had a pretty rough time. He had to carry a sleeping bag so he'd have a place to sleep in that country. Much of his transportation was by rail and he just had to go however he could, a scholarly man. His bearing was deceptive at first. You would think he was a rather difficult person but I didn't find him to be so. He was my 'official trustee' as well as my inspector.[22] I had to go to him for everything I wanted. I got a couple of blackboard brushes at the time and a box of chalk and things like that. We had a very difficult situation in the school district I was in. The secretary of the board was in jail and the chairman of the board wanted the books. But the secretary wouldn't give them to him, so the chairman went down and broke into the secretary's house. At the time, the secretary and his wife were in jail. So the chap in jail went ahead and laid a charge of breaking and entering against the chairman of the board. So, in the end, we didn't have a board and Mr. Gower was made the official trustee for that reason.

The secretary had been in the army and was partially deafened. He had to go down to Prince George for examination or a 'check-up,' and he used to practice being deaf for some weeks before he went down. When he went down, his wife let the loggers around know he was going out, and she would not mind a little entertainment. He would come in the middle of this and find them. So both of them were in for blackmail. That was my first year there.

We had a great spirit among the people for the teacher and the inspector. They thought the inspectors were out to get us, and they did everything they could to help us out. During my first year, the language that the grade 1's were using was very difficult to understand and they came with their own family. So Gower came in and realized the situation and he wasn't very happy when I was taking their reading. So, he suggested I let them go for recess and he said:

'Clay, you have one hell of a mess here.' I said I realized that I had and what I wanted him to do was tell me how to fix it. 'I want some help from you.' He looked at me for a minute or two and said, 'You can't do here what God Almighty didn't do.' And I said: 'Fine, as long as you remember that when you are making out my report.'[23]

1927: "The most important man"

Stewart Graham

Unlike many teachers who only knew the school registrar through correspondence, longtime schoolman Stewart Graham's relationship with J.L. Watson was personal as well as professional. Their relationship illustrates the closeness among professional educators during the first half of the twentieth century, as well as the closeness of a provincial society where "everybody knew everybody else" at the time. In the following reminiscence, Graham explains the origins of this relationship with Watson:

Dr. Willis was the provincial superintendent. He was actually the deputy minister. He had an assistant, D.L. MacLaurin. However, the most important man for the day-to-day operations of the education department was the registrar, J.L. Watson. A fabulous man, a man who, I think, could recite the name of every teacher in British Columbia. When I was married and came down in July, I went to see Mr. Watson and he said, 'I hear you're married.' And I said, 'Yes.' He said, 'Who did you marry?' I said, 'Olive Nordrow.' 'Oh, Olive Letitia Nordrow. She graduated in such-and-such a time,' and so on.

In retrospect it was J.L. Watson who phoned me and offered me a job in 1927. I was earning $9 a week running a mattress machine with Victoria Bed and Mattress and he phoned me at the Victoria Bed and Mattress during the noon hour. No one answered the phone. The phone rang several times and finally I went in and answered it and it was J.L. Watson and he asked me: 'Would you like a job?' And he described it. 'Could you bring your car?' I said: 'Yes.' He said: 'We'll pay you $2.50 an hour, double-time for overtime and you'll have to work the first of July,' because that's when the [examination] papers were distributed.

He had a son and a daughter. The son and I were very good friends, Don Watson. And if J.L. Watson thought you had any ability, if he thought you were a good type, he saw that you got a job. Later his son said to me, 'Father would like to have a car. Now you turn your car in every year. Would you consider selling your car? And I said: 'Yes.' And he said: 'Would you teach him how to drive?' And I said, 'Yes.' And I taught Mr. Watson to drive. In retrospect, I realized he was the second or third highest paid man in the education department but he was well into his 50s and never owned a car, never had enough money. One of my regrets was the fact that just a few months before I joined the department he died of cancer. I had been over to see him at Christmas that year. When I came down on my Christmas holidays I always dropped in to his home.[24]

1926: "Well, they can't laugh at the teaching...being done."

Alice Glanville

Regional historian, Alice Glanville, is known for her volume, *Schools of the Boundary, 1891-1991,* from which this brief but warm memory of a school inspector is taken:

Many will tell of the school inspector, Mr. Sheffield. I can't say enough in his favor. He was demanding, but so kind to many lonesome young teachers and we surely needed encouragement, not criticism. When I said that people laughed at my tiny school, he replied, 'Well, they can't laugh at the teaching that is being done.' And that answer was applicable to many one-room schools at that time.[25]

1927: Mildred McQuillan's diary

The entries in Mildred McQuillan's 1927 diary cover four months in the Orange Valley School, 10 miles from Fort Fraser near Prince George. They stand as a rare and candid record of the appalling living conditions that faced many young female teachers.[26] McQuillan's general disgust with her assignment and her bleak description of a schoolteacher's life is unmatched in content or style in any other writing of this time. Here in blunt term she describes her journey north and some of the ills that befell her. Samples from her diary penned during the autumn she spent at the school illustrate why many of the province's some 800 rural districts were obliged to recruit new teachers annually:

Sunday, September 11, 1927: Left home by stage for Fort Fraser . . . Got ticket. Lost four bones [dollars] to get to Fort Fraser.

Monday, September 12, 1927: Left Vancouver at 9:30 a.m. Mrs. Brunt came down to see me off. Advised me to stay a year. Had supper on train; no dinner, couldn't eat. Slept on train.

Tuesday, September 13, 1927: The porter calls at 4:00 a.m. to change trains at Red Pass Junction in the Rockies. Roll out, pitch dark: alone in the world. Five men and myself all go in the station for an hour: have a fire for a while and then nearly freeze, walk track to get warm. Got into hotel dump at 8:00 a.m. Have cold stale breakfast for 50 cents—horrors . . . Arrive at Fort Fraser at 11:30 p.m. Conductors and trainmen disturbed my sleep three times thinking they'd taken me beyond my destination. Mr. Moore and Dibbles meet me. Some cold burg! Have 10-mile drive in Ford; heart in my mouth all the way. Roads rough, narrow and crooked as a snake. Get to new home about 1:00 a.m. Boarding house. Enough said! Sleep soundly in new bunk.

Wednesday, September 14, 1927: Breakfast, couldn't eat, homesick, go a mile over trail through woods to school. All in, climbing the hills. Come in sight of little log school in middle of forest. No yard, no flagpole, no water, dirty kids, 16 in number. Little space and little equipment, dark as a cave. Growl at kids all morning. Homesick as the devil . . .

Friday, September 16, 1927: Crawl off to school, same as a snail. Boys blacken faces on black stumps after school. I don't give a hoot. Take myself to Fraser Lake at night, go visiting: some ride in the mud coming home!

Cheam School near Chilliwack was just one of hundreds of rural schools in the interwar era where pupils enjoyed little in the way of school sports, save what they could organize in the rough yards around schools. Photographs such as these testify to the immense differences in educational and social opportunities afforded rural and urban youngsters before 1950. Courtesy B.C. Archives I-00525.

Saturday, September 17, 1927: Sleep till 10:00 a.m. or at least stuck to bed. Finally, crawl out and have egg, toast, cakes for breakfast, refuse mush. Do my weekly wash in muddy water. Clean mud off shoes from night before and work at [embroidering] tea cloth to beat the dickens. Go to bed about 10:00 p.m.

Wednesday, September 21, 1927: Off to school, been here a week, seems like months. Smoke first cigarette in desperation, scared stiff in case some old woman pays a visit while doing so. Get home to find I've missed a car ride . . .

Monday, September 26, 1927: No better at getting kids down to work. Children go home now after being kept in an hour and made work . . .

Friday. September 30, 1927: Dr. Stone visited school. Tells of former happenings and people. Smoke cigarette on my way home, getting used to country. Make out reports and count days till Xmas . . .

Saturday, October 1, 1927: Sleep as per usual till late. Actually get my hair washed after being grey with dust, sew and wash. Get ready for grand dance at Fraser Lake. Leave about 8:00 p.m. Served supper out of grey enamelware. Get home 3:30 a.m., feel homesick . . .

Monday, October 3, 1927: Another week to pass by. Kids have awful colds, snows a little. Come home and write letters.

Tuesday, October 4, 1927: Wake up with devilish cold. Go to school feeling ill.

Saturday, October 8, 1927: Try my weekly sponge bath. No life for me. Two months and one week left. Went down to visit Mrs. Newman. Walk past trail to her place, about half mile too far, go back and finally find it, a shack in the woods. Lonesome, deliver me . . .

Tuesday, October 11, 1927: My 23rd birthday today. Horrors! Smoke cigarette on my way home, snow coming down thick and fast. Find five letters for me when I get home. I fall into a dream and read them. Played cards tonight for first time . . .

Sunday, October 16, 1927: Not a thing to do, rotten day, no chance of even going to Kirk. Got mail and cheque today. Feel like taking train out tomorrow night . . .

Thursday, October 20, 1927: Slept soundly for once last night. Ran out of matches so no smoke today. Tried to light one in stove while janitor was sweeping but he was too curious so didn't succeed . . .

Sunday, October 23, 1927: Eight more weeks and I'll be well on my way home. Wonderful, washed my hair in hard old water in wee basin, no bath. Finish a few letters. The Dibbles Jr. arrive. I get out some dough to pay my board and holy, dying catfish, church on fire! Suffering tomcats! Holy smokes! Ye gods! My stars! Dirty dying Dora! Damn. Absolutely robbery! Outrageous, I have to pony up 35 bones for this dive. Haven't yet got my breath back and am not Scotch either. I'll say I won't be rich when I get out of prison . . .

Tuesday, November 1, 1927: Ground white this a.m. but gone again. Heard coyotes calling tonight. They did a little butchering here today. Killed the old sow I was scared stiff of and had her liver for supper.

Saturday, November 5, 1927: Watched it break daylight this a.m. Arrived at Prince George at 8:00 a.m., then made a beeline for Prince George Hotel and got a room with bath. Three bones a night, too, but worth it to me. Had a 20-cent breakfast and rolled into bed nearly dead. I slept till noon, my head being better, I washed my hair and had a bath, the first in two months. It took me two hours to have a clean up, then I wandered out to look town over, and some place in the mountains. Cold as charity . . .

Sunday, November 6, 1927: Got up at 12:00 a.m., had a hot bath and then dined. Two meals a day is my limit. I went out for a stroll and nearly froze. Took a snap of schools and tried to locate Miss Milligan . . . Went out to dine and thought I was hitting a fair restaurant and it turned out to be some joint. Nothing but Chinese restaurants here. Too many hobos roaming the streets, so I returned to the hotel PDQ and will now proceed to write letters, read, sew, and wash my hair once again and then sleep till noon tomorrow . . .

Tuesday, November 8, 1927: Ten degrees above zero, nearly freeze. Get to school and I am first there so I lit the fire. Being a smoker I had matches; anyway I told janitor to step around earlier after this. Kids sit around fire while I read a chapter of *King Arthur* . . . I get home nearly frozen . . . I get a notice saying school closes December 22 but I don't give a rip. I'm closing a week or more earlier . . .

Friday, November 11, 1927: Get to school this a.m. to find one pupil crying with cold . . .

Monday, November 14, 1927: Thank heavens in a month's time I'll be ready for train . . .

Tuesday, November 15, 1927: Real cold with a wind, have to hold my mitt over my big nose today . . . Got a supply of notepaper today so just took great pleasure in writing out my resignation . . .

Thursday, November 24, 1927: More snow today. Came home and had hot dinner. After school I went for mail and got back after dark tired out. Scared stiff in case I'd meet a coyote or two. Bears should be denned up so didn't worry about them . . .

Saturday, December 10, 1927: Darn near froze last night, only 27 or so below. Got up and we all went to Fraser Lake. The coldest day I ever witnessed. Had blankets over us, and straw as well . . . Have four more days to put in . . .

Tuesday, December 13, 1927: Prepare for concert tonight. Let kids go home early to get ready. I sew a big grey blanket up for a curtain, and stuck sacks of candy on tree . . . Got concert started at 8:30 with seven spectators. Nine arrived in all. Some of the kids bawled and wouldn't do their bit . . . I strolled home feeling happy to think it was my last night in Orange Valley . . .

Thursday, December 15, 1927: Feeling like the dickens. No train . . . Train finally comes at 5:45 a.m. and I say 'Goodbye' thank heavens! Train had been delayed because it couldn't get steam up. 'Twas so darn cold, cold, cold. Train goes along slowly. I get a sleeper but was roosted out so I crawl out about 9:00 a.m. Go and dine. Great to get something tempting to eat. Go slowly along our way. Snow has to be cleared off track. Scenery is wonderful, loads of snow, icicles. Get to Pacific at foot of mountains at 2:30 p.m. and are told a big snow slide ahead of us 20 ft. deep so would have to wait at Pacific . . .

Friday, December 16, 1927: Still at Pacific, 150 miles from Prince Rupert and boat is to leave at 9:00 a.m. CNR wired through to say boat would wait till 3:00 p.m. for us. None of us wanted to miss the S.S. Prince Rupert for it would mean some old Union tub to travel to Vancouver on and I knew them from Valdez Island trips. Snow was finally cleared away and we leave this hole at 10:30 a.m. or so, all very much relieved.[27]

1927: "Help, what do I do now?"

Bernard Gillie

Long before the advent of a modern health care system and the establishment of routine inoculations to prevent serious contagious diseases, the outbreak of epidemics forced school closures and terrified communities. Here, school principal Bernard

Gillie describes the outbreak of a polio epidemic in the Okanagan Valley during the second half of the 1920s, an event that led to the community being quarantined:

> When I went to teach my second year at Ellison, which was a two-room school just outside of Kelowna, I . . . took over as principal. Let's face it, I'd never been principal of anything until I got there. Being principal of a two-room school is not exactly a position of great prominence, and it so happened that the year I went there . . . the girl teaching in the primary class was a girl I'd gone to normal school with, and that helped a lot, because we knew each other and worked well together.
>
> But about the end of September, an infantile paralysis epidemic, a polio epidemic, broke out in Kelowna and the regions surrounding—and a very serious one. The school was closed before the end of September. They closed all the schools in the Okanagan valley. A number of children and other people died. A very significant number suffered serious impairments and so on. It was really tough. We didn't open again until after what was Armistice, or Remembrance Day. So it was a period of nearly two months the schools were closed. Obviously, it wasn't easy to run a school or try to build anything. You couldn't leave the district. You weren't allowed to. I couldn't go.
>
> Anyway, as a further complication, the very first day that school opened, at 10 o'clock there was a knock at the door. I went to the door and here is this chairman of the school board, I knew him very well, and he had 18 young people with him. 'Mr. Gillie,' he said, 'These youngsters are a group of Austrians who have just come, imported into Canada, into the Okanagan from Austria. Their parents are working in the tobacco industry.'
>
> In those days, the Kelowna valley was a center for a big tobacco industry. There were tobacco barns and tobacco fields all over the place. But these youngsters from Austria were scared out of their wits. And he said, 'Here's a list of their names.' Not being Austrian, I couldn't even pronounce their names. He said, 'They'll be with you for this year.' And he said, 'They don't speak any English.' Here was I, with a classroom of grades 5, 6 and 7, and a primary room [some 40 students], and here I've got these 18 new Austrian youngsters speaking no English and I didn't have a clue as to what to do.
>
> So I lined them up, the smallest one at that end and the largest one at that end and I divided them down the middle, and said 'You people, you're in the primary room, and you people are in my room here. And it happened that the oldest ones, there were a couple, two youngsters from one family that were about 15, and they had obviously been in a couple of years of high school in

Austria. Anyway, my point is that I didn't know what to do. I hadn't any idea, and the only person I could think of who could possibly give me some practical help was C.B. Wood, who taught me in normal school. So I sat down that very first night and I wrote a letter to C.B. 'Help! What do I do now?' sort of thing. And within the week, I got back several books and he wrote a long letter setting out in practical form things that I could do about handling this situation.

It was just a lifesaver. And we got through the year. It was difficult, but we made it . . . But this was an example of the kind of support that teachers wanted and in so many instances never got.[28]

The School Inspector

Riding the river to inspect schools in the spring. **Courtesy Bill Plenderleith.**

From 1900 to 1925, the number of new schools and the size of school enrollments grew rapidly. This led to an increase in the number of provincial school inspectors and the size of the territories they would patrol. Completion of the Grand Trunk Pacific Railway between Edmonton and Prince Rupert meant that the Peace River area was now open to settlement. As settlements grew around mills and agricultural communities, new schools were established as soon as 10 youngsters of school age could be rounded up. Local schools were governed by an elected three-person school board, charged with providing a school and maintaining its upkeep. To ensure a crude measure of educational quality and compliance with provincial regulations, school inspectors were expected to examine all schools in their territory at least once a year. This usually involved travelling by rail or by car over muddy or snow-choked roads to visit schools, and to encourage communities to improve school buildings and the teachers' living conditions. At times, school inspectors were also expected to sort out local quarrels that sometimes went beyond schoolhouse doors.

1927: "My first inspector was a tremendous gentleman"

Stewart Graham

Although school inspectors were frequently regarded as fearsome individuals who could make teachers and, sometimes, entire schools tremble, this was not always accurate. Here Stewart Graham recalls school inspector Ray McLeod, a kindly man greatly affected by wounds he sustained in World War I:

> I went to work for the education department on July 1, 1927 but that was as a student, working in the summer . . . I worked all summer with the inspectors of schools. I joined the department as a full-fledged, full-time member, went to work on August 15, 1945. In the meantime, my first job was principal of a school in Dawson Creek, a new school, a four-room school when the railway went in. Then I was in Creston, which was the first voluntary consolidation of seven or eight school districts. Max Cameron [author of the 1946 finance report that led to the amalgamation of hundreds of school districts] used that as one of his ideal models.[29] Max was a close personal friend of mine. We worked, played bridge and talked things over together.
>
> [As a principal], I had four first-year inspectors and they were all new brooms, and I hoped that when I was appointed that I didn't act like a new broom. There was Ray McLeod, a cripple, who should never have been sent into the Peace River. He died up there. Bill Plenderleith, J. Elmer Brown, and K.B. Woodward were the others. McLeod was a husky man, gray wiry hair, horribly wounded in the First World War. I can describe his first inspection of mine. It was in wintertime. The school was about three blocks from the main street in Dawson Creek, a town of about 400 people, and Mr. McLeod had come up the night before and stayed in the Dawson Hotel that was another two blocks up

Peace River school inspector Bill Plenderleith in a sled making his school rounds in the mid-1930s. **Courtesy Bill Plenderleith.**

Main Street. Now he did that because it was political to bring business. In 1932 no one had any money. Mr. McLeod came around the corner, three blocks away, and started up in the snow. He had an artificial leg. It took him close to . . . an hour to advance three blocks, the piece he had to walk. By the time he reached my school I was sort of a sweating wreck.

My first inspector was a tremendous gentleman. One thing he helped me do was organize the first local of the BCTF in the Peace River. And at our first convention, I proposed the toast to the Department of Education and Ray McLeod replied. We stayed until about three o'clock in the morning in the lobby of the Hart Hotel in Pouce Coupé talking. About two weeks later he was dead. The work was impossible for him up there. You see, to get from Dawson Creek to Fort St. John by team and cutter, and that was a fast team and a good cutter, took two days.

McLeod lived in Pouce Coupé. He was the first resident school inspector in the Peace River. There was seven miles of gravel in the Peace River, from Dawson Creek to Pouce Coupé. The reason was that the liquor store was in Pouce Coupé and Dawson Creek was the largest town. So they put gravel on the road so they could get through under most adverse conditions. The rest was gumbo. I can best illustrate the condition of northern roads by describing a trip from Progress to Dawson Creek. Progress was 25 miles west of Dawson Creek. I spent a full day in my car in 1946 or 1947 when I went back there to cover those 25 miles . . . And that's the type of thing that Ray McLeod had to do when he drove his car [in the 1930s]. And that's the reason, incidentally, why the teachers had such a dreadfully lonely life. Travel was almost impossible most of the year.[30]

1927: "You already know how to handle this situation"

Gerry Andrews

Gerry Andrews, who would later become surveyor general for British Columbia, began his career as a schoolteacher in the remote outpost of Kelly Lake in the Rocky Mountain Trench, a posting that could only be reached by several days of grueling travel by cutter or on horseback. In this brief piece, Andrews' impressions of the inspector, G.H. Gower, are considerably different from those registered by Bernard Gillie during his time at Hutton Mills. In contrast to Gillie, who claimed Gower to be incredibly unsympathetic to the problems faced by young teachers, Andrews regarded Gower as "a fine and helpful friend:"

In many of British Columbia's interior settlements, the cheapest and easiest forms of local construction were log buildings with a pole roof covered in sod. Although this particular building at Kelly Lake was abandoned when the school inspector photographed it, the flagpole was still standing, although the chimney was not. The tiny windows and low ceilings were subjects of concern to the school inspectors who called repeatedly for improvements to lighting and ventilation in their annual reports. Courtesy Bill Plenderleith.

The school inspector's visit finally materialized about the end of February . . . The Peace River district was then served by G.H. Gower, based at Prince George. He had an enormous territory to cover, much of it by primitive and arduous travel. He arrived at Kelly Lake late one afternoon quite unexpectedly, having come in a light cutter with a driver via Swan Lake and Brainard's. Bed and board . . . were no problem. Jim was away, so his cot was vacant. Mr. Gower spent most of the next day in the school and then left for Swan Lake in the evening, probably having late supper at Mrs. Brainard's.

He was friendly, sympathetic and helpful, and the evening gave us a chance to get acquainted. In the morning he had me go through my usual routines with younger and older-age groups both separately and together. After lunch he took over with his own questions and routines. Asked to describe the action of putting out the light, one boy responded, 'Kill the light.' This amused Mr. Gower, who thought it entirely logical.

I sensed that the inspector's reactions were favorable. I remarked to him that, at the beginning, I had thought of writing to the normal school in Vancouver for advice. 'Forget it,' he replied, 'you already know how to handle this situation better than anyone there.' He also expressed admiration for my wholesome way of life—baching, getting firewood, water, caring for and exercising my saddle horse, my evening classes for adults, pinch-hitting in Jim's store, and [continuing] my senior matriculation studies. He strongly urged me to return for a second school year, so our good start would not be in vain. I was encouraged and gratified. I had won a fine and helpful friend.[31]

1927 and 1928: "Dear theacher [sic]"

George Emmila

George Emmila was a Métis pupil at Kelly Lake. In 1927 and 1928, he wrote two letters to his former teacher, Gerry Andrews, who was then attending the University of Toronto. Emmila's letters are interesting in two respects. First, they reflect the profound difficulties many aboriginal children faced when it came to writing in one language, English, while they continued to speak their own native language every day out of school. Second, the letters also illustrate that the attendance of aboriginal children in rural schools was interrupted by the adherence of aboriginal families to traditional practices, such as hunting or fishing in the autumn months:

> You donte know wow happy as I am when I get your letter come. My Father he sick bad, But he getten better. He is gone to the mountains. They kill lots of fur But fur diden worth nothing. A big coyot cost $4 and rats 90 c. That is good prise and mink is good prise to. My Grande Father is not hom now. He will com sune I think teacher. He kill not very much fur. That is all for my Grande Father.
>
> The ice is not very strong. It is not frozen hard this winter. But we have skating all winter. It is very good to skate now at Kelly Lake. I have a good pair of skates Teacher gave me and she gave hus knifes. She gave tgen boys. Mr. Young [the trapper whose trading post doubled as a school] is not home to he go to the grande Prairie he will come back last of this week. I ask for a suite of clothes for me. It is no snow in here. It is gone be summer soon. We will play ball soons. Now that you left Adolphus lost the ball. I like this teacher. Adolphus get abnout six whipinygs. I get one times strap. Theacher hit me both hands about five times each hand. That is all for today Theacher so good-bye. Send me a letter soon as you get my letter Please. Your loving boy George Emmila.[32]
>
> Letter Two:
>
> Just a few lines to let you know I am going to mountains tomorrow morning. I have been at mountains twice with my brother so I dinent go to school not very good this winter. But I am going to school when other teacher comes, so I and not good writer yet. I am excuse with my writing I am sorry I cannot write good, mabe you will trow away my letter. That is all for that. My dade dinit kill much fur this winter because my little sister was sick. She is juss a bow two

months old. She isn't very strong yet so goodby. If you write me I will tell you lots of things about Kelly lake now. Please send me letter soon as you get my letter. I am very loonsome with you. Your strolly Mr George Emmila.[33]

Life in British Columbia's interior was difficult. The climate was harsh, the winters often brutal, and roads were usually poor and, sometimes, non-existent. In such places, the life of the teacher was far from genteel. So, too, was it challenging for inspectors to get from school to school as many found out first-hand. **Courtesy Bill Plenderleith.**

1928-1930: "Many nationalities and only one flag"

From public education's earliest beginnings in British Columbia, the province's schools were characterized by youngsters from diverse social, cultural, and linguistic backgrounds. By the early years of the twentieth century, immigration's effects were evident in city and village schools alike. As the following discussion shows, nowhere was more culturally diverse than east Vancouver and, in particular, the area around Strathcona School, a neighbourhood that became a melting pot for immigrants from Eastern and Western Europe as these teachers from the school recall:

> Gertrude Doyle: There was no stage in the school of any kind but we had all this talent, and we needed money, so they put all the tables together, right in the end of the hall, and their dressing room was the staff room. The performance was put on top of these tables, swaying as they were. There were Ukrainian dances with costumes, Japanese costumes, all sorts of little plays and skits and things like that, and it was a howling success. It must have been 1928 to 1930, right in there somewhere. And then every Friday, we'd have a half an hour in the auditorium, and sometimes it would be a Japanese program, sometimes a

Chinese program, sometimes Jewish, sometimes blacks. They took their turns and it used to run overtime.

Jennie Schooley: One of these concerts that we had was 'International Day.' Miss Roberts put it on and she taught all the children the chorus of all the national anthems. She had all the Italians in one section, all the Ukrainians in another, all the Chinese in another, all the Japanese in another, and all the various nationalities in groups. And then, the people of that nationality would sing the first verse of their national anthem in their own language and the whole senior building would sing the chorus, and then they'd go on to the next national group. That was just thrilling. I can never remember when I was there in the 1930s and 1940s any discrimination of any kind. We never thought, this one's Chinese, this is Japanese, this is something else. We just thought they were all children, and they too, they all mixed together.

Eileen Farrington: It was the school of many nationalities and only one flag. That was our motto.[34]

This 1931 Ganges grades 1 and 2 class illustrates a long tradition of youngsters from multicultural backgrounds in British Columbia schools. Visiting one such class in an urban school, an inspector casually noted: "Ten of the pupils come from homes where a foreign language is spoken." **Courtesy Ivan and Sue Mouat.**

1927: "A considerable rivalry"

Stewart Graham

During the early decades of the twentieth century when high schools were confined to a handful of cities and large towns, responsibility for their inspection rested with two long-serving government officials, Albert Sullivan (1909-1943) and J.B. DeLong (1913-1946) who became legendary in educational circles because of their influence over the province's high schools. Stewart Graham, who became an inspector himself in 1945, recalled the differences between the two men and how their particular personal characteristics shaped their approach to school administration.

When I went to work in 1927, the operation of the 'departmental' examinations was divided between J.B. DeLong and Albert Sullivan, two gentlemen who didn't like each other. There was a considerable rivalry. I guess stemming from the fact that they were the only two high school inspectors . . .

Now, this was the division of work. Mr. DeLong was in charge of the high school matriculation examination papers and the processing of them in the Parliament Buildings. When they came into the free textbook branch; my job was to take them out and distribute them to the people at Victoria College where they were marked under the supervision of Albert Sullivan. When they were marked, I brought them to the Parliament Buildings, where teams of three—an inspector, and a couple of high school principals, or university professors—entered the marks on huge bookkeeping sheets. You see there was the 60-40 method of being successful. You needed 50 per cent to pass, but if you got an average of 60 per cent, you were allowed to drop to 40 per cent in one or two subjects. So these marks were all entered on this big sheet of paper, added without adding machines, and the average taken and decision made whether the pupil passed or not.

I can illustrate the two men's character this way. Albert Sullivan called me in to his office, which was the principal's office I think at the college and he said, 'I want you to go to A, B and C, (naming three places in Victoria) where permission had been given for the men to mark the exams in their homes. Because I was trying to be efficient I just thought that instead of going from A and B to C, it would be much closer to go to B then to A and, finally, to C, and I did this and came back to the college. As I entered the college in the front hallway, I was told by a solemn-faced member of the Department of Education that Mr. Sullivan wanted to see me. And I walked into his office and he kept me standing while he did some work of his own. Then he looked at me and he said, 'Stewart, you took some papers out to be marked.' 'Yes sir.' 'Where did you go?' I told him. 'Is that the way I told you to do this?' I said, 'No sir, I thought . . .' 'I want no explanations. In future you will follow my directions explicitly.'

I said that three teams of three entered these marks and added them. Now, there was a fabulous character by the name of Jake Palmer, who was the principal of John Oliver High School and he thought that he was a whiz at arithmetic. He could add faster than anyone else, and he and a man by the name of Woodward, with another one, was the team of three.[35] DeLong found out that I was a whiz at mental addition, so he took the third man out and put me in with Palmer and Woodward. In all modesty, I beat him every time. DeLong would then come in and ride Jake Palmer. 'You're letting this kid beat you. You're not?' Now, that's about as good a picture of the two characters, both well educated, both highly respected: one rigid, 'this is the letter of the law and that's what you do;' the other with a Puckish sense of humour who was always looking for a joke.[36]

1930: "A particular liking for my wife's muffins"

Carlyle Clay

A different portrait of high school inspector J.B. DeLong was provided by Carlyle Clay, whose Okanagan class DeLong inspected. Clay, who became an inspector himself toward the end of his educational career, explains that the kindly DeLong battled a serious stomach ailment throughout his life that gave him a "lean and hungry look" that unnerved teachers:

The sleigh used by nurses to visit schools, farms, and ranches in the Peace River was also used at times by the school inspector to make his rounds. Occasionally, it was also used by local law enforcement officers to track down miscreants. Courtesy Bill Plenderleith.

I went to Rutland and T.R. Hall was my inspector. He was not English but he was a very cultured person, very fair and interested in teachers. Hall was very approachable and his office door was open every Saturday. Then I had J.B. DeLong and he and I got along fine. He was tall and thin. [He looked like} an undertaker. Paced back and forth. I had him in Rutland for a little while. The first year I was in Rutland we had an epidemic of polio and we didn't open school until November 12, although it was a superior school.[37]

The principal was having a pretty heavy load and I had a fairly heavy load but my subjects weren't as heavy as his. I only had a second-class certificate, but I took part of the grade 10 class, which I wasn't supposed to do. One morning, when I came in, my class was all seated and it was very quiet. I couldn't quite see it, as it was a bit dark in one corner. When I finally looked down, there was J.B. DeLong sitting in one of the seats down at the back. The class was out for recess. He mentioned my teaching grade 10 with only a second-class

In almost all parts of the province, getting to school was difficult. Here Peace River youngsters in the 1930s used skis (above) and toboggans (below) as transportation. **Courtesy Bill Plenderleith.**

certificate and said: 'however, you are doing very well at it and we won't say anything about it. We'll just leave it.' He and I became very good friends. He was so thin and pale because he suffered terribly from stomach trouble. We had him up for meals once in awhile and he had to be very careful of what he ate. He had a particular liking for my wife's muffins.[38]

1930s: A principal's work at Woodfibre

Dorothea Stafford

In the following story, former schoolteacher Dorothea Stafford provides a glimpse into the professional life of her husband, Harold Stafford, during his days as a principal at Woodfibre School on Howe Sound and at Kimberley in the East Kootenays during the 1930s:

Woodfibre . . . was a 'company town' with a three-room school. The school board members were proud of the school and were not afraid to spend money.

Many of the workers in the pulp mill were Japanese. The town was comprised of two distinct sections with the mill in the middle. By the time the Japanese children reached grades 7 and 8 they spoke English fluently. However, in grades 1 and 2, where they equalled the number of English speaking children, there was a language problem. But the expression 'ESL' hadn't been invented! Teachers managed as best they could.

The only way to reach Woodfibre was by Union Steamships or privately owned boats. We knew that the inspector of schools would come on one of the two days of the week when the Union Steamships boats would stop at Woodfibre before proceeding to Squamish. On its return trips to Britannia Beach and Vancouver it called in again at Woodfibre. The school inspector was L.J. Bruce, a tall, soft-spoken gentleman with a well-trimmed beard who came once a year to make reports on the teachers. He told us that children were in awe of him. They would go home and tell their parents that the King (or God) had visited their classroom. Thus, Mr. Bruce would be at the school for no more than two hours after he had climbed the steep flight of steps to the school on the hill. It was remarkable how quickly a messenger would arrive at the door of the principal's classroom with the word that we would soon have a visitor. We always had advance notice!

Many people in the province's vast inland empire made a living in lumber.
Courtesy Dorothea Stafford.

Harold went to Kimberley in mid-term, January 1930. The annual reports show the total number of classrooms but fail to mention that three of these rooms were located away from the center of town. There was a one-room school at the Top Mine about a mile or more above town. It was closed after a few years. The two-room school at the concentrator site, Chapman Camp, was a more modern building than the big school. It was a two-mile walk away and we had no car.

It is interesting to note that some reports mentioned the salary received by a principal. One very vivid memory of those years was a decrease in salary in 1934 and 1935. In 1936 the salary returned to the amount in 1933. At the time of the decrease one staff member, a single man, said: 'They can't do that to us' before he resigned. It was several years before he could get back into the profession. The secretary of the school board was an accountant in the office of the mining company. I do not know the basis for the salaries, but I knew that a decrease played havoc with a household budget that was already strained to the limit . . .

At no time did Harold have clerical help in his office. One afternoon a week I looked after the records for the 'Penny Bank' project. I spent the afternoon in the office but I cannot recall how many years this program continued. The clerical help I was able to give was helping with the marking of standardized tests and easily marked subjective examinations. Harold typed his letters and reports on his own typewriter which cost $70, paid for at the rate of $7 a month . . .

> In the nine and a half years we lived in Kimberley, Harold's life revolved around the school . . . He was also the representative from Kimberley for the BCTF . . . Later, he was a delegate to a meeting of the provincial executive in Vancouver. At one meeting he was called out by a secretary to receive a telegram announcing the birth of our eldest son. He remembered the return trip by train as two of the longest days in his life, made even longer by delays when the train was caught between rock slides.[39]

1930s: "Because I was so rich"

The Great Depression devastated British Columbia. Reduced demand for goods saw laid-off workers from mills and farms scrounging for municipal work, mainly road repairs and building. Those hired, more often than not, owed their good fortune to the preferential hiring practices that favoured married men with children. For the others, hope lay in cobbling together enough odd jobs to eke out a living or to become part of the barter economy that emerged as "regular" jobs vanished. On farms and ranches, hired hands were the first to be let go and even well-established agricultural businesses such as seed companies were forced to cut labourers' wages from $3.50

The lean years of the 1930s were apparent in photographs of youngsters in schools. Especially in rural British Columbia, photographs show children poorly-clad with many reduced to wearing overalls and torn sweaters. Hand-me-down clothing, sometimes cut from an older brother or father's suit, was commonly the order of the day. The clothes of the senior students in Merritt's grade 11 class in 1930 appear threadbare. Even women teachers found it difficult to maintain a smartly-dressed appearance or to project a professional image when their salaries had been slashed. **Courtesy B.C. Archives F-01110.**

to $1.50 a day. In the Peace River, by one estimate, seven out of 10 families sought government relief. The poverty of many Depression-era families was evident when children came to school. Rather than see their charges go hungry, principals and teachers often dipped into their own pockets to provide pupils with something to eat. Of a 1930s Salt Spring Island school without electricity, indoor plumbing, or water, a teacher recalled:

> In the winter time when it was cold and we had the fire going, we used to put a kettle on the heater to boil water and then the older girls would make hot cocoa for the students. I thought because I was so rich, being paid $70 per month, I could afford it.[40]

1930s: "Expected to provide the soup"

A Depression-era teacher from Nanaimo looked back on her training at Victoria's Normal School and observed:

> Apart from sewing, we received lessons in health and cooking. We were specifically taught how to make soup because if you were put into a rural school, where the children were not able to go home for lunch, you were expected to provide the soup for their dinner.[41]

1932: "I could see Canon Hinchliffe . . . Minister of Education wincing noticeably"

William Gibson

Under pressure from the business community, Conservative Premier S.F. Tolmie appointed a committee of non-partisan businessmen during the darkest year of the Great Depression to investigate the state of government finances and make proposals. The committee, headed by B.C. Electric president, George Kidd, issued its report the following year, calling for, among other things, the abolishment of the provincial grant to UBC and reduction of free public schooling to children six to 13 years.[42]

In the following letter written to educational civil servant, Cliff Conway, on July 22, 1970, UBC medical professor, William Gibson, recounts the role his father, J.W. Gibson, known as the "father" of agricultural education in British Columbia, played in alerting *Victoria Times* editor, Benny Nicholas, about the implications of the Kidd report and the dangers it presented to public education:

> I can well remember one Saturday afternoon when we had taken a picnic supper to Willows Beach [in Victoria]. It was at the time that George Kidd, president of B.C. Electric had filed his 'businessman's report' on the future of the university and had recommended that it be closed, in the depths of the depression . . . Suddenly, who should appear walking along the sand with his light-coloured and very beautiful cane but the rotund editor of *The Victoria Times*, Benny Nicholas. He soon had my father by the arm and you could see them most of the afternoon strolling way down in the distance in very active conversation, and every so often Ben would take his cane by the tip and would come down with a resounding crash on the sand. In my mind's eye I could see Canon Hinchliffe, then Minister of Education, wincing noticeably.
>
> The upshot of this was that Ben Nicholas and *The Times* came out strongly for the university and against closing it. This, among other things, sparked the great debate which was held in the university auditorium one Saturday night where Professor Henry Angus had a debate with George Kidd. I felt sorry for

In rural British Columbia, distance and difficult terrain made medical inspections of pupils far more difficult than in towns and cities. Here a Peace River nurse in the 1930s prepares to make her rounds.
Courtesy Bill Plenderleith.

> Kidd though I disagreed completely with his thesis, because the poor fellow seemed to be alone on the stage, very nattily dressed, with a hostile audience of well over 1,200 people crowded into this structure that normally would hold 900. When Henry Angus came on he was cheered to the rafters, and this ascetic little professor soon found that this was very heady stuff. He started by saying that he must discount of course, any prejudice that he might have in the matter, such as being a native son of British Columbia. More cheers. As he went on with this call for complete objectivity by the audience and his possible biases, he got further cheers. It was about that same time that Dr. George Weir [UBC's first professor of education] took up the cudgels . . . So George Weir whaled into the subject everywhere that he could.[43]

1933: "The education department's 'unofficial' official representative"

Stewart Graham

Because of the difficulty in finding individuals willing to serve as school trustees, the education department customarily appointed school inspectors or, on occasion, senior principals, to serve as government representatives in local school districts without a board of trustees. Here, Dawson Creek principal, Stewart Graham, recalls the circumstances surrounding such an assignment in the Peace River region in 1933, just before inspector Bill Plenderleith consolidated a number of the small districts into larger and more efficient administrative units:

> Dr. Willis wrote me. No telephone in those days. He wrote me and said that there would be some time before a replacement [for school inspector Ray McLeod} would be sent—and, as principal of the largest school and because he knew me personally—he would like me to be the unofficial official representative of the department . . . So for a period . . . I did do certain things for the department as official trustee for all of those schools . . . from the Alberta boundary, and from the northern boundary of Prince George electoral district to the Yukon, and out to the Pacific Ocean. There were three school districts. Dawson Creek was a school district. Rolla was a school district. Fort St. John was a school district and the rest was the Peace River administrative area. I had to sign every cheque, every work order. I had to buy the ice, the wood, pay the janitors. Sometimes the janitor was the teacher, in which case we paid them $5 a month extra. I would often spend Sunday at home with my wife checking to see that the cheques were issued. I had one person working with me, a woman who was my secretary and bookkeeper. In addition, I had a branch of the correspondence department. A lot of paper work, a lot of hours. Tremendous hours of work,

including going out to the country and rescuing a young female teacher, getting her out of there and sending her home to her family.

I spent 10 to 15 per cent of my time travelling, getting from here to there. I put 25,000 miles on my car. I used airplanes. I used horses. And one time, just for effect at Fort Nelson, I went by dog team, but that was for effect. Just to say that I'd done it. Inspecting, oh, it really . . . I hated the word inspecting. We had to write reports and my report had to include the icehouse and the barn, and the teacherage.

During the Depression, the government did two things: first, they took the only snow ploughs out of the country and brought them south; so we had no roads open in the winter time. Couldn't afford to run them. Not enough votes up there. Get them down into the country where the votes were. Second, they took the cars away from the B.C. Police. They only had two cars, one in Pouce Coupé, where there was a three-man detachment that covered the whole South Peace, and one in Fort St. John where there was a one-man detachment. Now they needed more than one car, particularly because the sergeant in charge slammed into a car in Pouce Coupé.

My landlord, where I boarded, had the only taxi license in the north, and he was a lazy guy and he knew I liked to drive, so I used to drive taxi on the weekends. And I drove the police. A couple of times I was sworn in as special officer. I covered the country and I got to know the people. I got to know the hazards of living up north. I got to know what our teachers were up against.

The most heinous crime in the north at that time was to steal a window. In these log cabins, if a door was stolen, you could get some boards and you could board it up but you couldn't get light in if you put boards over the windows. The windows were always four or six-pane. Many of the people were on relief. The men got $17 a month. A married man got $35. I think it was $5 for each kid. Bureaucracy wouldn't mail the cheques to them, so they established an office run by a policeman, a member of the B.C. Police, in Dawson Creek. And every month, every person in the north had to walk into Dawson, or come to Dawson Creek to pick up their cheque.

Teachers paid $25 a month board, out of a salary of $78. It cost $76 dollars to go from Vancouver to Dawson Creek, the end of the railroad. And that didn't include meals or a sleeper, or anything. Just the train fare. Seventy-six dollars there and $76 back. They got $780 a year. They paid their $25 in advance for their accommodation because that's the only money that the family had. For food, they bought some shells for the best shot in town who would go out and shoot some game. Their desserts were Saskatoon berries.

That's why when I went back there in charge of all the schools, I had what we called a helping teacher and he had a car, I would take the teacher out to see what sort of place they were going to stay. When I went out north of Doe River to one of these little log cabins, it had just a partition. It also had an attic . . . Now, there was a double bed in the bedroom where the guy and his wife slept. The kids, I don't remember where they slept. The teacher was assigned to the attic. To get to the attic he had built a ladder along the wall from the head of their bed, so that if she stayed there, the teacher had to climb over their bed where the two of them were sleeping and climb up this ladder. I took her back to our place in Pouce Coupé and she stayed with us, and I got word to the person responsible for that school . . . that they had to find more suitable living quarters. Another teacher told me that they . . . hung a blanket on a wire around the bed and that was her bedroom . . . and she said: 'You know, those little devils of boys! I was taking a bath and I looked and they had a tear in the blanket and there was an eye . . . But, you see, I get emotional about this. That's what those goddamn teachers had to put up with.[44]

During the first half of the twentieth century, people made a living however they could across British Columbia's expansive interior. Here is the season's catch c. 1934, worth hundreds if not thousands of dollars. **Courtesy Bill Plenderleith.**

Anyway, one day in April or early May 1933, at about 9:00 a.m. or 9:30 there was a terrific banging at my bedroom door. My residence was a small woodshed that had been converted into a bedroom. I'd been out Friday night at a party and I was sleeping in Saturday morning. Anyway, I said: 'Come in!' The door opened, a big husky, red-faced, red-haired guy with a hat on, and a cigar this long, walked in. 'I'm Plenderleith, the new inspector of schools. Dr. Willis said for me to see you; that you'll help me. Now I want you to take two or three days off. We'll get a substitute and you're to show me the ropes around here.'

1933: "You don't have the job until . . . the letter of appointment"

Christopher Wright

By gentlemen's agreement in the legislature, education remained a subject generally beyond party politics throughout the first half of the twentieth century. Nevertheless, as school commissioners Putman and Weir pointed out in 1925, politics and patronage was often alive and well in appointing teachers in school districts stretching from cities like Vancouver to small rural settlements. Superintendent Christopher Wright recounts the political and other influences at work even within parties when he obtained his first teaching post in Darlington in 1933 and, later at the Chase Superior School, where, by his own admission, he was appointed principal "over a much better qualified applicant:"

After graduating in 1929, I worked for two years before returning to Kamloops High for senior matriculation. Then came a year at Victoria Normal School . . . In 1933, I graduated with an interim first-class teacher's certificate.

The depth of the Depression was in 1933. Teachers were not quitting jobs. Any school district, anywhere in the province, could count on 100 or more applications. I wrote over 40 letters, pestered Mr. Matthews [the school inspector] for news of vacancies, and visited several schools in the Kamloops area. August ended and I still had no job.

On the first day of school, Mr. Matthews telephoned me that the Darlington School, 50 miles up the North Thompson River from Kamloops, had no teacher and that, if I could get there, I could have the job. The Darlington trustees were having trouble with finances and it was thought that the board might be dissolved and the school, like many others, placed under an official trustee. Usually in the Thompson valleys the official trustee was Mr. Matthews.

My father, who for the first time since 1920 had a steady job, hired a taxi for $10 to take me to Darlington, now called Darfield. I had directions to take me to the secretary, Mrs. O'Connor. I said that Mr. Matthews had sent me and asked that I be appointed. She replied that if Mr. Matthews had sent me, I must be the teacher. I said that I had to be appointed. So Mrs. O'Connor, with the help of my taxi driver, got hold of the other two trustees, Hubert Janning and Arthur Bryan. A meeting was held, I was appointed and I insisted on getting a letter of appointment. It was arranged that I would board with the O'Connors.

Now 1933 was an election year in British Columbia and Alan Matthews was a staunch Liberal. One hour after I was appointed, the Liberal candidate, R.H. Carson arrived and said, Mrs. O'Connor, I would like to introduce your new teacher.' In the background was Don Rankin, a classmate from both Kamloops High and Victoria Normal schools. I hung tightly to my letter of appointment, breathing thanks to Harold Campbell and C.B. Wood, who both had emphasized, 'You don't have the job until you have the letter of appointment.' Then I learnt that Mr. Janning was the President of the North Thompson Liberal Association, and Mrs. O'Connor the Secretary! Later, I heard of much moaning in Kamloops Liberal circles: 'Poor Don, his father couldn't afford a taxi.' Rankin senior had a much better job than my father.

Pleasures were simpler then: a popcorn vendor in front of South Park School, Victoria in the 1930s. **Courtesy B.C. Archives I-20781.**

That autumn I had my first inspection as a teacher. Mr. Matthews inspected the pupils' work very thoroughly. He complimented me on the excellent spelling of the grade 8 class. At that point, I made a mistake and said, 'I was surprised that two boys did so well.' Two weeks later my report came, very satisfactory, but with the remark, 'Spelling could be improved in two cases.' I learnt my lesson, never to volunteer such information to an inspector.

I received favourable reports at Darlington for the next three and a half years. In December 1936, Mr. Matthews then told me I should see Mr. A.C. McCurrach, official trustee for the Chase Superior School; the principal and one teacher had quit amid public uproar. I was appointed principal over a much better qualified applicant. (His mother was a prominent Conservative). Later, I heard that, in the tea party gossip of Kamloops, Mrs. McCurrach had said that it was a case of sending 'Chris Wright or two policemen!'

I was at Chase for six and a half years, teaching grades 7 to 12. Mr. Matthews inspected regularly. Being much more at ease in the high school grades, he liked to take over lessons in mathematics and Latin. In my last year there, the grade 12 Latin course had changed. Before his spring visit, I made sure that the class was studying a section of Julius Caesar that had not been in the old curriculum. The inspector took one look at what I was teaching and let me carry on.

In 1943, I was appointed to Kamloops High School. Mr. McCurrach said to me, 'Well, Chris, you won't have Mr. Matthews anymore.' He was wrong. That year, the department retired the high school inspectors and turned their duties over to the local inspectors. A second inspector took over Mr. Matthews' outlying districts. Once again he visited my classes. In grade 9 mathematics I was teaching a new concept of positive and negative numbers. Mr. Matthews took over the lesson. He had a different concept than the textbook; it took me the next two weeks to get that class straightened out.[45]

Rural youngsters sometimes came to school on horseback. **Courtesy Dorothea Stafford.**

The Women's Welfare Officer

Miss Lottie Bowron outside a rough school in the Peace River country c. 1930.
Courtesy B.C. Archives H-2682.

By the 1920s, teaching was well established as a career for independent young women newly minted from the normal schools in Vancouver and Victoria. Their training in academic subjects and educational methodology, however, did little to prepare them for life in remote rural communities where their very presence sometimes aggravated communities already divided by deep cultural and linguistic differences. With few local entertainments, unattached females, smartly dressed and attractive, often became the focus of attention and gossip. Both the education department and local communities held teachers to rigorous expectations of moral behaviour. After one young teacher was murdered on the north coast, and another committed suicide on Vancouver Island following harassment by a female school board member, the education minister saw fit to appoint a Women's Welfare Officer to support female teachers in rural schools in the person of Miss Lottie Bowron, former personal secretary to Premier Richard McBride.

Between 1929 and 1934, the indefatigable Miss Bowron travelled the length and breadth of the province visiting hundreds of young women in isolated rural schools. Whatever the difficulty, Bowron overcame it with tact and good sense, followed by blunt speaking and the full force of an indomitable personality backed by the prestige and power of the education department, sometimes in the person of the school inspector. In addition to her visits, Miss Bowron also wrote encouraging letters to young school mistresses, and frequently sent small parcels of art materials or books to brighten a poorly-equipped classroom or to bolster an inexperienced teacher's spirits.

Report on Blind Channel, Thurlow Island

Lottie Bowron

Evidence of the impoverished social conditions that surrounded generations of educators in British Columbia's hinterland is confirmed in a report by Miss Lottie Bowron dated 26 March, 1929:

> Living Accommodation: Miss Cook is living alone in a little house which is provided by the community. I do not believe there is any other place for the teacher to live as there are very few houses and all small ones.
>
> Remarks: Miss Cook has written to me asking for advice in regard to certain difficulties, gossip being one of them, another being the effect of an unruly small boy in the school. When I arrived matters had improved a little. The boy had left the community and the feeling was that he was not coming back, nor did the people wish him to for he had a very unsettling influence on the other children.
>
> Blind Channel is in a very isolated position. There are no industries going on, the men whose homes are there are going to logging camps for employment and coming home occasionally, i.e. the majority of them. There are no roads away from the community and the only walk is along the beach. No social life at all. The school seems to hold the place together and some of the children are sent there on account of it. I would consider Blind Channel a hard place for a teacher unless she had many resources within herself. I believe that the present teacher has made the best of a hard position. I do not think it is a place for a young teacher. It is just possible that there may not be a school there next year as the people do not seem very settled.

> I called upon the secretary of the board, Mrs. Dykes, whom I had heard seemed not very satisfied with the teacher. I gave her an opportunity to discuss matters with me in this regard but she did not take it. I also called upon Mrs. Carroll, another trustee, these two women seem to constitute the board.[46]

Getting Around the Province: "Trust to Luck on the Weather"

Getting around the province in the period between the wars was the first and most serious occupational challenge faced by teachers, principals, and inspectors who worked in rural and isolated schools. By 1929, nearly 60 years after Confederation, there were still only 29,000 kilometers of roadway, most of it unfinished, connecting a province of some 950,000 square kilometers. Many parts of British Columbia could only be reached by rail. For example, a normal school graduate from Victoria or Vancouver who was offered a job in an up-country school had first to travel by rail to either Red Pass Junction in the Yellowhead Pass, or to Edmonton, Alberta, before taking a train to central or northern British Columbia—a journey that could easily cost a month's salary each way. The Queen Charlotte Islands, and the scattered communities that dotted inlets along the coast could only be reached by the boats of the Union Steamship Company with such peculiarities of scheduling that it was impossible to stop for more than a few moments in each village. Some communities, Kelly Lake for instance, could be reached only by foot, or on horseback requiring several days' ride.

This meant that travel itineraries were carefully prepared in advance. Inspectors in the Peace River region, for example, could only reach isolated schools by rented car using Rolla and Fort St. John as staging points for sorties throughout the high plateau. Following a rail trip, young teachers with little money usually had to rely on someone giving them a "lift" to various communities and, more often than not, walking the remainder of the way to their schools. In some cases, the schools at settlements such as Forfar and Hudson Hope "could only be done," as one inspector put it, "by saddle or riverboat," the latter usually in the form of an open flat-bottomed scow.

The travel difficulties and dangers besetting educators in rural British Columbia are clearly confirmed in the following two letters—the first, in 1933, written by school inspector Ray MacLeod to Miss Lottie Bowron, the welfare officer for women in rural schools; and the second written in 1939 by W.R. Dunwoody, the official trustee of Nelson area schools to S.J. Willis, education superintendent:

Ray MacLeod's letter to Miss Lottie Bowron

Pouce Coupé
January 6, 1933

Dear Miss Bowron:

I wish to acknowledge receipt of your letter of enquiry regarding weather and road conditions here . . . This winter has been even worse than last, very considerably worse. And as you know last winter was considered the worst in many years. Added to this is the fact that none of the roads are being kept open by the Public Works Department this year. All travel is by sleigh. Cars have not been able to make even Dawson Creek for two months. Although the weather has been cold it was only just before Christmas that the Peace was frozen solidly enough for crossing; which was on account of the fact that no 'chinook' came to raise the river and cause the ice to jam. The channel in the middle was swift enough to prevent freezing. Points north of the river were getting very low in food supplies by the time traffic could be resumed. Mine was the last car to come back by ferry on November 2. It took three hours to make the crossing, instead of the usual ten minutes; and I was chilled to the marrow when I got to Feenie's on this side.

The snow came early this year—October 10—and has been with us almost ever since. It is pretty well packed now and is about two feet deep. Of course, it is drifted too, in many parts. There have been no 'chinooks' yet: the temperature usually is about –20 degrees, but is often colder. Conditions of travel are probably as good now as we can expect until summer. In the spring there will be the mud to contend with and that is much worse than the snow. I have just checked back over last year's record: snow continued a hindrance to travel right into May and until the end of June there was terrible mud.

It strikes me interesting that it takes as long to make the trip from here to Fort St. John as it does to go to Vancouver: three days by sleigh if one goes with the mail carrier. I think the only thing for you to do is to come when it is convenient for you, and to trust to luck on the weather. But do not wait till the spring thaw . . .

With best wishes, I am
Yours sincerely,

W. Ray MacLeod
Inspector of Schools[47]

W.R. Dunwoody's letter to education superintendent, S.J. Willis

November 6, 1939

Dear Sir:

Following closely on my recent report of a fatal automobile accident which cost the life of Miss McKinnon, a teacher at Gibson Creek School, I now regret to report a further automobile accident wherein Miss Clara Stewart, our teacher at Kamanoe and Miss Helen Lentsmann, teacher at the recently-opened Cay Creek School lost their lives last evening.

It appears that these two teachers, together with Miss French and Miss Jardine of Ootischenia, were proceeding to their schools last evening and the car left the road near Brilliant and fell down the precipice 150 feet into the Kootenay River. The driver, a Mr. Sweeney, and the above named lost their lives. Miss French and Miss Jardine however were fortunate in escaping. Both are suffering from shock however. Miss Milne, also a teacher at Ootischenia, is rather in a nervous condition over the occurrence and consequently it will not be possible to reopen these schools for at least a week. Our supply of teachers in the Nelson district is now exhausted and I am writing to Mr. Watson, Registrar, asking him to endeavour to secure me the services of two teachers to fill the vacancies.

Respectfully yours,
W.R. Dunwoody
Official Trustee[48]

Not for the faint hearted, the inspector travelled in all weather. **Courtesy Bill Plenderleith.**

A Plan for the Peace River

As education superintendent C.C. McKenzie's report in Chapter 2 illustrated, even before the beginning of the twentieth century, provincial authorities in Victoria were considering how to consolidate small school districts to save money. The 24 school districts that the province's first school superintendent, John Jessop, visited in 1872 jumped to 257 in 1902 as the province developed. By 1932, British Columbia consisted of 830 school districts.[49] More significant was the fact that these 830 districts were comprised of only 1,163 schools, more than 1,000 of which taught only the elementary grades.[50] As historian F. Henry Johnson reported: "The case against the small school district was that it was inefficient and over-administered (three school trustees for one teacher) and that the calibre of trustees left much to be desired. The chief fault with the rural school district, however, was that it was far too small an area with too slender a tax base to provide modern educational facilities."[51]

The first ambitious experiment to reorganize rural school territories in British Columbia was conducted under the direction of Bill Plenderleith, school inspector for the Peace River region. Plenderleith recommended to the education department that 39 small rural districts be amalgamated into four larger administrative units. The consolidation plan, as well as Plenderleith's appointment as the government's official trustee, provoked a sharp reaction among many Peace River residents. Some called the government's action "arbitrary, undemocratic, coercive, despotic, fascist," and, even, "un-British."[52] In the following memorandum of December 13, 1934 to Premier Pattullo, education superintendent S.J. Willis details school inspector Plenderleith's concerns and the reasons why the education department had already consolidated 14 small school districts into a larger governance unit known as the Central Peace:

> On August 30th, 1934, I received a letter from the inspector of the Peace River Block containing the following statements:
>
> 1. The present system of local administration in our rural school districts is very unsatisfactory for the following reasons.
>
> In the majority of these districts there are only two or three persons who are legally qualified to hold the office of trustee.
>
> That in many cases those who are legally qualified to hold office as trustees are absolutely unfitted for such office from an educational standpoint.
>
> That in many districts the direct and indirect authority wielded by the trustees over the teachers amounts to tyranny.

And, that the majority of rural trustees are not familiar with the B.C. *Public Schools Act,* and in many cases willfully make no attempt to enforce it. This is usually because of fear of stirring up ill feeling with a neighbour.

2. That the present division of the inspectorate into small school districts is unsatisfactory for the following reasons.

That it engenders sectional jealousy among contiguous districts because of differences in tax rates and differences in the attitude of the people toward educational activities.

That it limits the possible selection of trustees to a very small section of the population.

And, that once the school district is formed, the members of the school board are usually unwilling to give up any portion of it to accommodate the needs of a new school district. In many cases the local boards, in this way, retard educational progress instead of assisting it.

3. That, in the majority of cases in this district, neither the secretary-treasurer of the school board nor the auditor is qualified to keep or audit account books. This general carelessness which I have found in accounting is not because of deceptive intention but because of lack of knowledge.

On October 9, 1934, one group of 14 small rural school districts were united on the recommendation of the inspector into one large rural school district to be known as Central Peace, and placed in charge of the government agent at Pouce Coupé as official trustee.[53]

1935: "H.B. King and the 'new curriculum'"

Bernard Gillie

H.B. King, a World War I veteran and former principal at Kitsilano Junior High in Vancouver, became technical advisor to the minister of education in 1934, a position only slightly less influential than that of deputy minister, S.J. Willis, principally because of King's longtime association with the education minister, George Weir. Known commonly by his army rank, "Major" King was the chief advocate for the "new education," or what was more generally known as progressive education. In 1939, he was appointed chief inspector of schools, a position created in 1925 but unfilled. King retired in 1945 and was succeeded by H.L. Campbell (1945-1947), who later claimed that King was "the worst practicing psychologist he had ever met."[54] In the following interview, longtime provincial educator Bernard Gillie, who also knew King well, recalls King's didactic manner and its crippling effects on teachers and administrators in schools:

> I knew H.B. King quite well, having worked in the B.C. system virtually all the years that H.B. King was here. He was a rather portly gentleman with a very pronounced paunch. He'd come here to the school [at Oak Bay] occasionally . . . It's true to say that many of us avoided going down to see him in his office for anything in particular, because, once he got you in there, he expounded his theories in education for hours at a time.

H.B. King, educational progressivism's chief advocate in British Columbia, and likely the most powerful individual in educational government from the 1920s to the end of World War II.
Courtesy City of Vancouver Archives, CVA 371-1676.

When he got talking to an individual or a class you realized in a very few moments that he wasn't talking to you at all. He almost forgot you were there. He was laying out his whole thesis and, if you stuck around long enough, you would get the whole thing. But, by the time you got to the end of it, you weren't sure where the beginning had been. The way the words flowed out of the man. And he disdained any word that had less than seven syllables, we all swore to that. You just went away completely stunned. I remember seriously thinking, 'I'm in the wrong racket! I just don't know what this is all about!'

It is my personal opinion . . . that H.B. King had a more profound effect on what happened in classrooms in this province in schools than anybody else that was ever in the system. Well, of course, he was a disciple of the great Dewey. After he wrote a report, the 'King Report,' which was a pretty influential document, his personal impact on teachers . . . and what they did was tremendous.[55] He almost single-handedly undertook to change the approach of teachers to their job of teaching in a classroom. He accepted the Dewey theory of instruction and dealing with young people almost holus bolus. Carried it perhaps . . . to an extreme. [In adopting] the child-centered curriculum . . . the education department made a colossal mistake, and probably King was responsible for it, but they produced what they called the 'new curriculum' in about 1935.[56]

There were all kinds of new concepts of how to teach in a classroom. One of the ideas was the development of a 'project' method, the project method of instruction, whereby your youngsters were to learn in the classroom by undertaking various projects. In the course of working out this project, they developed the learning, the understanding, the skills and so forth that they needed. They did it that way, rather than by having a teacher stand up in front of the class and say, you know: 'This is how you do it, step-by-step.' But the mistake that was made, which created a great disservice to the whole idea that the Dewey system espoused, [was that] somebody came in with a thing that's two inches thick for elementary curriculum, and tells you how to teach everything under the sun, and teachers were totally unprepared for it. Confusion reigned . . .

I can remember it so vividly. I was teaching here at Oak Bay High at the time, and the teachers in this area, as they did all over the province, used to meet afternoon after afternoon in self-defense. There would be a social studies section, a mathematics section, and an English section. The teachers of those subjects got together trying to figure out ways of implementing what this new curriculum espoused. And it was a gorgeous case of the blind leading the blind, because none of us knew . . . And I know our teachers, I know men individually, principals, particularly, who were driven out of the profession because they simply could not interpret what he wanted put into effect in their schools.[57]

1937: "The department should not be feared!"

H.B. King

Although King remained the chief architect and most strenuous advocate of a "progressive" curriculum for the province's schools, this curriculum was not altogether favoured by some of the department's conservative-minded inspectors nor, indeed, by many teachers, as Gillie suggested above. Provoked by a comment that the education department was somewhat tyrannical in enforcing the "new curriculum," King issued the following response that certainly illustrates something of the high-handed way with which he treated his educational colleagues:

> I do not understand your suggestion that the rank and file of members of the teaching profession keep a discrete silence upon matters having to do with the curriculum from 'fear of the Department.' The Department of Education does not employ the instrument of fear and coercion. Teachers are not prohibited in any way from expressing their opinion upon education, though it is expected that persons of education will express their opinions in appropriate language. The amount of weight attached to their opinions will vary with individuals according to their ability, intelligence, general education, experience, and good judgment. Most teachers with the 'progressive ideas' that you refer to will have their time well occupied in trying to catch up to the progressive ideas in the program of studies. However, this Department appreciates progressive ideas in education which are based upon careful thinking and sound professional knowledge. It even regards with sympathy erroneous ideas if these ideas are symptoms of growth and the holder of them is open-minded and ready to change his convictions with fuller knowledge.[58]

1939: "If it's a boy, we'll call him John"

John Burnett

The diminutive Colonel John Burnett, a distinguished veteran and a school inspector from 1939 to 1965, was generally well regarded for his kindness toward teachers and children. He was known at times to overlook departmental regulations that required a minimum enrollment of 10 children to keep a school open in rural communities. In the following passage from an interview, Burnett recalls a delicate situation in the Lower Mainland that required his help:

Sitting in a school late one afternoon, I was approached by a young female teacher who quickly disclosed that that she was expecting a baby and that she intended to get married to her boyfriend. 'You and your boyfriend go to Bellingham [Washington State] and get a permit to get married,' I advised. 'Then, the day you wish to get married, tell your principal that you are coming to see me. When the baby begins to show, tell the parents of the kids at school. I guarantee there won't be any difficulties,' I promise. As the young teacher was leaving, she turned around in the doorway and said, 'If it's a boy, we'll call him John.'[59]

Across Canada, children between the wars and after commonly completed homework assignments, or other school exercises, in workbooks such as these. **Courtesy Greater Victoria School District Archives.**

1940: "This thing with you and King"

Carlyle Clay

A.S. Matheson, who served the education department as a school inspector from 1936 to 1956, was but one of numerous inspectors who occasionally ran afoul of the bombastic chief inspector H.B. King who, despite a reputation for pomposity, was not without a sense of humour. Legend has it that a parent of a student at Sir James Douglas in Victoria complained to H.B. King that his child's teacher had told him to go to hell. King replied: "And that teacher told you to go to hell. This is the wrong place, you have reached the Department of Education."[60] In the following discussion, Carlyle Clay, at that time an elementary school principal in Armstrong, recounts the story of how King would use information gathered casually to check that the department's "boys in the field" were on their toes.

My inspector at Armstrong, where I was principal, was a man named A.S. Matheson. He was a very religious man, a Baptist. He was death on liquor and that sort of thing. We were very good friends and I found him very fair. I was coming home from Vancouver from a teachers' federation meeting. The train started out and I got into the observation car and I noticed King sitting there reading the paper and I hoped he didn't see me. However, after dinner he caught me. He wanted to know about Matheson and I knew that he and Matheson were not getting along very well because Matheson had been fired from his position as official trustee in Armstrong.

He wanted to know how I was getting along with Matheson. So I told him. I told him a few things that Matheson had done and I mentioned the fact that Matheson used to get out Saturday mornings at 7 a.m. and go up some of the valleys and pick up teachers and have workshops in reading for them. He'd pumped me a little bit more about it. So when Matheson was in the next time, I told him what I had done. Couple of weeks later, he was in and said, 'You're a great friend, you are!' I said, 'Why?' He said, 'This thing with you and King.' He said, 'You realize because of you and your big mouth, every grade 7 youngster in this province is going to have to write an exam in reading.' 'Well,' I said. 'Why?' He said 'Because of your blabbering to King. He had nothing to do and he was looking for something and this was just up his alley.' So, sure enough, along came the test in grade 7 the following spring.

The following spring, the teachers' convention was in Vancouver. I was coming down the steps at Kitsilano High where the convention was being held and King was going up. We spoke and I kept on going down. He said, 'Hey! Clay!'

I said, 'Yes, Dr. King?' 'You know what you told me on the train about Matheson and his reading? You were correct. I gave a test throughout the province and his class was head and shoulders above the rest of them.' He had just wanted to check what I had said about Matheson was correct.[61]

First period in the afternoon for a "mixed" class in Armstrong during the early 1940s. Allowing for individual differences and interests, commercial and technical students work at the table in the rear of the class while Carlyle "Mike" Clay teaches desk-bound "academic" students.
Courtesy Carlyle Clay.

1940: Report on the Mennonite settlement at Burns Lake, B.C.

Harold Stafford

On occasion, school inspectors would be asked by the education superintendent to write special reports on educational or social problems in their jurisdictions and to submit them to the minister of education. One such report was prepared in May 1940 by Harold Stafford on the progress of Mennonite families from Saskatchewan who had relocated to the Burns Lake area for economic reasons. In this instance, Stafford's task had little to do with schools and much more with an economic analysis of the Mennonites' situation and the resources at their disposal for farming as they tried to establish new lives in British Columbia:

Large scale farming, the economic depression, and drought were among the factors which made it imperative that Mennonite farmers in Saskatchewan seek new homes . . . Representatives of the sect visited lands in British Columbia situated between Francois Lake and Ootsa Lake. The report given on their return was so favourable that steps were taken to arrange for the migration of families living in districts adjacent to Swift Current and Saskatoon.

The economic status of the people was such that special aid was obtained from the Saskatchewan government . . . [and] the first of the families arrived at Burns Lake on May 7, and the last of the group reached its destination on June 18, 1940 . . . No sooner had the train stopped than the Mennonite people were busy preparing for the final stage of their journey to new homes. This was an overland trip to Francois Lake, across the lake by ferry, and thence by difficult stages to the actual ground where their new life was to begin.

Army tents and temporary quarters were utilized while land was located, cleared, ploughed and planted. Haste was necessary, the growing season was well advanced, and delay would mean lack of food for both man and beast . . . The fields of grain, crops of vegetables as well as the construction of log buildings tell how each man has solved new and difficult problems. As could be expected the first comers have made greater progress than those who arrived late in June.

The Mennonites are farmers at heart and, in loving the soil, realize that life on the land holds little material reward. As a group they are industrious and thrifty. It can be observed that they have laboured long and accomplished much. This knowledge of achievement is reflected in their attitude . . .[62]

1940: S.J. Willis: "The kingpin around here"

Bernard Gillie

From the time S.J. Willis was appointed principal of Victoria High School in 1908 at the then-princely sum of $166 per month, until his death in 1945, he remained one of the most powerful figures in provincial schools. From 1920 until 1945 he served as education superintendent and deputy minister of education and, with little political oversight, governed the educational affairs of the province as he saw fit. Although generally known for his sympathy towards teachers, he obviously did not impress BCTF representative, Bernard Gillie, with his sense of collegiality:

I remember going to see S.J. Willis on several occasions, when he was deputy minister. This was after I'd become active in federation work . . . and who I knew personally, and whose home I visited from time to time, because I'd gone to school with his son, Bill. He and I had been in Oak Bay High School together and he always met you very courteously and all the rest of it, but I think that the thing that impressed me most about him was that his office was not that large, but it had an enormous table in it, which he apparently used as a desk, and he sat at the end and . . . it was 20 feet away. You sat or stood at the other end. Never wasted a word, right to the point. Polite, interested and so forth. He would stop and think for a while and then give you an answer, but no sense of friendliness, no sense of treating you as an equal. No sense of 'We're in this together' but, rather, 'I am the kingpin around here, and you are one of my minions.'[63]

1942: "These were all Canadians, you know"

Nobue (Margaret) Shiga Minato

Nobue (Margaret) Shiga Minato was born in Vancouver in 1911. For reasons of national security, she and her family was part of the 1942 removal of Japanese-Canadian families to internment camps in British Columbia's interior in the months following the Japanese attack on Pearl Harbor on December 7, 1941. Nobue has written the following about her wartime experience:

Japanese families from coastal British Columbia were uprooted and moved inland for security reasons after the 1941 attack on Pearl Harbour, Hawaii, a decision later generations of British Columbians would regret. Here, school-age youngsters attend a Sunday school sponsored by the United Church in Kaslo. **Courtesy B.C. Archives B-01080.**

I was so worried about the children's education. They didn't start any school in September, and we'd arrived there about May, and they played all through summer and September. So I wrote to the head of the correspondence department at Victoria, and I said, 'I have a son who's in grade 7 and a daughter who's in grade 8, and they had good grades in Vancouver, and I don't want them to miss a whole year. So is it possible that I could teach them by correspondence?' and she said, 'Certainly.' So, I got all the things for grades 7 and 8, and then I started teaching our two. My son was 11 and he said, 'Everybody's out in the Fraser River swimming, and I have to go to school!' So I went around to the neighbours and said, 'Are there any grade 7 boys?' and there were, luckily, two, and they were willing to have them educated too. So then I got another little girl to come, the same age as my oldest daughter . . . The Japanese community built a school. And there were a lot of people that were university and high school graduates . . . So we didn't have to worry. The children took their exams in Lillooet . . . and they all passed.[64]

At Telkwa School near Smithers c. 1940, the space in the school was used both for academics as well as table tennis.
Courtesy Dorothea Stafford.

1943: Memorandum from Education Minister H.G.T. Perry to Premier T.D. Pattulo regarding "educationally underprivileged areas"

Across North America, the Depression brought into sharp focus the impoverished state of rural schools and the vast inequities in educational quality and opportunity between youngsters in larger centres and those in remote settlements. Here the education minister summarizes the state of affairs in the world of rural schools:

> In British Columbia, as in all other parts of the North American continent, the rural areas are the educationally underprivileged areas. It is the country school that is most often housed in a primitive building with inadequate lighting, heating, ventilation, and sanitary facilities, lacking the supplies and equipment necessary for carrying out a modern educational program. It is the country teacher who, on the average, is the least well trained, the least experienced, and the lowest paid. It is the country pupil who is most likely to be receiving a stereotyped and textbook-centred type of instruction . . .
>
> Underlying the educational problem is a financial problem. If rural districts had as much money to spend on their schools as urban districts have, equality of opportunity for education would be nearer realization than it is . . . It is essentially incorrect, of course, to speak of the rural education problem. There is no such single problem; there is rather a host of inter-related problems of all degrees of complexity.[65]

1945: "Find out if administration is your cup of tea"

Ray Williston

Save for the position of deputy minister, an appointment traditionally made at the pleasure of the government in power, the educational civil service generally remained professional and apolitical during most of the twentieth century. One of the few educational civil servants to become directly involved in politics was Ray Williston who resigned from the school inspectorate following his 1953 election as an MLA for Prince George. In 1954, Williston would become the first senior educational civil

The families of many children attending rural schools still worked the land as this photograph of a sheep farm west of Prince George in the early 1940s illustrates. Courtesy Dorothea Stafford

servant to serve as minister of education in the Social Credit Government of W.A.C. Bennett. Later, he recounted the nomadic paths he followed to become a teacher and, thereafter, a school administrator:

> My father was killed when I was 13 or 14. I went to work at 14 and have been working ever since. I graduated from normal school in 1934. I was working in a grocery store in Salmon Arm. A teacher in Salmon Arm was resigning to get married. The folks for whom I was working were on the school board and 'whispered' to me to apply for Hendon School outside Salmon Arm. I got the job.
>
> I went through school during the Depression, borrowed money and won a scholarship ($150) for the third year and got married on the basis of that. I taught from 1934 onwards. I wrote 500 applications. It was almost impossible to get a teaching job during the Depression. There were many individual school districts in those days. I was appointed to Rossland, a grade 5 job. The school board got 4,000 applications, and with no paid staff to sort them, they made a random selection of 25 letters.
>
> There were 16 youngsters in eight grades: four were in grade 8 and wrote provincial exams. All four got through. I went from there to Surrey and moved from Grandview Heights to a school on Scott Road, then an opening came in Princeton. Three popular places to teach from a salary point of view were Vancouver, Trail, and Princeton because there was employment in those areas and therefore a tax base. Trail had the smelter. In Princeton, the mines were going.
>
> I was in the air force during World War II, trained as a pilot. Afterward, I put in two applications to Prince George as a principal, but was so intimidated by the interviews, I decided it was useless and started post-graduate studies at University of Toronto in the fall of 1945. I just got nicely started when, on the same day, got letters from both boards offering me the position in Prince George. I went to the dean and he told me: 'Go out and find out if administration is your cup of tea then come back and we will make you a better one.'
>
> I was asked to apply to be an inspector [after serving as a supervising principal in Prince George] but I didn't do it . . . Got a phone call, 'apply or else.' So I applied. Initially I served as a 'roving superintendent,' a 'hatchet man.' I was sent into secondary schools where there were difficulties. I was sent north of the Peace and Prince George, first up the Alaska Highway. I inspected secondary schools in Peace River South. I had to get rid of the principal in one school. Then I was appointed to Prince George. I had problems there and all over.[66]

1945: "A deserted gas station was turned into a classroom"

K.F. Alexander

Ken Alexander was born in Fernie in 1910. At 23 years of age, he joined the staff at Fernie High where he remained for 10 years. Following two years at Nelson High, he became principal at Princeton Elementary High from 1945 to 1952. He joined the education department in 1955 as school inspector, working out of Smithers, and, in 1961, he became district superintendent for Mission-Agassiz. During his career as an educational officer, he spent considerable time in rural and remote parts of the province. Here, he recalls one humourous incident from his days in northern British Columbia:

> South of Burns Lake near Ootsa Lake, shortly after school opened in September, it was discovered that a whole community of Orthodox Mennonites . . . had started a settlement. When contacted about school they informed us that they were in favour of education but they wanted it in German. We told them this was impossible. Since there was no school in that area the school board found a deserted gas station and it was turned into a classroom and teacherage. The next problem was to find a teacher at a time when they were very scarce in 1945 and 1946.
>
> Luckily I found a fellow who had been training for the priesthood and he had been advised to take one more year before his final vows. He had no teaching certificate but was well educated so he was hired. After his appointment we found that he could speak German! He had an English accent and when I visited the school later he was teaching fractions to three pupils at his desk. He took a piece of paper, folded it in half and asked what he had. The three in unison replied 'one hoff.' Later on he became interested in the public health nurse and I became hopeful that I could talk him into getting his teaching certificate but, unfortunately, he decided to continue his training [for the clergy].[67]

Notes

1. J.H. Putman and G.M. Weir, *Survey of the School System* (Victoria: King's Printer, 1925).
2. Although the position was titled, "Chief Inspector of Schools," King's assignment had less to do with the supervision of the department's inspectors in the field and more to do with providing technical advice on curriculum and policy development to the minister. According to inspectors who served under King, the special personal relationship that King shared with education minister, George Weir, meant that King, rather than deputy minister S.J. Willis, was the minister's chief confidant and most influential advisor.
3. Jean Simpson Mann, "Progressive Education and the Depression in British Columbia," unpublished Master of Arts thesis UBC, September 1978, 40.
4. James P. Spradley (Ed.), *Guests Never Leave Hungry: The Autobiography of James Sewid, A Kwakiutl Indian* (Montreal and Kingston: McGill-Queen's University Press, 1969), 21-27, 31, 45, 53-55, and 63.
5. Christopher Wright's manuscript is courtesy of Terry McBurney and Barbara Naef.
6. Daphne Marlatt and Carole Itter (Eds.), *Opening Doors: Vancouver's East End*, 94.
7. Ibid.
8. Duncan Lorimer, *Memories: Victoria High School,* mimeographed booklet, 3 February 1972, 38.
9. ARPS, 1920-21, 26.
10. Interview with C.E. Clay, Princeton, 29 December 1988.
11. *B.C. Teacher,* "Best Educated Farmers Get the Biggest Return," November 1923.
12. Stafford, "A History of Burnside School."
13. Marlatt and Itter, *Opening Doors: Vancouver's East End*, 91.
14. Gower's report on Gerry Andrews was dated 12 March 1924 and, in it, he also noted that Andrews had 13 children in his class, nine boys and four girls. See Gerry Andrews, *Métis Outpost: Memoirs of the First Schoolmaster at the Métis Settlement of Kelly Lake, B.C, 1923-1925* (Victoria, B.C.: Amity Press, 1985), 246.
15. Hutton Mills is situated between Prince George and McBride and serviced at the time by the Grand Trunk Pacific Railway.
16. Interview with Bernard Gillie.
17. Putman and Weir, *Survey of the School System.*
18. Ibid., 43-44.
19. Watson was a graduate of the University of Toronto and, before enlisting for service in World War I, worked as a teacher at Greenwood before heading the department's textbook branch. In 1921, he was appointed as teachers' registrar. Watson also acted as departmental secretary to the Strathcona Trust, a philanthropic foundation that funded physical training and cadet work in provincial schools.
20. Interview with Bernard Gillie.
21. William Burns, "Reminiscences of an Ex-Inspector," *B.C. Teacher,* March 1926, 161.
22. Official trustees were usually school inspectors, appointed by the education department to administer a school district when a trustee board had been suspended.
23. Interview with Carlyle Clay.
24. Interview with Stewart Graham, Burnaby, 18 and 19 December 1988.

25. Alice Glanville, *Schools of the Boundary: 1891-1991* (Merritt, B.C.: Sonotek Publishing, 1991), 127.
26. In 1873, when the first *Annual Report of the Public Schools* was published, 16 of the 33 teachers in the province were women. By the 1920s, 80 per cent of British Columbia's rural teachers were women, many of them young and fresh from normal school. In 1927, approximately 700 women teachers served in the rural schools, the vast majority of whom were unmarried and close to the lowest end of the salary scale.
27. Mildred E. McQuillan, Personal Diary, BCA, Add. MSS. 1252.
28. Interview with Bernard Gillie.
29. Maxwell Cameron, *A Report of the Commission of Inquiry into Educational Finance* (Victoria, B.C.: King's Printer, 1945).
30. Interview with Stewart Graham.
31. Andrews, *Métis Outpost*, 51.
32. Ibid., 257.
33. Ibid., 260.
34. Marlatt and Itter, *Opening Doors: Vancouver's East End*, 94.
35. The Woodward referred to here in all likelihood was K.B. Woodward who served as a school inspector from 1935 to 1941, when he was appointed as an instructor in the Victoria Provincial Normal School.
36. Interview with Stewart Graham.
37. Lottie Bowron, "Report on Blind Channel, 26 March 1929, BCA Add. MSS. 347-2/27.
38. Superior schools were the first institutions in rural areas that were permitted to offer instruction to grade 10.
39. Interview with Carlyle Clay.
40. Correspondence D.M. Stafford to Thomas Fleming, 14 November 1989.
41. Corrine Langston, "Life of a School Teacher During the Great Depression," unpublished paper, University of Victoria, 1993, 6.
42. Interview with Mrs. Inglin, Salt Spring Island, 25 February 1993.
43. George Kidd, *Report of the Committee Appointed by the Government to Investigate the Finances of British Columbia* (Victoria, B.C.: The Committee, 1932).
44. Correspondence William C. Gibson to C.B. Conway, 22 July 1970, C.B. Conway Personal Papers are courtesy of Mrs. Ellen Conway.
45. Interview with Stewart Graham.
46. Christopher Wright's manuscript is courtesy of Terry McBurney and Barbara Naef.
47. Correspondence, W. Ray MacLeod to Lottie Bowron, 6 January 1933, BCA Add. MSS. 347-2/27.
48. Correspondence, W.R. Dunwoody to S.J. Willis 6 November 1939, BCA, British Columbia Department of Education Correspondence, GR 451.
49. British Columbia Department of Education, *One Hundred Years: Education in British Columbia* (Victoria: Queen's Printer, 1972), 87.
50. Ibid., 76.
51. F. Henry Johnson, *A Brief History of Canadian Education* (Toronto: McGraw Hill, 1968), 110-111.
52. Alan H. Child, "A Little Tempest: Public Reaction to the Formation of a Large Educational Unit in the Peace River District of British Columbia," *B.C. Studies*, 61, (1972), 24.

53. Memorandum from Superintendent S.J. Willis to Premier Pattulo, 13 December 1934, BCA, GR 1222, Box 2, File 2.
54. Interview with Harold Campbell and John Meredith, Victoria, 16 November 1983.
55. H.B. King, *School Finance in British Columbia* (Victoria: King's Printer, 1935).
56. The major curricular revision was concluded in 1940. See Johnson, *A History of Public Education in British Columbia*, 165.
57. Interview with Bernard Gillie.
58. Correspondence H.B. King to W.E. Houlder, 11 October 1939, BCA, GR 452, Box 1, File 2.
59. Interview with Colonel John Burnett, Vancouver, 13 December 1983.
60. Interview with Don Smyth, Sidney, 10 March 1989.
61. Interview with Carlyle Clay.
62. Harold Stafford's papers are courtesy of Dorothea Stafford.
63. Interview with Bernard Gillie.
64. Marlatt and Itter, *Opening Doors: Vancouver's East End*, 90.
65. Correspondence H.G.T. Perry to Honourable John Hart, Premier and Minister of Finance, "Report on Rural Education," No. 30/43, 1943, 1-2.
66. Colin Chasteneuf, interview with Ray Williston, Victoria, 28 January 1993.
67. K.F. Alexander's manuscript is courtesy of Terry McBurney and Barbara Naef.

The great escape: School's out for grades 1, 2, and 3 youngsters at Beacon Hill School, Victoria, c. 1962. **Courtesy Greater Victoria School District Archives.**

CHAPTER 5

Schools in Boom Times: The Era of Consolidation and Expansion, 1946-1971

The quarter of a century from 1946 to 1971 marked one of the most dynamic periods of growth in provincial education. War's end brought demobilization and the beginning of a new prosperity. Standards of living rose and so did social expectations, including the belief that high school education was within everyone's reach. The Great Depression and the war that followed had stifled developments in secondary, technical, and university education. Now, these demands returned, making education one of the largest "growth industries" of the 1950s and 1960s, driven in large part by the rising birthrates of the post-1945 "baby boom." Growth of both elementary and secondary school populations led to the construction of more than 650 new schools as well as severe teacher shortages as new industries developed province wide and as postwar levels of immigration increased from Europe and Asia. To meet the need for new teachers, the education department mounted a vigorous teacher recruitment program in Great Britain and Australia, among other jurisdictions. To promote greater equality of educational opportunity and access, the 800 or so school districts that existed in the interwar era were consolidated into 89 larger districts in the 1946-1947 school year, a move that made educational structures more efficient by making schools and school districts larger.

By the 1960s, the government of British Columbia, like other provincial authorities, was forced to expand its post-secondary educational sector to accommodate rising public demands for higher education. Newfound emphasis on the value of education made schooling a much more important public policy and political issue, particularly in light of the fact that educational expenditures had increased 35-fold between 1947 and 1971 and, as the 1970s began, constituted almost 30 per cent of all provincial expenditures.

Certainly, not all factors shaping education in the postwar decades were provincial in origin. International events cast their own shadow over provincial schools. In particular, the advent of the "Cold War" between Western and Eastern-bloc nations that followed the end of World War II, as well as the launching of the Soviet satellite, Sputnik, in October 1957 provoked new concerns about the quality of high school education, as well as severe criticisms about progressive education practices across North America.

Like a trellis in a cottage garden, the collection of stories that make up this chapter offer an extravagance of colours and textures, each providing small but vivid portraits of life in and around schools during the vibrant postwar era. Through these stories we see a province still largely shaped by its frontier character. Even in the second half of the twentieth century, British Columbia remained a place where log schools and teacherages still existed in many communities and where self-reliance and resourcefulness on the part of young teachers determined their survival and success in remote outposts far more than their academic competencies or the state of local schools.

Within such settings, small occurrences such as the construction of a school dormitory, the presence of an American army base, or even a toothache, could and did become events of consequence for people in and around schools, sometimes with far-reaching effects. Running through many of the stories of this time is the theme of equality or, more to the point, the lack of it. From scholarly pronouncements that no true equality could ever be secured between urban and rural regions to the plight of aboriginal peoples eager to free themselves from the yoke of poor quality schools, the idea of redressing past inequities is paramount. So, too, is inequality apparent in the experiences that marked the lives of immigrants. Altogether, these stories illuminate part of a historical record showing that British Columbia offered different challenges and possibilities to those who were English-speaking and British-born than to those, such as the Doukhobors, who were deemed "foreigners" in almost every respect. Women teachers, too, found themselves in the role of outsiders, particularly those who carried the stigma of being "married women," or those who aspired to leadership positions in urban schools. Their stories reflect the profound changes that were taking place in British Columbia's social fabric at this time, as well as their own struggles to free themselves from the shackles of custom, tradition, and past inequities.

Other themes are also evident here. Several stories disclose the hotly-contested and continuing struggle between progressive-minded and traditional-minded educators for control of the school curriculum and, de facto, control over the goals of public education. Changes in pedagogical fashion, we learn, were shaped by both time and historical circumstance. Sputnik's launch a continent away would sound the death knell for progressive education in British Columbia and would encourage provincial authorities to return schools to "the basics." Along with the political conflict over the curriculum, these writings also illustrate the growth of special interest politics as practiced by lobby groups for "special education" and French language instruction. These political developments will become even more evident in the materials found in the final chapter of this volume.

Consolidating several small schools into one was the principal solution to make schools more efficient and to provide youngsters with greater educational opportunities in the form of a more comprehensive curriculum. Here Salt Spring Islanders flock to the opening of the Consolidated School at Ganges in the spring of 1940. **Courtesy Salt Spring Island Archives.**

	No. of Schools	No. of Teachers	Official Trusteeships
Brown, J.E.	51	122	12
Burnett, J.N.	39	126	9
Calvert, F.G.	35	80	5
Daniels, E.G.	33	118	4
English, J.F.K.	38	163	9
Frederickson, C.J.	42	144	20
Jewett, F.A.	54	101	26
Manning, V.Z.	36	98	3
Matheson, A.S.	37	143	10
Matthews, A.F.	52	95	17
Morrison, H.M.	47	123	2
McArthur, H.	51	69	29
MacKenzie, H.H.	33	137	2
McLellan, F.A.	57	85	4
Plenderleith, W.	49	127	1
Robson, T.F.	34) plus 18) 52	45) plus 18) 63	35
Stafford, H.D.	46) plus 7) 53	74) plus 7) 81	27
Thorsteinsson, B.	27	78	9
Towell, A.S.	16	55	2
Turnbull, A.	64	103	16

As this rota of inspectors' duties in 1944-1945 shows, 241 small districts were functioning without school boards and were being managed by individual inspectors. The fact that the province's school governance system was not working properly led government to enlarge the size of school districts by reducing some 650 school districts to 89 in 1946 and to 75 a decade or so later. **Courtesy Dorothea Stafford.**

1946: "The equality . . . must be rough, but . . . substantial"

Maxwell Cameron

Emboldened by the success of the Peace River experiment in the 1930s, and with similar reorganizations in the Fraser Valley, the British Columbia government in 1944 appointed Max Cameron, a UBC education professor, to investigate the state of provincial school finance and governance and to address administrative concerns raised two decades earlier by Putman and Weir's 1925 inquiry into provincial schools. Translation of Cameron's recommendations into legislation in 1946 marked a watershed date in British Columbia school history.[1] It reduced what was once more than 800 school districts to 89, ensured that a standard assessment rate was levied against all property for school support and, in time, led to the emergence of a more powerful BCSTA and, later, to the local appointment of school superintendents.[2] As the following passages from his report illustrate, Cameron was extremely concerned about what might be lost if educational control was completely centralized:

> Nature, with an irritating disregard of the problems of school administration, has decreed that no system will produce perfect equality in British Columbia. Good schools can exist or can be placed within the reach of the majority of our children, but the children in the vast and sparsely settled hinterland will continue to be at a disadvantage, no matter what system is adopted . . .

Urban schools offered many opportunities for physical education. In rural schools, the situation was entirely different. Here youngsters in the Okanagan-Similikameen region struggle in 1945 to perform calisthenics on an uneven schoolyard. **Courtesy B.C. Archives I-00529.**

There are some obvious advantages in complete centralization, or the placing of the whole school system in the hands of the provincial government. In the eyes of the province the child in Telegraph Creek is as much entitled to a good schooling as the child in Vancouver, and everything possible would be done to see that he got it. The great merit of centralization is the equality it can produce . . .

Against these advantages of centralization . . . must be placed some dangers . . . Complete centralization is almost certain to result in some loss of local interest in schools. Experience has demonstrated that the most strenuous efforts to enlist local interest by means of local advisory boards are futile. Many citizens will not serve on a board which is merely advisory . . . It would be a great tragedy if our school system were to lose the services and support of our school trustees, who for the most part have done excellent work, often in spite of very irritating obstacles. The administration of schools by local boards has other merits . . . Because local control results in greater public interest, because it enlists the voluntary services of an army of citizens, and because the local people can feel that, in

Boys washing clothes in a Prince George school dormitory shortly after the end of World War II. While the movement to consolidate school districts and schools was underway, youngsters from areas surrounding Prince George were "boarded" so they could attend high school classes not offered in rural schools. **Courtesy B.C. Archives, 1-00677.**

part, they possess the schools, that they are doing things for themselves rather than having things done for them, it may be proper to call decentralization more democratic.

In the informal discussions accompanying the public hearings of this commission it became clear that the majority of our citizens wish to retain local management of schools . . . We must have more equality than we have; if we cannot have it without complete centralization, we shall have to have that too; if we can have it and still preserve local control, let us by all means do so, and let us do so even if equalization is not complete, as long as it is substantial.[3]

1946: "Changing the north through the schools"

Stewart Graham

We changed the whole life in the north through the schools. At the end of the war there were tremendous supplies and buildings up there that were put under War Assets. I had a letter from Ian McKenzie, the Minister of National Defense in Ottawa, [and Member of Parliament] for Vancouver Centre. This letter stated that I had preference for all materials that were being handled by War Assets. The War Assets people were so crooked that letter didn't mean a thing till I caught a guy helping himself. One of the dock guys, and I blackmailed him. So I bought a lot. I bought a whole flock of American Army H huts.

I bought the huts . . . because I was the trustee. I bought the Royal Canadian Air Force Officers' Mess in Dawson Creek. I built schools out of the H huts, but the Officers' Mess I turned into a dormitory, under the Cameron Report. It had running water, bathrooms, electric lights—the whole business. At the end of the first year of living there, they gravelled the road from Dawson Creek to Rolla, 14 miles north. That meant we could put a bus on. And the kids rebelled. They weren't going home to the barrel of water, the outhouse, and no electricity.

And do you know what happened then? The mothers rebelled. Now the farmers had all made money. They had worked on the highway. They had their crops. The prices had gone up, and all at once they discovered that in the scoop-outs that they had for watering their cattle and so on, they could put a pump, and pump water into the house. They didn't drink it but you could wash in it and I guess they did. It would flush a toilet and by the gods of war, it wasn't long until the farmhouses in the Peace started to have modern conveniences. So I say that, in that respect, the schools changed the mode of living.[4]

1946: "Making good citizens"

George Weir

In the February 1946 issue of *British Columbia Schools,* George Weir, Minister of Education, reminded British Columbians of the new and progressive educational road they had been travelling since the publication of Putman and Weir's survey in 1925 and H.B. King's curriculum reforms from 1935 to 1940. World War II, which had been waged to "make the world safe for democracy," had prompted new concerns about the capacity of human society to behave in civilized ways and, again, brought into sharp focus the critical importance of the school's role in promoting good citizenship. Here is the crux of what the minister said:

> Let us remember that the most important business of the school is that of making good citizens. It may turn out scholars. It may produce successful men of business. It may educate for culture. It may enable its graduates to make a better living. These and other things it may do, but the real test of its accomplishments is the kind of citizen it produces. [5]

Victoria youngsters twirl around maypole in 1940s. **Courtesy Greater Victoria School Board Archives.**

1946: "High school methods course was a waste of time"

J.B. DeLong

The British Columbia education department had long thought of itself as forward-looking. The department had pioneered distance education in Canada during the 1920s through its correspondence schools and, during the following two decades, likewise led the nation in its advocacy of school radio programs, as well as innovations in domestic science and citizenship courses. In an attempt to ensure that school inspectors and other educational managers were up to date in their training at the end of World War II, the department encouraged its officers to enroll in educational courses that would enhance their professional knowledge. Here the senior inspector, J.B. DeLong, describes his experience at a prominent American university with his friend and departmental colleague, Alex Lord:

> Alex Lord and I took a six weeks' course at Columbia University, New York—expenses paid by the B.C. Government. I took the following courses:
>
> 1. High school methods by Professor Clark of Chicago University.
> 2. Tests and measurements by a teacher of the Horace Mann School of New York.
> 3. A 7 a.m. lecture course by prominent educationists.
>
> The high school methods course was a waste of time. The lecture course was very interesting. I was particularly interested in the course on tests and measurements as some people in B.C. had gone crazy over intelligence tests and objective tests.[6] The instructor gave us an intelligence test. He told us he had written the test himself and made a much better mark than we made, but remarked that did not mean he was more intelligent than we but that he had written so many similar tests that he knew just how to handle them. He said a pupil should not be judged on one test but should be given a battery of three tests and that the final rating should be based 50 per cent on the teacher's judgment.
>
> Mr. Lord went to the theatres. I attended the big league baseball games. One day I persuaded Lord to go with me to Coney Island. He was so disgusted with the ladies in their scant attire that we remained only a few minutes.
>
> In 1948 Mr. Lord and I, along with six others, were given the honorary degree of LL.D. at UBC. The reason I was included in the list has been a mystery to me. I was official trustee of the University Hill School for 18 years. I managed to get

excellent teachers and paid them the Vancouver scale of salaries. I made out a very generous budget each year, sent it to the Education Office and got the full amount asked for. I retired about 1946 having spent more than 30 years with the education department. These were strenuous years. Some years I had no holidays. While my work was trying I was very happy in my job.[7]

As a vibrant postwar era began, British Columbia's schools were still managed by a brigade of inspectors and other educational officials, in effect a pedagogical old guard consisting of men and women who had served in schools across the province before becoming senior educational civil servants.

Front and centre are Harold Campbell, assistant superintendent of education and his boss (in the light coloured suit) F.T. Fairey, deputy minister. The woman in the third row (centre) is Dr. Edith Lucas, director of the secondary correspondence branch. To her right is Miss Bertha Rogers, director of home economics. The two women in the second row (right) are probably Miss A.B. Miller, director of elementary correspondence and Miss A.F. Adamson, acting director of school and community drama.

Courtesy British Columbia School Superintendents Association Active Retired Members.

1946-1950: "You don't know how good a fire it was"

Carlyle Clay

Among the challenges facing school inspector Carlyle Clay was the task of supervising schools attended by Doukhobor children. To protest provincial policy insisting that Doukhobor children be educated in public schools, some members of the Doukhobor community set fire to local schools from the 1920s to the 1950s, prompting school authorities to employ watchmen to oversee the safety of teachers, children and the buildings themselves. In some cases, however, the causes of school fires, as Clay explains, lay as much in poor building design and shoddy construction than in the actions of this religious group:

> We had a school district that was rather an interesting one. We hired a crooked architect in the Castlegar area. I couldn't persuade the board that he was crooked, so I had to let the board go ahead. The deputy minister said that it was the school board's business, not ours. 'Go ahead and carry on. We just have to have something more definite to go on.' So anyhow, we were building

Wooden school structures were susceptible to fires. For many years the Department of Education in Victoria refused to carry fire insurance on small rural schools because of high premium costs. They preferred to rebuild schools whenever necessary as in the case of the school at Palling, north of Burns Lake, which burned to the ground in 1940.
Courtesy Dorothea Stafford.

a series of schools in Thrums. The previous school had been burned down. So we are building a school in Thrums, and we got one started. We were told that as soon as we got this one going, it would never be used. It would be burned down before it was used. So we put a watchman on seven nights a week, as during the day it was all right.

We got the school all finished at Easter. We had a bit of a social affair on Sunday afternoon. The books were moved into the school. It was a two-room school, and we were quite happy with it. The building period was over and everything was going fine. At seven o'clock that night, the watchman was coming to work and was 100 to 200 yards away from the building when the thing blew up in his face.

So they had to have an investigation about the school and the crooked architect at the same time. I was asked to meet with the Architectural Institute of B.C. and I did. I had a set of plans for the school and I told them what had happened there and what went wrong. A couple of the fellows took the plans away for a closer look. After they had looked at them for a while, we got on with the meeting. I said it was a good fire. They said, 'You said it was a good fire?' I said, 'I did say that but I don't want to be quoted.' 'Well,' they said, 'You don't know how good a fire it was because that school wouldn't have been standing in two years.'[8]

1950s: "They used to just send old missionaries"

James Sewid

Prior to the transfer of responsibility for aboriginal schooling to the province in the early 1950s, the Dominion Government operated a system consisting of both "residential" and "day-schools" in which authority for the education of aboriginal youngsters was delegated to church officials on a fee-for-service basis. The day-schools, which grew in number between the 1920s and the 1940s, were located on reserves, allowing aboriginal children to remain with their own families and to speak their own languages while attending school. The quality of day-schools, however, was generally poor as James Sewid recalls here:

We talked to the people in the Department of Education and I thought that education was one of the most important problems at that time. When we first moved to Alert Bay the older kids went to school there, but they had to stop when they were 15 or 16 and several of my children had already reached that age. In those days when they were 15 or 16 they would just tell the Indians: 'That's that. You go now. You're finished.' That was the ruling of the white man over the Indian. No matter how hard you tried to keep them in school, when they reached that age they just told the Indians to go home. Not only that, but all the Indian children had to go to an Indian day-school in Alert Bay that was separate from the school for the white children in the other end of the village. The teachers there were often unqualified to teach. They used to just send old missionaries to the village to try and do the best they could. The effect of that wasn't always too good for the children in school. We asked the education department and the Indian department to get rid of the day-school system. Also I felt that if there was a white settlement nearby then the Indian children should be transported there by bus to go to that school which was better qualified.

The native brotherhood had been fighting for integrated schools for a long time and that fall they decided to integrate the [high] school at Alert Bay. They had just finished building a new high school there with the help of the Indian department [Department of Indian and Northern Affairs] and these students who had reached grade 7 were to start going to that school. My daughter Daisy was among the first ones to be sent up there. She came home crying a few days after school started and said she didn't want to go back to that school. I asked her, 'Why don't you want to go back to school?' 'Well,' she said, 'the kids make fun of the way I dress and the way I talk.' So I told her, 'You dry up those tears and go back up there. Don't come and tell me those things. I want you to stay there.' So she went back and pretty soon she started bringing non-Indian kids to our house. She even brought some home for supper and it was proven that integration could work. She was my first child to get a better education and go through those higher grades of school. I hadn't been able to help any of my children very much with their schoolwork because I didn't know very much. I felt bad when they didn't do very well in school and I used to give them prizes or money if they got good marks. I used to give Daisy so much for every 'A' that she got and she really did well in her schoolwork.[9]

1951: "The problem of private schools"

H.G.T. Perry, The Prince Rupert Daily News

Even before the public school system was organized in 1872, British Columbia families enjoyed the option of sending their children to private schools. The advent of a free and universal system of public schooling, however, did not extinguish parental demands for different and, sometimes, more elite forms of educational provision.

Department of Education photograph of a Sir James Douglas class, Victoria, c. 1948. **Courtesy Greater Victoria School Board Archives.**

From the 1870s to the 1950s, a modest number of so-called "private" schools operated mostly on Vancouver Island and in Vancouver, along with a small number of denominational schools dominated by the Catholic School Trustees' Association. After war's end in 1945, however, growth in the non-public school sector became more vigorous and, between 1945 and 1978, 65 additional private schools were added, bringing the total size of this sector to 180 schools with some 24,000 pupils enrolled. Passage of Bill 33, *The Independent Schools Support Act*, on June 13, 1977 provided funding for non-public schools up to 30 per cent of the costs of public schools operating in the same jurisdiction, providing that the non-public schools taught the provincial core curriculum and met certain other requirements. In the following editorial, newspaper chief and former Liberal education minister (1941-1945), H.G.T. Perry, raises important postwar questions about equity and cultural pluralism as they applied to an emerging public demand aimed at extending public assistance to non-public sector schools at mid-century:

> A function of government is to find solutions to problems that disturb the body politic—the people. The art of high statesmanship is to so modify the will of the majority that the rights of minority groups are protected to such a degree that they do not override the will of the majority, and receive consideration and protection.

It is on these foundations that political liberty and democratic government rest and continue . . . It is fitting therefore to emphasize that political democracy is expressed by legislation and law as the will of the majority qualified by fair consideration and recognition of the reasonable rights of minorities . . .

The question arises in many minds as to why private schools exist and continue to flourish notwithstanding there is a comparatively good public school system in B.C. One explanation is that some of the private schools are patterned on the British grammar schools and that they give a better all round education, especially as to classics, discipline, good manners and sports, than the public schools. Parents who can afford it are those who send their children to private schools of this type. Students matriculate from there in the same examinations as public school students.

The problem of this type of school is not very pressing and it is disputable between the governors of such schools as to what aid, if any, should be accorded them by the province. But there is another type of private school maintained by religious groups, due to their conscientious objections to the strictly secular education of the public schools. With strong conviction they believe in a religious atmosphere pervading the classroom. Or at least they object to a few parts of the public school curriculum, especially as it affects history and biology.

This situation is not peculiar to British Columbia. It exists in every province, but in other provinces the difference appears to have been composed . . . This objection is not applicable to the B.C. public schools where no denomination or indeed hardly any religious influence is permissible. An accusation against our public schools is not that they are denominational or even religious, but that they are so extremely secular as to be actually pagan.

Hence we have our fine public school system supported by the state, supplemented by our high school grammar school type of private schools, and in addition our private schools supported by religious groups, mainly Catholic in B.C. . . . The crux of the problem is on the question of how much, if any, state support shall be given to such schools. For the cost of maintaining these schools entirely, without any cost to the state at all other than for certain free textbooks and matriculation examinations, has become too heavy a burden for religious bodies to bear. One cannot say the problem does not exist. It will become more acute later unless dealt with in the near future.

There is, of course, the powerful majority in B.C. who are committed to an exclusive type of secular education in our public schools. On the other hand, there is a powerful minority who conscientiously desire their children should receive an education tempered with religion.

Up to the present, this minority (not entirely Catholic) has provided the entire education of their children without any cost whatever to the state. In this respect, they have saved millions of dollars to the taxpayers. In addition, they have, as property-owning parents, paid their school taxes to support the state public school system from which their children derive no benefit.

As law-abiding citizens we should abide by the law. But conscience knows no law but conscience. Hence, in democratic states legislation has been provided on many matters for conscientious objectors. Legislation should be by the will of the majority, but in a truly democratic society the majority should realize and exercise its high responsibility of being fair and reasonable towards the claims of the minorities . . .

No solution can ever be complete or satisfying in full to either majority or minority opinion. No gratitude can be expected. But something could be done to compose this different viewpoint and heal this festering sore, in part, of the body politic that might otherwise become a dangerous cancer . . . This article is written by a Protestant to provoke serious thought and tolerant consideration of a problem on the horizon.

At the risk of being misunderstood, misinterpreted, calumnied, pilloried, ostracized and damned, we venture to propose as an immediate step that the Government appoint a Royal Commission of one or of three persons to inquire forthwith into this problem and to make recommendations.[10]

Planting a school garden at Sayward School, Vancouver Island, in the 1940s.
Courtesy Dorothea Stafford.

1951: "From logs to steel"

Harold Stafford

Max Cameron's 1945 plan to consolidate schools had many far-reaching effects. Most noticeable, however, was the postwar school building program it promoted. Here, school inspector Harold Stafford describes the primitive conditions of the school at Surge Narrows in the 1950s on the eve of its replacement by a new and much more modern building. The old Surge Narrows School typified the conditions found in many small and rural British Columbia school districts before Max Cameron's consolidation plan was put into effect by government after the end of World War II:

> The Surge Narrows School is on Read Island in School District No. 72 . . . on the eastern coast of Vancouver Island, where lumbering and fishing are the basic industries. Within the school district boundary are included many islands and a portion of the mainland of British Columbia. The log-school was built by settlers in 1924 to provide an eight-grade education for their children. It operated for several years, then was closed for a time. By 1946 the board of school trustees considered the school building a distinct liability rather than an asset.
>
> The building had been constructed of hewn logs with the spaces between rudely chinked with clay and moss. The windows were as large as the low ceiling would permit and yet were most inadequate, the floor was uneven, and the 'shake' roof leaked. Water was carried to the school from a near-by stream, and the sanitary facilities were most primitive. In the dull rainy winter months, to keep themselves warm, the children huddled together over the wood stove as the wind whistled through opening between the logs, and on these dismal days as they tried to master their studies they grouped themselves beneath a single suspended oil lamp.[11]

1951: "Settling into the teacherage"

John Calam

Emeritus UBC Professor John Calam, a noted educational historian, began his distinguished educational career teaching in the province's small schools before attending graduate school at McGill University and Teachers' College, Columbia in New York. In the following story, told in fine detail, Calam recounts his experience converting a teacherage, moved from Barrett Lake to the schoolgrounds of the Telkwa Superior School in 1953, into a home for his expectant wife, Renée:

Monte Lake School in the Thompson-Nicola region was built in 1952 and was but one of many post-1945 school buildings in British Columbia constructed using the new international style of architecture. To some critics such buildings reflected a stultifying conformity and represented little more than "egg carton" design. **Courtesy B.C. Archives I-22644.**

In early summer 1953 I accepted the principalship of Telkwa Superior School with its incomparable prospect of the tree-lined Bulkley Valley and towering Hudson Bay Mountain. On behalf of School District No. 54 (Smithers) local trustee George Shepherd offered Renée and me a choice of living quarters—either a suite attached to the Anglican church, or the teacherage. 'May we see the teacherage?' we exclaimed in unison. 'It hasn't arrived yet,' replied the unflinching Mr. Shepherd. Renée and I exchanged glances. Was this some country put-on at the expense of city folk? 'When do you expect it, then?' I enquired, going along with what I took to be a joke. 'Maybe tomorrow,' Mr. Shepherd replied in all seriousness.

How right he was! The following afternoon on a low-deck truck there hove into view a wooden hut measuring perhaps 10' x 16'. At length we learned something of its provenience. Recently abandoned by the shifting demographics of the district, the old Barrett Lake Teacherage had been displaced 25 miles northwest to Telkwa for two years, Mr. R.J. Adams having been paid $650 as an advance on the moving contact. Set up on cement blocks and furnished with a wood and coal stove, it became our home for the school year.

Though small and roughly constructed, its two miniature rooms and storage loft at the time seemed adequate for our modest belongings. Hollow exterior walls filled with wood shavings augured well of cold weather ahead. Granted, its situation on a gravel plateau near where the old and new school buildings stood would submit Renée during school hours to the hustle of school bus arrivals and departures, as well as to the spirited cries of children romping at recess or noon-hour break. After hours and on weekends, though, it would afford us a degree of privacy and on school days shorten my commute between home and work to 40 paces either way, a blessing during severe weather. As well, rent appeared exceptionally attractive at $20 per month against my salary of $3,550 per annum.

Advantages aside, though, further scrutiny confirmed that certain city amenities were sadly lacking. There was no electricity. Nor was there running water. Indeed, not only would water have to be carried in from the school; as things stood, it would also have to be carried out. Moreover, neither chemical toilet nor outhouse were anywhere in place. Such being the case, Renée and I would have to use hot water and toilet facilities at the school, a reasonable arrangement for the time being but impracticable throughout the lengthening nights of Renée's burgeoning pregnancy. As well, despite the stove's promised heat no provisions were yet in place for dry storage of the wood and coal that would generate it. All things considered, though, the teacherage appeared a better bet than the church annex. So we said we'd take it.

In rectifying perceived shortcomings of this one-time Barrett Lake teacherage, we received assistance from the Smithers District School Board which in late August moved to furnish us with lumber, a sink, hardware, and paint. With these supplies in hand Renée and I agreed to improve the building by constructing cupboards, shelves, a wood and coal shed, and an outhouse, as well as to redecorate inner walls and outer trim. Accordingly, with all the confidence of the uninitiated we flung ourselves into the project.

For some of our home improvement problems we found only partial solutions. Water supply was a case in point. On the one hand, with a baby on the way we were likely to use more and more water as the year progressed. On the other hand, with hot and cold running water already on tap over at the school, and bound by the limitations of a two-year building permit for the teacherage, it appeared unlikely that the Smithers School Board would extend school water lines to so temporary a dwelling as our provisional domicile. Carrying water from school to teacherage thus established as a necessity, we resorted to a time-honored simplification. At the Telkwa lumber yard we bought a 2" x 8" pine plank about four feet long which I fashioned into a serviceable yoke. Two short lengths of sash cord, two large snap hooks, and a couple of buckets completed the rig which enabled me, pioneer style, to keep us in water with comparative ease.

The domino effect of an abundant water supply nearby can easily be imagined. A small hot water reservoir built into the stove contained several gallons of water for heating. But as a holding tank for substantial back-up quantities it was far too small. Nor, once cold set in and darkness descended early, were our inclinations likely to include fetching two buckets of water whenever they were required—at 2:00 a.m. on a frost-hard night for example. Instead, yoking in enough water for at least 24 hours (at times up to a dozen buckets) had to be

Everyone's at work in this 1951 Williams Lake Elementary class. **Courtesy B.C. Archives I-00693.**

done all at once under optimum weather and lighting conditions that day. But where to store it all? The answer lay in an oval-shaped copper container with a handle at either end, kept permanently filled on top of the stove, together with several auxiliary buckets placed wherever there was room on the kitchen floor. This plan prompted purchase of more buckets, which, together with our two round galvanized bathtubs brought with us from Lac la Hache, made possible our practice of bathing according to the so-called two-tub system. Following this procedure you sit in one tub, put your feet in the other, crook your knees over adjoining rims, and have your partner ladle warm water down your back affording a sensation we declared well worth the bother. For the time being these hot water arrangements also enabled Renée to do hand laundry, prompting installation of a clothesline from the rear porch to a convenient tree and a drying rack within the teacherage itself. So far so good.

Thankfully, a regular enameled sink arrived one day from the dealer. Without benefit of a drain trap we installed it at the end of a counter with a down pipe leading outside to the rock pit and insulated against approaching November chills. On account of abundant gravel thereabouts the pit drained admirably. A second problem was learning to operate the stove efficiently. Not that it was faulty. On the contrary, it performed very well indeed. Its stovepipes and chimney drew vigorously. Jumbo matches, scrunched newspaper, dry kindling, and seasoned stove-length wood fired it up in a jiffy. And with the correct air intake and flue adjustment, local coal held it steady for considerable lengths of time. Since, however, the hot water cauldron encroached on that flat area of

Youngsters in the Okanagan Mission School outside Kelowna in the 1950s do "board work" in spelling. **Courtesy B.C. Archives I-00516.**

the stove top one customarily deploys for making pancakes; and assorted pots, pans and kettles crowded one another on what remained of the iron-ringed heating surface, we accidentally dowsed the fire once or twice, and a few times came close to scalding ourselves.

Throughout this phase of our settling into the teacherage, fortune smiled on us albeit selectively. The good news was that shortly before school reopened the board electrician wired our little house and hooked it up to the village power grid. In the weeks following we revelled in the use of a new Frigidaire and an Easy Spiralator washing machine, plugged in an old radio permanently tuned to the Smithers' CBC repeater station, enthused over our own electric toaster and a vacuum cleaner occasionally borrowed from the school and, most of all, relished late-evening reading near any one of several 60-watt light bulbs. Here was gracious living indeed. But the bad news was my miscalculation of the time and drive required for resetting the school in motion, preparing lessons, completing the promised renovations at the teacherage, badgering Carson's Truck Lines to deliver three crates of household effects from Vancouver, and establishing professional prenatal care and counsel for Renée and the child she was carrying. In the event we pressed on piecemeal as opportunity permitted. I installed shelves and devised simple drying racks for clothes and winter footwear. Renée sewed up the first of a married lifetime of heat-reflecting curtains, concealing valances, and draft-defying room dividers. She tackled the painting, too, not to mention day-to-day housework. As August ran its course, though, preparation for the new school term began to whittle down my hours at liberty.

What a transformation the tiny Barrett Lake building had undergone since its arrival—a diminutive empty shell—not two months before! Now warm and dry, surrounded by familiar fixtures, implements, adornments, and facilities, we realized that whatever the year held in store for us, we could at least enjoy each other's company in a place we called our own. Quickly, too, we grew to appreciate that other component critical to community newcomers—local people supportive of our work and sympathetic to our outlook whose children so agreeable graced the scene. Meanwhile throughout our novitiate, like hermit crabs in their borrowed seashells we seemed to wear rather than inhabit the teacherage. Psychologically at least it became our portable sanctuary. And when in January 1954 our firstborn Marie entered our lives, she imbued it with radiance worthy of a palace.[12]

1952: "A great start as new immigrants "

John Burdikin

Severe teacher shortages in British Columbia following the end of World War II encouraged many teachers from Great Britain, Australia, and other Commonwealth countries to relocate in Canada. Two such individuals were John Burdikin and Art Holmes who became superintendents of schools in the 1980s following long and successful careers as teachers. In the following story, John Burdikin recalls their early days in British Columbia, the support they received from school inspector Grove Carter, and the close relationships that continued to characterize the educational community in the postwar years:

> Art Holmes and I arrived at the Main Street Canadian National Railway terminus [in Vancouver] late in April 1952. A few months earlier we'd decided to emigrate to British Columbia to check out 'business' opportunities. The plan was to send back to England for Molly, Art's wife, and Evelyn, my fiancée, if we were successful and liked things here.
>
> After a few days at the YMCA on Burrard Street, it became apparent to us that though we liked Vancouver, there were no 'business' opportunities there for us and, even worse, we were so short of money (at that time we could bring only 50 pounds sterling each with us) we would soon have to go to the Immigration Office for support and work our passage home on the next available ship. We had arrived in B.C. at a time when several unions were on strike, and university students were looking for summer jobs. The day we learned that we weren't even in the 'top 100' on the waiting list for dishwashers at the Vancouver Hotel, we went in search of teaching appointments and forgot about 'business.'
>
> We were interviewed by Inspector Grove Carter at the Birk's building on Granville Street. This proved a turning point in our fortunes. He told us of teaching positions he thought might be suitable for us in his inspectorate. He mentioned Quatsino, Delta, University Hill, Powell River, Howe Sound and others, giving us the impression he was inspector for all of B.C. By the time we were leaving his office, we had provisional offers of jobs. Art was to go to Winter Harbour (a one-room school), and Evelyn and I to Stillwater (three rooms) in Powell River district beginning September 1952.
>
> We were elated until it suddenly dawned upon us that we couldn't survive to take up these positions unless we found interim paying employment. We explained our dilemma to Inspector Carter, who suggested we apply for jobs

with the forest service by going to the Granville Building Forestry Office. We did so. We got jobs as dispatchers although we were not sure at the time what they were.

An idyllic summer followed. From our salary of $176 a month we saved enough to help pay for Molly and Evelyn's fares. I had discussed plans for our wedding with Evelyn. One matter settled early was that it was to be a church wedding. I learned that a brother of the engineer on the Forest Ranger's boat at Madeira Park was a warden at St. James Anglican Church in Vancouver. He arranged for us to be married there. At this time, Mr. Carter had spoken to Mrs. Carter of our plans. She invited us to have a wedding reception at their house on Cypress Street, Vancouver. Also, she wrote to Evelyn's mother to discuss such an arrangement, which was well received by her. In the afternoon of August 15, 1952, Evelyn and I were married at St. James by Reverend David Somerville, who, years later, became the Anglican Archbishop of the province . . .

In those days, school inspectors, as exemplified by Grove Carter . . . provided educational guidance to their teachers. When I became a district superintendent of schools, I reviewed my collection of the monthly newsletters that Mr. Carter sent us. They dealt with the 'basics' which have not really changed fundamentally over the latter half of the twentieth century—one more legacy and gift from an inspector who was both a mentor and a friend.[13]

Times changed but the province's geography did not. Inspectors continued to reach schools in out-of-the-way post-1945 coastal communities using whatever means available to them, in this case a supply boat.
Courtesy Dorothea Stafford.

1952: "What the hell are you doing . . . in a government car?"

Stewart Graham

To offset the longstanding problem of modest salaries, government's education officials were granted a few special "perks" by the province's chief education officers, deputy minister S.J. Willis and his successor, F.T. Fairey. Here, inspector Stewart Graham explains how this "unofficial" system worked and how it eventually came to an end:

We were taken down to Victoria to mark papers. Now there was a reason for it. I spoke a while back about the number of principals who got more money than inspectors of schools. When I joined, Dr. Willis said to me, 'Stewart, the car is yours. If you go to California for a holiday or something like that, let me know so if there's a question I can say permission has been given.' When we went to mark papers we lived in a hotel or, in my case, I lived with my family. And I got $5 a night and an eating allowance, $3.50 a day. And I got, I forget whether it was $250 or $350, too, as an honorarium for marking papers. So we went.

Nineteen fifty-two was the date. The government took away the honorarium for marking papers. They also issued special license plates . . . so we could be identified as driving government cars. At two o'clock in the morning, returning from a school board meeting in Agassiz, a carload of adults drew up beside me and yelled, 'What the hell are you doing out at this hour of the night in a government car?'

When I was assigned to the Peace River, I lost one license plate in a mud hole. That was so successful, I took the other one off. Then I was called to Victoria. I drove all the way to Victoria, through Spokane and Seattle to get to Victoria. I drove all the way back without any license plates. Bill Straith, the minister of education, noticed this, coming out of the Parliament Buildings, just before he said, 'Stewart, what happened to your license plates?' 'Oh,' I said, 'Sir, I lost them in the mud at Peace River.' 'Oh,' he said, 'You'd better get them replaced.' But I drove the car anyway. I never was stopped. I drove the whole year without any license plates, because I hated those red and white license plates so much. Then they put a decal on our cars, on the sides, on both doors. Just the Province of British Columbia, it was a huge decal. So we said to the department, 'Can we own our own cars and go on mileage?' And they said yes. And I organized a co-operative scheme through Brett Motors in Chilliwack, and bought eight Pontiac cars for the guys. But, you see the change in attitude? Not only were our salaries going down relative to the union teachers and administrators, but these little perquisites were taken away from us. Small-minded, small-minded people, I think.[14]

1950s: "Not for you people"

Harry Assu

In the following story, Chief Harry Assu illustrates that the overall rising expectations of the postwar generation for higher levels of schooling, and for a better quality education, were shared by minority groups, especially aboriginal peoples:

We got our start on education through the church school on the reserve here and in the home-schools run by the churches in Port Alberni, Chilliwack and Alert Bay. The trouble was that Indians were only allowed to go to grade 9, and then they had to get out. A man who came here told me the missionaries didn't want us to have much education, but I don't know about that. I wanted my boys to go to high school, so I went to see the Indian agent, M.S. Todd, and told him so. He said to me, 'Nothing doing.' I asked him, 'Isn't it for everybody?' and he answered me, 'Not for you people.' We were really treated rotten in those days. It has pretty well changed now.

When I got home I was very angry, and I went straight to Rev. Moore and told him how the agent had said, 'You're lucky to get public school!' Rev. Moore said, 'We'll go tomorrow to see the head of the school district.' So we went and talked to this man for a while, and I told him what the agent had said to me: 'If an Indian student is 16 years of age, he's out!' I asked the school administrator, 'Can I get my kids into high school?' He said 'sure. But we'll have to by-pass the Indian Affairs Department. Could you pay $125 each? Yes? Then send your boys to Heriot Bay High School on Monday morning.'

So two of my boys were the first here at Cape Mudge to get a high school education. Rev. Moore coached them at nights, and they got on well with their work. Later in the same year, I attended a Liberal party meeting in Courtenay, and a young man came over to sit by me. He was the first lawyer in Campbell River. He asked me what had happened over getting a high school education for my sons. I told him about the struggle I had had to get those boys into high school. Luckily, the Liberal party representative was leaving for Ottawa right away, and he was told about it by the lawyer, and about three weeks later word came back that native kids could attend any public high school. That is when it opened up for our people.

That fall my boys went down to King Edward in Vancouver to finish their high school. They were the first native Indians to attend that school. The principal there, Mr. Wilson, welcomed us. He told us that they had students from every other ethnic group in Vancouver, and he had been looking forward to having some of our people. He said, 'Kids here don't make any difference between races. They are all one here.'

Now our people can pretty well attend any school, college, or university of their choice. My grandsons have attended a private school for boys on Shawnigan Lake. People didn't think education was so important for girls in the early days, but we sent our youngest girl to Pitman's Business College.

In the 1960s when the Evans were serving the church here, my daughter-in-law, Cissy Assu, helped Mrs. Evans get the nursery school going for kids. After Mrs. Evans left, Cissy volunteered to keep the school going, and she kept it going for another year. It is still going.

A lot of young people from Cape Mudge have a high school education now, and some have university. They are trained in teaching, social service, secretarial work, government, law, business, museum work, and nursing. When visitors come here to Cape Mudge and say how 'lucky' we are to have so many able people in this band, I am thinking to myself, 'Well, we are not all that 'lucky' you know! Our people went ahead by standing up for our rights.'[15]

1953: "So little for the mind: An indictment of Canadian education"

Hilda Neatby

Dissatisfaction with the allegedly "soft" character of progressive education was nowhere more forcefully expressed in the postwar world than by University of Saskatchewan professor, Hilda Neatby. In her 1953 volume, *So Little For the Mind*, Professor Neatby, an historian and the only female member of the 1951 Royal Commission on National Development in the Arts, Letters and Sciences, provoked enormous controversy in British Columbia and elsewhere across the country about the state of Canadian public education, an institution she argued, that was dominated by the vapid ideas of school professionals and wooly-headed instructors in teacher training institutions:

In English-speaking Canada, as in the United States, there are signs of unrest and dissatisfaction . . . on the part of parents and teachers, who, although they may be branded as 'traditionalists,' are in no sense reactionary . . .

The Dick and Jane books were basal readers written by William S. Gray and published in the United States by Scott Foresman between the 1930s and the 1970s. They were published in Canada by W.J. Gage and were used as springboards to reading by several generations of youngsters in British Columbia. Gates and Huber's Work-Play books were also popular readers in the province and across North America between the 1930s and the 1960s.

[Progressive education] is frankly anti-intellectual. There is no attempt to exercise, train and discipline the mind. This is old-fashioned language, now forbidden by the experts, but its meaning is still clear to the literate person . . . The denial by the schools of the duty of intellectual training is neatly reflected by the current fashion of lightly dismissing in argument an unanswerable proposition as 'a question of semantics.'

Progressivism is anti-cultural. This is quite in keeping with the revolutionary, pseudo-scientific materialist fashions of the day . . . The result of progressivism has been effectively to cut off many if not most of our pupils from any real enjoyment or understanding of the inheritance of western civilization; and certainly from any sense that the achievements and values of the past are a trust to be preserved and enriched for the future. Culture in its traditional sense of intellectual and moral cultivation is as unfashionable as is scholarship . . . The sensible and fair thing is surely to let children know by experience in school that life may be difficult and disagreeable as well as delightful and simple; that theirs is a world for workers, and that work demands their best effort; and to help them to acquire in school such firm habits and such clear principles as will enable them, whether they gain or lose the world, to do their duty in it with diligence and with intelligence. Nothing could be less practical or progressive than the current fashion of keeping those who should be achieving the age of discretion in ignorant, if contented immaturity.[16]

Post-1950 schools boasted impressive new facilities similar to this library in a Victoria school. **Courtesy Greater Victoria School District Archives.**

1953: "Mass secondary education presents a challenge"

Harold Campbell

Harold Campbell was one of the most prominent figures in British Columbia's educational development in the twentieth century. After stints as a teacher and principal, he was appointed municipal inspector of schools for Victoria in 1942 and, in 1953, was made deputy minister in the department of education.[17] Like many of his colleagues in educational government at the time, Campbell was progressive-minded and, while quick to advocate the democratic character of schooling, he also remained conscious that the democratization of the secondary grades imposed new challenges on educators to develop curricula relevant to all youngsters, including those with "superior minds" upon whom the world greatly depended:

During the past three years an extensive reorganization of the secondary-school curriculum has been under way. This reorganization has been designed to provide a program of studies which would challenge the interests and capacities of the able students, who are proceeding on to the professions, while at the same time meet the needs of the majority of young people, who now seek some secondary education. It is rare indeed in these days to find a parent who does not wish some secondary education for his child, and in ever-increasing degrees the commercial and industrial world is insisting upon it.

Mass secondary education, however, presents a challenge. Can the school provide adequate cultural and vocational training for the many, and at the same time treasure and develop to the full those superior minds to whom society must ever look for the solution of its problems? In other words, can the modern composite secondary school so train the great majority of youth that, in addition to cultural development, it will enjoy and be capable of doing the arduous physical tasks of drawing fish from the sea, logs from the forest, minerals from the mines?[18]

1954: "Minister of education with 10 minutes notice"

Ray Williston

Former school principal and school inspector Ray Williston was elected MLA in 1953 and, following Robert Bonner's brief tenure as education minister, Williston was appointed to this position in W.A.C. Bennett's Social Credit government which he held from 1954 until 1956. Here, he tells the story of becoming a government minister and the joys and frustrations that went with the job. Of particular importance are his comments about the departmental politics that surrounded the establishment of the University of Victoria and Simon Fraser University in the early 1960s:

When the House retired, W.A.C. Bennett told me he was going to make me minister of education. All the warning I got was 'Ask Bob Bonner about it.' Bonner said he had a speaking engagement in Nanaimo and couldn't tell me anything. I was going home to Prince George and had to phone my wife to say I was staying in Victoria. Rumours that W.A.C. had picked me out as future minister of education when I ran for election weren't true. W.A.C. didn't know me from a bale of hay.

When I was minister of education, I didn't report to anybody. I didn't have to report to a committee, unless I was seriously going after money. Nobody knew what I was doing . . . I wanted to professionalize teacher education, get rid of the normal school, align teacher training with the university and have a university certificate. During the fall, [the province] announced that all teacher training would be at the university level from now on.

[UBC president] Norman McKenzie was a very strong individual and had secured an agreement with Harold Campbell and Judge Clearihue [from Victoria College] that there would be only one university in B.C. and that would be UBC, and that they would have direct say [in determining] the affiliated campuses outside the university.[19]

It was not what I had in mind at all. Rather than have McKenzie have complete domination . . . [I wanted] the Board of Education established in 1955 [to be] in control. By consolidating the normal school with Victoria College under UBC initially for accreditation [we] intended there would be a separate university in Victoria. We set up our own teacher training and advertised for a headmaster.

[At UBC] Dean Scarfe was brought in from Manitoba as dean. Harry Hickman was placed over top of Victoria College. A one-year [teacher training] course was not enough. We wanted a two-year course for elementary teachers and a B.A. and one-year of teacher training for secondary teachers . . . We encouraged elementary teachers to go on for a B.Ed. We ran into trouble. We didn't have enough teachers and the extra year training meant a gap of another year until new ones were in the system. We recruited in England and canvassed for married teachers to come back for one year. It was a resounding success.

I was put in as minister of education with 10 minutes notice. I got pitchforked out of education with 15 minutes notice . . . I was moved over to lands and forests but still had an interest in a university in Victoria. I was looking for lands for a campus . . . General Pearkes was minister of defense for the federal government and was in charge of military lands [including those in Gordon Head outside Victoria]. Pearkes turned those lands over to the province . . . and they came to the department of lands. I was the minister of that portfolio but still couldn't get any cooperation from the education department. Les Peterson had taken over as minister but had no background in education. I was completely dependent on Harold Campbell and Campbell still had an agreement with Norman McKenzie regarding UBC. Every time I asked Les Peterson to come and discuss it, Les would go back to Harold and it would get cut off . . .

When I got the endowment lands, Judge Clearihue was chairman of the board of Victoria College. Even though he also had an agreement with McKenzie, he finally was persuaded about the need for a university in Victoria, separate and distinct from UBC. One day in October [1962], Clearihue, Harry Hickman, Harry Gilliland, Hugh Farquhar and three or four more of the old instructors from the normal school got out on the lands out here near an old administration building. Hugh Farquhar got an old shovel. They dug a hole and said: 'This is the start of the University of Victoria.'

It was not until recently that Harold Campbell admitted that he crossed me up every way he could because he had an agreement with McKenzie. He admitted it was one of the stupidest things he had ever done in his life and he regretted it.[20]

1956: "The total enrollment was American"

K.F. Alexander

Ken Alexander grew up in Fernie and attended the University of Alberta where he earned a B.Sc. degree and a B.Ed. degree. He taught at Fernie High and Nelson High before becoming principal of Princeton Elementary-High School and Mission Junior-Senior High School. In 1955, he was appointed as an inspector of schools and, in 1956, as district superintendent for Prince George. In the following story, he reminds us of the relationships between Canada and the United States that continued after the end of World War II and the educational effects of the Distant Early Warning Line (known popularly as the DEW line) on local communities in central and northern parts of the province:

There was an American army base called Baldy Hughes some distance from Prince George. It was part of the 'Distant Early Warning' system and was located at a place called Baldy Mountain. It was approximately three miles from a lumber mill where we had a one-room school with propane heat and lights and an outdoor privy. The parents at the base were driving their children each day to attend this school. Suddenly the mill closed and all the local residents left so that the total enrollment was American.

Shortly afterwards, I had a visit from two army officers from the base who asked if there was any possibility we could move the school to the base. They told us they would install electric lights and proper heating and would build a properly heated washroom outside with indoor plumbing. I asked them if they would be happy with a B.C. teacher and a B.C. curriculum and they assured me they would. I took the offer to the school board that was most enthused with the idea so the move was taken and the Americans did everything they promised.

I visited the school sometime later and couldn't help smiling to myself when the teacher had them singing 'O Canada' and 'God Save the Queen.' There was only one minor problem that arose early in November when the two same officers appeared at my office asking if the school could be closed for Thanksgiving. I had to turn them down since the school had already been closed in October for Thanksgiving.[21]

1956: "Modern education superior to old-time teaching"

The Vancouver Province

Dr. Harold L. Campbell, B.C.'s deputy minister and superintendent of education, took 'a backward glance at education' Monday and intimated the present stacks up well. Teachers of 50 years ago, he told the 37th annual BCTF convention in the Hotel Vancouver, 'would have laughed' at the suggestion of a philosophy of education. 'The teacher was no guide, philosopher, and friend,' said Dr. Campbell. 'Nor did he attempt to gently mold or press children into desirable patterns. He chopped them down to size or pattern. None of your soft pedagogy.'

'The old education assumed that all answers were known; that there was little for the pupil to do but listen and learn. There was no research in teaching and learning,' he said. 'Mechanical repetition, recitation, and rote learning were the order of the day,' he said. 'There was little in the way of a formal curriculum.' In 1906, there were 28,000 children in B.C. schools, said Dr. Campbell. Only 68 per cent attended on the average school day and only four per cent were in what are now grades 9 to 13. Dr. Campbell felt a major reason for so few pupils going to high school was the philosophy that 'only the very bright were worth bothering with.' It was policy then, he said, to fail every child in every grade in which he did not achieve an arbitrary standard. Average failure rate was from 20 to 50 per cent.[22]

Before and After Sputnik

The progressive dream that schools could be liberated from the old classical regime remained mostly undisturbed until the late 1940s and early 1950s. In the post-1945 era, the British Columbia education department formally endorsed the progressive view of schooling that had been circulating in the province's educational circles since Putman and Weir's report in 1925, or even earlier. This view held that character, education, and citizenship were the paramount goals of public schooling as a departmental bulletin in 1957 illustrated:

> The people of this province have established schools for the primary purpose of developing the character of our young people, training them to be good citizens, and teaching them the fundamental skills of learning necessary for further education and adult life . . . A good school program develops children in two ways—as individual persons and as citizens. Since this development begins long before the child comes to school, the program must build upon a foundation already well defined. It should be so planned that it helps the child to become an individual who has confidence in himself because of what he is and what he knows. At the same time it should guide him into becoming a person who is respected and trusted by his fellow man. A school program that neglects the child in either of these respects fails to fulfill its responsibilities.[23]

However, the October 1957 launching of the Soviet satellite, Sputnik, greatly changed the educational climate in the province and, indeed, across North America. Sputnik's success indicated that the "high ground" of space had been won, at least temporarily, by the Soviet-bloc countries because of their prowess in science, mathematics, and engineering and also suggested that schools in Canada and the United States—especially the high schools—were deficient in the way they taught the basic subjects. In Sputnik's wake, enormous amounts of public and political attention turned to the public schools that had allegedly failed to keep pace with international educational developments, specifically those of the Eastern-bloc nations. Amid this educational crisis, four Canadian provinces, including British Columbia, turned to their own time-tested oracles for help and convened royal commissions of inquiry. Sperrin Chant, UBC's dean of arts, directed the British Columbia 1958-1960 royal commission. In their 1960 report, Chant and his colleagues strongly advised educators to abandon their progressive approach to education, arguing that many progressive goals were too diffuse for schools to pursue and that the public school system should restore the intellectual development of youngsters as the school's primary goal.

1960: "Intellectual development . . . is essential for human survival"

British Columbia Royal Commission on Education

> Intellectual development is chosen as the primary aim because, in the first place, it is essential for human survival, and the future of both the individual and the race depends upon it. In this period of the world's history, more than ever before, the survival of mankind will very largely depend on learning more intelligent ways for dealing with problems that threaten to annihilate the human race.

Over the course of human history, methods have been worked out and applied for such purposes as extending the use of the human intellect by the development of language and number systems; the continuous accumulation of knowledge; the refinement of the Arts and the Humanities; the devising of scientific procedures; and for deliberate study in every field of human endeavour . . . The transmission of all of this intellectual accomplishment from generation to generation is indispensable to human progress. Modern life, with its complexity and the speed and magnitude of its undertakings, places an ever-increasing premium upon mental competence, and intellectual development has become a necessity for all who are capable of profiting from instruction . . .

Intellectual development implies many things, but as the major emphasis for a modern school system its principal features need to be described. In the first place, it means the acquisition of skill to use the basic methods for dealing with intellectual matters—namely, the accurate use of words and numbers. In the modern world, illiteracy is a severe handicap to intellectual development and a persistent hindrance to participation in modern affairs. Moreover, an illiterate population lowers the general standard of living and impedes the progress of any community.

Intellectual development in the modern sense implies also an understanding of man's heritage of knowledge concerning both human achievement and what has been discovered about the universe. Furthermore, it includes an appreciation

Until the end of the 1960s, urban high schools were renowned for staging elaborate costume dramas to entertain pupils, their families, and the community around the school.
Courtesy Victoria High School Archives.

of the human values and principles by which the affairs of life are judged to be worthy or otherwise. Ignorance, as does illiteracy, curtails intellectual development and restricts the scope of human endeavour.[24]

1960: "Now, as always, the school is an agency for intellectual training"

J.F.K. English

Chant's report substantially changed the official rhetoric about the purposes of school inside the education department. It also allowed more than a few inspectors and other department officials to voice their own conservative and traditional views of education. One such individual was J.F.K. English, who was appointed deputy minister and superintendent of education in 1958. In the following passage, English distanced himself from the ideas of the educational progressives and asserted the fundamental importance of mastering the basic subjects, a view long shared by educational traditionalists:

> No doubt the question is often asked, what is the primary purpose of elementary and secondary education and what should the schools be trying to do? It might be said that a school's main function is to prepare pupils for good citizenship, to produce effective citizens by equipping them in various ways through experience in the classroom, including basic training in certain fundamental skills and the inculcation of such ideals as honesty, co-operation, and consideration for others. It should be the aim of this program to have pupils take their places in the world of today, which we know, and that of tomorrow, which we must envision; and it should be the object of any current society, of which the schools are a part, to have each generation of young people become more effective citizens than those of any previous time.
>
> It is my firm belief that an indispensable function of all schooling at every level today, as in the past, must be to provide sound instruction in the fundamentals of language, in mathematics, science, and history, and in the other disciplines which may have been developed in the course of mankind's quest for usable knowledge. Let us accept the primary fact that now, as always, the school is an agency for intellectual training. Schools exist to teach pupils something—the subjects in the curriculum and, in addition, good habits and healthy attitudes toward life in general.[25]

1961: "Weaknesses in the existing system"

Frank Levirs

One of the best-liked officials in educational government during the middle decades of the twentieth century was Frank Levirs, a man who was associated with the provincial system for almost 60 years as student, teacher and administrator.[26] He was appointed inspector of schools for the Omineca region in 1946 and, in 1965, was made superintendent of education, an office that dated back to colonial days. In the following speech, Levirs, like his colleague J.F.K. English, acknowledged the excesses of progressive education and endorsed a renewed emphasis on basic intellectual development as the key goal of schooling, in line with what the Chant commission had recommended:

> The present reorganization is based on the recommendations of the report of the royal commission on education which carried out its investigations throughout 1958-1960. That commission conducted the most exhaustive survey of education in British Columbia since the Putnam-Weir commission 35 years earlier. It was on the findings of the earlier survey that British Columbia's school system of three and a half decades was built; it is probably true that reference to the recommendations of the 1960 survey will be made for at least the decade to come and probably much more.
>
> When the commissioners viewed the secondary schools of 1958, they showed sympathetic understanding of the problems that had been encountered and the attempts meant to meet them . . . They dealt with such problems as external pressures on the curriculum, the explosion of knowledge, experimentation, the doctrine of interest, [and] individual differences . . .
>
> They also pointed out the weaknesses . . . in the existing system. Programs have become overloaded in an attempt to meet every pupil's real or fancied need . . . In identifying and making provision for individual differences, some schools have fallen into the extreme position of catering to every whim or every demand. The doctrine of interest has been misinterpreted to assume that pupils should learn very little in which they are not immediately interested.
>
> Schools have sometimes tended to neglect their basic task of fostering intellectual development in order to cover certain areas of training which are in reality the primary responsibility of other agencies. The separation of pupils into two streams has not been wholly successful in producing either a good 'university' or a good 'general' program. On the one hand, the 'university' program has failed to demand enough because too many pupils of inadequate ability are

taking it, these pupils either dropping out after failure or reducing the prestige of the 'general' program by transferring to it before graduation. On the other hand, the 'general' program, already designed for pupils of inferior ability, has no high standards, is far too general in that (except the field of commerce) it apparently leads nowhere, and is unfavourably compared with the 'university' program by parents and employers and even the schools themselves.

The commission felt that the root of all these evils was the organization of the school program itself. They therefore recommended a reorganization 'designed to provide more adequately for pupils of different levels of ability . . .'[27]

1963: "Maternity leave"

The B.C. Teacher

As teachers' educational credentials rose in the early 1960s, particularly in the form of completed university degrees, they began to see themselves in more professional terms and to demand better salaries and working conditions. The great expansion of the K-12 system in the two decades after 1945 was accompanied by the appointment of much larger numbers of married female teachers, women who had been discriminated against in earlier decades because of their marital status. Efforts to improve the quality of working conditions for married women were celebrated at the time in professional magazines for teachers, as the following article from *The B.C. Teacher* illustrates:

> With the increasing demand for, and occurrence of, married women working in general, and teaching in particular, it is increasingly important to have provisions for maternity leave. With the shortage of qualified teachers, married women must not be discouraged from teaching. School systems must establish adequate policies with regard to maternity leave.
>
> In the United States, as in Canada, there is no nation-wide policy for maternity leave. In most of the states the local school boards have the authority to give or withhold leave and pay. Only California, Delaware, Kentucky, Louisiana and Tennessee have specific state laws relating to maternity leave for teachers. In Canada, the provision for and the length of leave vary from province to province . . .
>
> In both countries there is strong resistance to the employment of married female teachers. It is common for single women to be given preference, although this discrimination has lessened somewhat in the last ten years. The North American countries are behind the times compared with some European countries. The

Scandinavian countries have legislated social insurance, which covers health and maternity programs, as a public service for citizens in general.

All natal care in Sweden is given free of charge. Mothers are also entitled to special maternity benefits. These benefits are coordinated with the health insurance scheme and are administered by the sickness funds . . . Sweden also gives eight months' leave of absence for caring for the new child. It is usually taken after maternity leave. The teacher receives no pay during this period, but is reinstated in her position at the end of the period of leave . . .

The International Labour Organization has shown concern for maternity leave and protection as part of its larger effort to provide adequate social security for the world's workers . . . Forty countries and five territories under United Kingdom administration grant maternity leave on full pay . . . As mentioned before, practice varies considerably in regard to maternity leave in Canada, and for the most part, leave is without pay. The cost of confinement and doctor's care may be covered by the many hospital and medical insurance plans across Canada, although the type and extent of coverage vary.[28]

1968: "I married and settled down never to teach"

Frances Fleming

Frances Fleming's career in education, like that of so many others, was delayed by the Great Depression and it appeared for a while that she would never teach. In time, however, she became an important figure in provincial schooling. Fleming was the first woman to be appointed as a superintendent of schools in the post-1945 era. She followed in the footsteps of Margaret Strong, superintendent of New Westminster schools from 1911-1914 and the first female to be appointed as a school superintendent in Canada. Here, Frances Fleming sketches out the circuitous route that led her from the normal school to the superintendent's office:

In 1932 I graduated from Vancouver Normal. There were no vacancies —750 first-class teachers out of work in B.C. I worked at the old *Commonwealth Weekly Newspaper* for $5 a week until, in 1935, I married and over the next several years had three children, and settled down never to teach professionally.[29]

In 1944 to my surprise I was appointed to teach at Stave Falls School by the now defunct Mission School Board who had learned there was a qualified teacher living in Stave Falls. It was great fun. I did an article on remedial reading for an educational journal, borrowed books from the BCTF lending library and from Victoria, and really enjoyed myself. The inspector, H.H. MacKenzie, gave me an excellent report and a letter of dismissal, saying that 'the boys' would be back from war and would be taking over their own jobs, thank you.

My husband's work took him to Burnaby, and to my surprise, C.G. Brown, superintendent there, asked me if I would start Burnaby's first special class at Kingsway West. I said I would try. At the end of the year, C.G. Brown gave me a glowing report. He wanted me to take some courses. I asked him about tenure. The board, he said, still did not want married women teachers on staff. I resigned. I could not see any future in education for me.

We moved away for two years. When we came back to Burnaby in 1948, I did some long term substituting for Vancouver and was offered a one-year contract to teach special classes. For six years I received an excellent report in May, was fired in June, rehired in August [to circumvent the policy against hiring married women]. Because I was not on permanent staff, I could only pay dues to the BCTF not participate. Reluctantly, I started to take summer school to upgrade my certification. If I had not loved education, I'd have given up every year.

In summer, 1954, a scout for West Vancouver School Board, impressed by my artwork, offered me a job and a permanent appointment at West Vancouver. It was August and I had not yet received my annual appointment. I accepted, and wrote to Vancouver saying I had been fired so many times I thought I should take the hint and go. Vancouver then removed married women from the banned list and invited me back. I taught at West Vancouver for the year and returned to Vancouver on permanent staff. What an incredible feeling, after all those years.

In 1958, my husband moved to Sechelt. We did not want to be separated. I resigned from Vancouver and applied to Ann Burns at Gibsons' school board office for a teaching job. 'You will be teaching at Pender Harbour,' said Ann Burns. I argued. I had only elementary qualifications, no secondary degree. Ann lost her patience. 'Degrees, hell!' said the Secretary of the Board. 'What we need is teachers and you have the best record I have ever seen!'

I enrolled for correspondence at UBC and hit the long trail of summer courses again. Meanwhile, at Pender, we had a sequence of disastrous principals. I was asked to take over. I was not interested in administration. I loved teaching. After three requests, I agreed, and kept right on teaching full time, doing the administration after school. In 1965, Pender became the smallest accredited secondary school in B.C.

My husband moved back to the power dispatch office in Vancouver. I resigned from Pender and applied once again to Vancouver. Yes, they would be pleased to appoint me to Templeton, teaching art, typing and some occupational.

In 1966, I quit Vancouver again, drew out my pension money and took my masters degree at UBC. I was never going back to teaching. But in the spring there was a nasty incident at Templeton that I knew I could have averted. My heart went out to the kids involved. I phoned the principal, Ken Waites, to ask if there was any chance of my coming back.

'Don't be silly.' 'Hmm, don't be silly yes, or don't be silly, no?' 'Come down tomorrow at 10 o'clock and I'll have your papers ready to sign.' So I re-established my pension, and went back to work. In 1969, I was asked to attend the applicants' class for administrators. I was then appointed vice-principal of Magee, being the first female administrator in Vancouver secondary education in living history.

From there I was appointed to be superintendent at Quesnel. Women were treated so strangely all those years. It seems like a different world. They are still not well received as top-flight administrators. They will have to look to themselves to see what reasons can be found that they are still, as a group, somewhat ineffectual. They cannot claim any of the barriers that held me back for a good quarter of my professional life.[30]

1968 and 1969: "The corpse above the classroom and a teacher with a snake-skin covering"

Donald Campbell

A graduate of Mount Allison University and a naval gunnery officer during World War II, Donald Campbell joined the education department in 1968 as a district superintendent and was assigned to manage several districts in the province's largest and most northern territory, the Stikine. While student protests, "sit-ins," and other counter-cultural events disturbed the normally tranquil face of Canadian life in cities around the country, Campbell was faced with his own cultural difficulties adjusting to life in the northland, as the following two stories show:

Telegraph Creek! Is there any place in British Columbia that is more remote, difficult to reach, to depart from, or historical in background? Not likely, and especially so during mid-winter with temperatures seldom soaring to the heights of 10-degrees below zero Farenheit. The single-track road connecting Telegraph Creek with the outside world via the Alaska Highway is (or was in 1968) very dangerous and hazardous to one's health, often closed by weather conditions of snow, ice or mud, and the single telephone line connecting with Dease Lake was out of operation as much as in operation. One always checked carefully at Dease Lake as to the estimated whereabouts of the postal delivery truck before starting out, for the driver seemed to have a charmed life with no regard to the icy narrow roads where two vehicles could not pass, steep 80-degree cliffs along the Stikine Gorge, or any vehicles on the road coming towards him.

Historically, I was told that there still remained some scattered remnants of the telegraph wire and reels, two or three miles west of the small community that were originally stored for the proposed telegraph line from lower British Columbia to Dawson City during the gold rush bonanza days of 1897-1899. When the gold rush ended, the telegraph enterprise collapsed and the wire and supplies were abandoned. All that remained in Telegraph Creek were a Hudson's Bay trading post, a two-room school, a few small business entrepreneurs and a scattering of houses. There was also a small wharf along the side of the river where a floatplane could tie up if it successfully flew the river gorge.

On one visit to the school and community during late winter, I sat in the classroom after school talking with the female teacher who lived nearby with her husband. I asked about her husband. He was not the other teacher but sort of worked and helped around the community. The teacher continued drinking her tea and with her free hand pointed up to the ceiling. I didn't think much about this but after swallowing her mouthful she said 'he's up there—dead, and frozen stiff.' Well, that was a real bit of a shock and surprise but, after recovering and asking about it, she explained in a very cool, unemotional manner.

The explanation was as follows: It appeared that her husband had taken ill, and with no doctor, hospital or medical services in northern B.C. or even communication with the outside at the time, he died. What to do then? Phone line down, roads impassable, total isolation. No inkling as to when transportation or communication would be restored, and even if restored, the teacher would not be able to drive the body out to civilization for transport or burial in the Fraser Valley where their regular home was located. The first thing required of course was to somehow preserve the body and this was done by laying it on a flat surface in the back porch of the house where it froze solid overnight while still protected from the wolves and coyotes. However, the body could not remain there because of continual in and out traffic and, since there was space with a trap door above the classroom, a decision was made to pass it up and leave it there until the teacher could drive out during the Easter holidays. And there the corpse remained. It seemed to me to be a sensible solution to the problem since the northern attitude was always 'to make do as best you can.' Who was I to upset things, or a decision that had already been made? However the story and event did not end at this point. It continued.

It seems that it is a very serious crime to transport a human corpse from one province to another without a death certificate and proper clearance certificates—and a still more serious crime to transport a human corpse from another province or territory into B.C. And since the road from Telegraph Creek leads only out of B.C. to the Alaska Highway at Mile Post 649 in the Yukon Territory, then eastward to finally re-enter B.C. and head southwards, there was no alternative available to the teacher when a warm spring period came along just as the Easter holidays began. The body of her husband began to thaw so she got help, got the corpse down from the attic storage area into the station wagon and headed out towards Watson Lake and the south. By the time she arrived in Watson Lake the thawing process was well under way and becoming serious, so she drove directly to the airport, attached a delivery and address tag to the body and, by some means or other, talked the Canadian Pacific Airlines into shipping it south by the next plane. Still no certificates or clearances.

Late next night in Fort St. John the phone rang, waking me up only to hear an irate agent at the airport telling me that there was a corpse there with no papers and wanted to know what I wanted done with it. By that time I was puzzled

Inspectors reached remote Vancouver Island schools and schools up along the Sunshine Coast by using float planes borrowed from provincial ambulance services. **Courtesy Dorothea Stafford.**

but very wide-awake and eventually realized just what had happened. What to do and what could I do! I knew nothing about such things or requirements. They were not in my mandate as district superintendent or official trustee but, fortunately, I knew that my good friend the government agent in Fort St. John would definitely know and give solid advice. Sure enough, on awakening and considering all circumstances he said that he could look after the problems, provide the necessary certificates on a temporary basis so that the teacher could get her husband to Vancouver the same night, and enable her then to get the body from there to a mortuary in Langley.

At this point and seeing that the pathway was cleared, I figured my duty had been done so I called up the elementary supervisor who had been told about the problem. He very graciously took the hint, and said that he would get the papers and deliver them to the airline agent and the teacher. Which he did and all ended quite satisfactorily at the time. To this very day I do not know if there were any after effects to the necessary but probably illegal method of transporting a human corpse without a death certificate or clearance out of British Columbia and then back into the province. And I don't want to know—but in the far north people just do what is possible with whatever is on hand according to the circumstances.[31]

The second story concerns a teacher in Lower Post. Lower Post is the most northerly community in British Columbia being only three miles from the border with the Yukon Territory, four miles from Watson Lake and located on the Alaska Highway. The two-room school there provides me with a number of remembrances but one of the most outstanding is that of the female teacher with the snake-skin covering.

The Lower Post population was 98 per cent Indian at the time—what we today call 'aboriginal' or 'First Nations'—but there was a combined hotel and store, a residential school for the natives, and a scattering of homes. There was also a two-room school divided between primary grades and intermediate elementary grades with a teacher for each room. Many of the pupils had had little or no contact whatever with white people other than the teachers, and often lived most of the year out in the bush. They were a wonderfully warm group and very familiar with nature and all the animals one would find in the wild. It is important to remember this point.

My predecessor in this superintendency had informed me that the school had no teachers hired for the next term so that the first duty I would have to perform was to hire two teachers. I was the superintendent as well as the official trustee in this district—the Stikine. The two that were hired were a young husband and wife team with one year of experience. I was quite pleased with their work in the first half of the year and everything appeared to be going along smoothly and reports from the community were favourable.

It was in late January or early February with the temperature hovering around -30 degrees Fahrenheit that I got the first inkling of a problem. The elementary supervisor called me in Fort St. John to suggest that it might be advisable for me to take a trip up to Lower Post but she wouldn't say just what the problem was. Now that is quite a long trip, two or three days at least by car and not to be taken lightly in mid-winter, so the only alternative was to fly to Watson Lake, rent a car and then drive back down the Alaska Highway. On checking with the secretary-treasurer and, informed that the budget was way over-spent, I decided to put the trip off for a while and let time heal the problems. However about three or four days later another phone call came and in very strong northern language I was advised to 'get off my butt and get up here in a hurry.' So, budget be damned—onto the plane and into the car to Lower Post and to the school.

The intermediate room and the male teacher were in full form but the primary room was a different matter with the teacher, supervisor, three or four parents and a few children gathered around them. One could cut the tension with a knife—and I had walked right into the midst of it.

The entire problem centered around a science class lesson involving animals, in this case snakes, and the class had discussed how snakes shed their outer skin layer each year by wriggling out of it. Then the teacher told me that to illustrate what the snakes did she kicked off her shoes, hiked up her skirt and peeled off her pantyhose. Now, refer back to paragraph two and remember that these six or seven-year old children had had very little contact with white people. In fact I learned later that this teacher was the first white person some had ever seen, so one can imagine what an effect this disrobing act had in their minds. It was traumatic to say the least, and even one or two of the parents weren't too sure about it at all. It seems that the children thought she was actually pulling off her real skin, that all white women did the same, and that they were possessed by a magic spirit that could harm the children. However, after a time and much lengthy discussion, the attendance problems were solved and the parents agreed to have the children return to school the next day.

The general atmosphere around Lower Post in general wasn't quite the same for some time after this episode but gradually eased off, although whenever in Lower Post I noticed that the pupils were friendly but sure did treat that teacher with care. The teachers finished off their year and then moved on to some place in the Northwest Territories.[32]

1971: "The most exclusive men's club in Vancouver"

Norma Mercer

Save for Victoria, the province's urban school districts had been resistant to the idea of female administrators since the late-nineteenth century. Norma Mercer and a handful of female colleagues were among the first women to break down the invisible barriers that had long prevented female educators from rising to senior administrative positions in schools and district offices in modern times. In the following stories, Mercer tells of her rise through the ranks and the awkward social consequences of joining the "old boys' club" in school administration:

I am purely a product of Vancouver. I graduated from Kitsilano Secondary School. I went to the provincial normal school and became a teacher at the age of 17. I then took time over the next couple of years to complete university. I went back to university full time for two years and completed an honours B.A. in history. Some eight years later I began working on my Masters degree in teaching at the University of Oregon. In the 1970s, I registered at UBC in the doctoral program. I did two years of doctoral studies.

I taught in Vancouver at MacDonald School. It's down on Hastings and Victoria, and at the time it was a fairly rough part of town, a rather bad tenement area. A lot of the kids came from very unfortunate kinds of homes. A room and bathroom shared by 10 families kind of thing. And yet at the same time we had families who had lived there for years and the community had grown up and had houses there. I was there for two years. I taught grade 3 and physical education as well. I also went overseas to teach with the Department of National Defense for two years in the 1960s in France and, when I came back, I went to teach at a high school in Vancouver, Kitsilano. This was most interesting because I had been there as a student and a lot of my teachers were still there. And it was while I was at Kitsilano that I made the transition and following five years there, I applied for and was assigned to an elementary vice-principalship. At that time there might have been only one [other] elementary vice-principal in Vancouver who was female and that was Jean Fraser.

When I got my first principalship in 1970, I was never interviewed for it, never applied for it. I was simply phoned when I was at the University of Oregon and was told that the night before I had an appointment to the principalship. Three men who were members of the quote 'old boys' network' were determined before they retired that they were going to have a woman in the principalship. [By this time], I had been in three schools and I think I had a high degree of credibility.

I had the experience. I was well known and well respected in a district that said, 'It's time women came into senior administration.' When I was appointed as a principal, I joined the most exclusive men's club in Vancouver, and that's the way it was. It was probably as difficult for them in many ways as it was for me. In fact I think it was probably more difficult for them because I knew what I was getting into and they were used to operating in a particular way.

When I was interviewed I was asked the question of why I wanted the job and I modestly said I thought I could make a difference . . . I really went in thinking that I could flatten that structure a bit. I could make it more humane and more understandable to people who are out there. I think there have been some strides made and it's not the same as when I first went in.[33]

Notes

1. Maxwell A. Cameron, *A Report of the Commission of Inquiry into Educational Finance* (Victoria, British Columbia; King's Printer, 1945). "We are justified in saying," Cameron reported the following year, "that costs per pupil still vary so widely as to indicate great differences in the quality of the schooling provided, and that differences in ability to pay for education, and in the burden of school taxes, are undoubtedly substantial (27)." To correct this difficulty, Cameron proposed re-organizing sparsely populated districts into administrative units "large enough to justify a reasonably adequate schooling from grades one to twelve (86)." "While few would be so optimistic," he wrote, "as to suppose that any system of school finance devised by man could, or even should, remove such inequalities altogether, all would agree that a good system should aim at reducing them (20)."
2. Thomas Fleming, "Our Boys in the Field: School Inspectors, Superintendents, and the Changing Character of School Leadership in British Columbia" in Nancy M. Sheehan, J.D. Wilson, and David M. Jones (Eds.), *Schools in the West: Essays in Canadian Educational History* (Calgary: Detselig, 1986), 297-298.
3. Cameron, *A Report of the Commission of Inquiry*, 36-37.
4. Interview with Stewart Graham.
5. G.M. Weir, "To the Teachers of British Columbia," *British Columbia Schools*, Vol. 1, No. 1 (February 1946), 7.
6. The "some people" mentioned here is likely a thinly-veiled reference to H.B. King's obsession with educational measurement. DeLong and other inspectors of more traditional views did not necessarily agree with King's progressive and highly psychological approach to schooling.
7. J.B. DeLong, "Memoirs," courtesy of Bill Lucas.
8. Interview with Carlyle Clay.
9. James P. Spradley (Ed.), *Guests Never Leave Hungry: the Autobiography of James Sewid, a Kwakiutl Indian* (Montreal: McGill-Queen's University Press, 1989), 191-192.

10. *The Prince Rupert Daily News*, "The Problem of Private Schools," Tuesday, 23 October 1951, 2. Harry G.T. Perry was managing editor of the newspaper.
11. Harold Stafford, *The Nation's Schools*, Vol. 47, No. 5, May 1951, 1.
12. John Calam has kindly allowed use of this material for this volume. Otherwise the material is Copyright © 2001 by John Calam.
13. John Burdikin's manuscript is courtesy of Terry McBurney and Barbara Naef.
14. Interview with Stewart Graham.
15. Harry Assu with Joy Inglis, *Assu of Cape Mudge: Recollections of a Coastal Indian Chief* (Vancouver: University of British Columbia Press, 1989), 86-88, 90, and 95-97.
16. Hilda Neatby, *So Little for the Mind: An Indictment of Canadian Education* (Toronto: Clarke Irwin, 1953), 11-19.
17. Campbell began his career as an assistant to David Wilson head of the government's textbook branch and the province's first school inspector. Following an assignment as teacher in a one-room Vancouver Island school, Campbell saw wartime service with the 16th Western University Battalion. After demobilization in 1919, he became the first assistant at the Lampson Street School in Esquimalt before taking the job of principal in Prince Rupert. In 1928, he was appointed to the school inspectorate with responsibility for the Kamloops region. Two years later, he was appointed to the position of assistant principal at the Victoria Provincial Normal School.
18. ARPS 1952-1953, N30.
19. Norman McKenzie was president of UBC; Harold Campbell was deputy minister of the Department of Education; and Judge Clearihue represented the interests of the Victoria Provincial Normal School.
20. Colin Chasteneuf, interview with Ray Williston.
21. K.F. Alexander's story is courtesy of Terry McBurney and Barbara Naef.
22. *The Vancouver Province*, 3 April 1956, "Modern Education Superior to Old-Time Teaching System: Soft Pedagogy Unknown," 16.
23. British Columbia Department of Education, "Administrative Bulletin 1957," 1.
24. Sperrin N.F. Chant, John E. Liersch, and Riley P. Walrod, *Report of the Royal Commission on Education Province of British Columbia* (Victoria: Queen's Printer, 1960), 17-18.
25. ARPS 1959-1960, X33.
26. Following his days as a student in Victoria's schools, Levirs earned B.A. and M.A. degrees in history at UBC before becoming a teacher at Ocean Falls and principal at Creston High and Kimberley High. Levirs was the last person to hold the position of provincial superintendent of education. After his resignation, all the superintendent's responsibilities were assigned to the deputy minister.
27. Frank Levirs, "The Reorganized Program in the Senior Secondary School: An address to the B.C. Council on Education, 3 March 1964," appears here courtesy of Dorothea Stafford and is part of Harold Stafford's papers.
28. *The B.C. Teacher*, January 1963, 159-161.
29. Frances Fleming's folio of notes on her career was sent as an enclosure to Thomas Fleming in 1987.
30. Correspondence with Francis Fleming, 1987.
31. Donald Campbell's manuscript is courtesy of Terry McBurney and Barbara Naef.
32. Ibid.
33. Interview with Norma Mercer.

British Columbia Legislative Buildings, Victoria. Courtesy B.C. Archives A-02772.

CHAPTER 6

Schools in Politics and Politics in Schools: Public Education's Baroque Era, 1972-2005

The year 1972 represented a watershed date in provincial education. It marked a century of public education in the province. It also signified a dividing line between a century-old tradition of centralized control of schools by the education department and the beginning of a new and decentralized approach that unhooked school administration from the overall governance of the system. Most of all, however, it marked the beginning of a new and political era in education, an era that began when the BCTF used its considerable human and financial resources to help unseat the Social Credit government, a government, by one account, "well into its dotage." This political activism on the part of the teachers' union would prove to have profound consequences for professional educators, government, and for parents and the public over the next three decades.

Long removed from the pitfalls of party politics, British Columbia's public schools did not become politicized overnight. Rather, their conversion to partisanship was a process that began in the early post-1945 era and gathered momentum throughout the 1950s and 1960s. Several factors were involved. District consolidation in the late 1940s gave rise to more powerful school boards and to a more influential trustee association that demanded greater local control over schools. The 1960s had also recast the province's social character, unleashing new expectations for personal freedom and individual rights. More than a decade of social activism that began in the mid-1950s prompted new challenges to the established social order and to institutional authority of any kind. Rapid growth in the under-30 population energized a many-sided movement for change and the expression of individual rights in all aspects of public affairs, including what historically had been society's most conservative agency—the public school.

Within this turbulent time of change, educational institutions found themselves subject to a new and vigorous public scrutiny. Viewed through the optics of a new age, British Columbia's education system did not seem particularly democratic in how it treated minorities, women, the handicapped, immigrants from other cultures or, for that matter, students and their parents. Schools, some argued, were the private domain of the senior bureaucrats in educational government, more specifically the deputy minister and his management committee, sometimes pointedly referred to as "Snow White and the Seven Dwarfs." As the 1970s began, even politicians concluded it was time to reorganize schools along more democratic lines and to redistribute authority more widely throughout the educational system.

Championing this new view of decentralizing educational authority was Mrs. Eileen Dailly, a former teacher and outspoken Burnaby School Board trustee elected in 1956 under the banner of the left-wing Co-operative Commonwealth Federation (CCF). Elected as a New Democratic Party MLA in 1969, she was appointed education minister in 1972 when the NDP came to power. In less than the three-year life span of the new government, Mrs. Dailly greatly changed the province's educational direction, as well as public expectations about what schools could and should do.

The longstanding tradition of strong central control over public schooling was "out," she declared. Decentralized decision making was "in." Administrative power, as exercised by superintendents, principals, and bureaucrats was something to be curtailed. The influence of students, parents, and local communities was to be expanded. Individualism, the great social creed of the day, was also "in." So, too, was an educational movement to customize school programs and services to meet specific student needs, a movement that greatly expanded the "social" agenda attached to the public schools. Sparked by rising public expectations, the provincial government now ordained that everyone's child was now capable of completing high school. In Mrs. Dailly's egalitarian vision, nothing less would do.

Meanwhile, a public school system designed in the nineteenth century to produce a rough-hewn educational equality between city and rural schools was beginning to groan under the weight of its vast new social and educational responsibilities, much like a medieval church later forced to support the adornments of the Baroque Age. The immense expansion of the school's social and educational mandate that took place between 1972 and 2005—embellishments never contemplated when public schooling began—justify the description of these decades as public education's Baroque Era.

Not surprisingly, many of the stories that comprise the final chapter in this volume are about politics, writ large and small. Some concern office politics inside the education department, or gender politics inside local school districts. Some involve party politics on the larger provincial scene or, in true British Columbia fashion, the activities of political personalities whose behaviours were sometimes as capricious as the weather along the coast. Some stories speak to the rising influence of special interest groups such as the BCTF and the BCSTA, along with the political gamesmanship that characterized a series of post-1972 skirmishes between government, the teachers' union, and other assorted special interest groups now self-appointed to the status of "stakeholders" in the provincial system.

Amid the tumult of recent years, one thing was clear. As public schooling became a growth industry after 1950, and as education became an essential part of public policy, the gentleman's agreement that historically existed among provincial political parties "to keep politics out of the schools and the schools out of politics" ended in 1972. No longer did the educational community appear to stand as a unified body joined by the idea of what constituted the common good in education. The cooperative spirit that bound school professionals and their institutions together in a small tight-knit community during the first century of public education was gone. Chief among the reasons for its disappearance was the staggering growth in size of the postwar system. But the close relationships that had long joined provincial educators to each other and to their community vanished for other reasons as a barrage of work stoppages, strikes, bitterly contested contracts, withdrawal of services, other job actions, and imposed arbitrations separated teachers from the public and from the administrators who directed schools. Such developments, along with an educational labour climate that was easily the worst in the country, led to mounting community discontent with public schooling and to a considerable loss of social status and community regard on the part of school professionals and educators in general.

Put simply, the stories that comprise this final chapter portray an educational house badly divided. It is a portrait that stands in marked contrast to images from earlier times when educators were lionized for their knowledge and for the important educational and social service they performed—and when British Columbians were quick to boast about their schools, teachers, and the great educational accomplishments that had been made since Confederation in 1871. The Baroque Era would prove to be a dark and fractious period in the province's school history.

1972: "The school system is organized like an industry"

Eileen Dailly

Mrs. Eileen Dailly began her educational career as a schoolteacher on Denman Island teaching 30 students from grades 1 to 8.[1] In 1972, she became the second woman to become education minister in British Columbia.[2] Her efforts to redistribute educational authority and to place teachers and students at the centre of the public school system met with stiff resistance on the part of some staff members inside the education department, as well as administrators in local school districts. The following passages are from the "White Paper," a document that Mrs. Dailly tabled in the Legislature to set out the educational directions she wished to take on behalf of the NDP Government:

> We believe that a major responsibility of the school system is to provide a measure of success for every student. The fact that it fails to do this in some instances calls for an examination of the whole structure within which the student is expected to learn.
>
> When we look at the structure, we discover the school system is organized like an industry, with the Department of Education as top management and classroom teachers as production workers. There are many levels of educational decision-makers between, who have diminishing responsibility and authority the closer they are to the products of the education system, the student. The student is often on the receiving end of a series of decisions that are made for him by people in the system who have no direct knowledge of his actual circumstances. Decisions with respect to curriculum, programs, and general policies of the school are decided in isolation of individual needs of students. Parents, in general, are not involved with these decisions . . .

The central relationship in education must be between the teacher, the student, and the parents. Professional educational staff must be deployed in the actual teaching situation or in supportive positions. The structure of the education system should be redesigned in such a way that authority and responsibility are distributed more appropriately, keeping in mind the principle that the primary relationship in education is between the teacher, the pupil, and the parent, and that other parts of the system must be in support of that relationship.

The current practice of segregating children into pre-school, elementary, junior-secondary, and senior-secondary schools must be re-examined. Encouragement must be given so that schools can operate on a year-round basis if advisable. Flexibility in school organization must be provided so that the social needs of children are more appropriately met. The present administrative structure may not recognize the supportive role of administration to classroom activity.[3]

Prior to the 1972 election, a 24" x 36" poster of deputy minister Joe Phillipson (top centre), and his senior management committee (top right clockwise: Les Canty, C.I. Taylor, John Meredith, Bill Reid, S.E. "Ed" Espley, Andy Soles, and J.S. White) adorned school board and principals' offices throughout British Columbia. The photograph's chief significance lay in the fact that no names were listed under the faces. It was assumed that everyone in the provincial system who "counted" knew who these men were. In a minor act of rebellion against the enormous power of the education department, officials in local districts humourously referred to the portrait of the senior management committee as "Snow White and the Seven Dwarfs."

1972: "The traumatic experience of meeting Mrs. Dailly"

Joe Phillipson

A "hold-over" from the previous Social Credit administration, deputy minister Johann "Joe" Phillipson was well known for decades in the educational community. After a distinguished career in the Peace River region, Phillipson was appointed as a school inspector and, later, deputy minister. In an interview he recalled his early days in the new NDP Government and his first meeting with the minister: [4]

Until I had the traumatic experience of meeting Mrs. Dailly as minister of education that first day in her office, I never thought of education as being a political thing. I guess I was terribly naïve. I had never played politics in education. Sure, I guess I played politics in education in trying to work a school board to do what I thought was the right thing, but I never played politics in the sense of working the Social Credit against the NDP. Education was a clean game as far as I was concerned, and I always thought that everyone played it in a clean way. I know that with a change of government, there was pressure from certain quarters among NDP supporters that the old guard in Victoria had to go—especially three or four of us, including myself and Ed Espley, our finance man. I found out I had been replaced one day when Eileen asked me to her office and introduced me to my replacement [Jack Fleming].

When Eileen Dailly took office, she was seen as a very nice lady who had been a school trustee and understood all the problems of school districts and teachers. And she was under tremendous pressure from the BCSTA, and especially the BCTF, who after all took much of the credit for getting the NDP into office. I think she was being pressured to paint the senior people in the office as the old enemy. Not all of us, but some of us. She was a very kind person and I believe she found the situation she was in very unpleasant.

The first thing she did was reassign Ed Espley, superintendent of finance, to accompany the newly-appointed commissioner of education, John Bremer, to tour the province.[5] Ed saw it as a graceful way out of a bad situation and a chance to end his career on a high note. She then brought in Jack Fleming as Ed Espley's replacement in finance. And, of course, Jack became deputy minister a few months later.[6]

1972: "School supervision in the north"

Terry McBurney

Terry McBurney was a teacher and administrator in British Columbia schools from Vancouver Island to the Stikine. He was later appointed deputy superintendent of schools for Surrey, British Columbia's and Canada's largest school district and was appointed as a member of the 1987-1988 royal commission on education. Here, he recalls his assignment in the province's most remote school district:

When I took a job in 1972 as school superintendent in the Stikine District 87 in northern British Columbia, I realized that it was geographically the largest school district in the province with a territory of more than 188,000 square kilometers. I also quickly realized after setting up residence in Fort Nelson just how far away I was from the mainstream of the province. The closest 'major cities' to this isolated district were Fort St. John, Dawson Creek, Prince George, and Whitehorse. Vancouver and Victoria seemed to be on another planet.

In the face of such distance, I was always grateful to Canadian Pacific Air (CP Air) for providing the principal link to the outside world—at that time Fort Nelson benefitted from two flights each way to Vancouver daily. I found out much later that this service would not last. During a visit to Fort Nelson in the spring of 1988, I learned that the airline service had been reduced to one flight each way to Vancouver on an every-other-day basis.

I was particularly aware of how much northern British Columbians depended on the Alaska Highway as the main artery—in fact, the only artery of ground transportation. In summer, driving hundreds of miles was made difficult by blowing dust (the highway was only paved at that time between Dawson Creek and Fort St. John). In winter, driving was made treacherous with blowing snow.

Also contributing to a sense of splendid isolation in the Stikine was the comparatively limited state of telecommunications with the outside world. During my first six months in Fort Nelson, television was during evening hours only on a one-week tape delay. The launching of Anik in early 1973 gave us the excitement of live TV! Thank God for CBC radio—Peter Gzowski and 'This Country In The Morning' saved our lives.

Distances were vast throughout the district. But the initial thing that struck me was the distance between schools. In Fort Nelson there were three schools. The next closest school was approximately 100 miles away at Summit Lake. The northern end of the school district was at Lower Post on the British Columbia-Yukon border. Schools were spread across the Stikine hundreds of miles apart from Good Hope Lake and Cassiar to Dease Lake and Telegraph Creek. Set off by itself was the two-room school in Atlin. Getting there for a visit involved flying from Fort Nelson to Whitehorse, where a car could be rented for a chancy 120-mile drive to Atlin.

Along with supervising district schools, I was required by the education department to inspect teachers requiring certification in schools that were affiliated with the Roman Catholic Church, such as Iskut, or teachers based in remote logging camps such as Mile 248 and Germansen Landing. In the latter case, the school operated for 14 consecutive days then was closed for a week so the teacher could join company personnel for a flight to Prince George or Williams Lake to enjoy whatever urban delights these communities could offer. Again, without CP Air and various small northern charter air services, none of these inspections could have been carried out.

Needless to say, as school superintendent, I was considered as part of the 'establishment' in the school district and in the town of Fort Nelson. This meant becoming involved in various community enterprises. During our time in Fort Nelson, my wife and I were instrumental in establishing the first community arts council. My wife became president of the council while I, along with the United Church minister and the local dentist, set up a film society under the council's umbrella.

One evening as we three film buffs were glued to the silver screen watching Orson Wells in 'Citizen Kane,' we were joined by two other souls who thought they were in a bar which wasn't decent enough to provide continuing service of cold beer! Community involvement also meant occasional speaking engagements at service clubs and other community organizations, as well as radio interviews. The guy who ran the local radio station was someone I had known in my life in central Alberta where I met him in his role as a playing coach of the 'Senior B' Red Deer Rustlers.

Recruiting and retaining teachers in the province's most northern and remote school district was a challenging task. When the government of the day reduced the pupil-teacher ratio across the province in 1974, I lost 75 per cent of my staff because they could find jobs much closer to the so-called civilized world. This was the best example of the 'double hit' that schools in the north took. Finding willing teachers meant participating in the annual 'meat market' sessions for graduates at UBC and UVic. Recruitment also involved interviewing respondents to our newspaper ads in Vancouver and even hiring teachers sight unseen, on occasion, following a positive telephone conversation.

Our ties to the 'mother ship,' the department of education that had sent us around the province, were sustained by the department's field services office as well as by zone meetings, the department's annual fall conference, and through service on government committees. Senior staff members in Victoria were hugely supportive of our efforts in the field by providing sound advice, budgeting assistance and even, as required, snow tires! The annual superintendents' conference convened by UVic was regarded as a mid-year treat of great proportions. The BCSTA, especially its branch services division, also gave isolated superintendents a chance to stimulate their professional and social connections.[7]

1972: "The Bremer commission"

Joe Phillipson

I was the deputy at the time [of the Bremer commission] and Minister Dailly had informed me that she planned to appoint a commission to study the issues in education. She asked me if I had any names to suggest to her. I took her request seriously and prepared a full report of individuals I believed had the appropriate stature to sit on such a commission—one such person was Dr. Bob Sharp who had recently retired as superintendent of Vancouver.

I have here my report but she never gave a response to it. One day, she asked me to talk to a person she was sending over to my office and wanted to know what I thought about his knowledge regarding educational issues. It turned out to be Mr. Bremer whom she had appointed as a one-man commission on education. I couldn't believe it.

When [Donald] Brothers was minister [1968-1972], I pressed for some resources for the ministry. We were short staffed in some areas and with, say $50,000, we could have resolved a lot of our staff problems and at the same time dealt with a lot of explosive issues facing us. But W.A.C. Bennett wouldn't budge. I know Brothers saw it my way but it was impossible to talk to the 'Old Man.'

When Mrs. Daily became minister, I conveyed the same message to her, but she just said she would think about it, which was her all-too-often response. Well then when we got into the Bremer thing, she asked me to develop a budget that would cover the cost of the commission. I thought if I pressed for $100,000 we would have enough for the commission and the initiatives that I thought were important. When I presented the proposed budget to her, she said in her opinion it was much too small and she made it $1,000,000!

> Well, the commission turned out to be a disaster. After a full year Bremer hadn't turned in any report . . . and Premier Barrett fired him while Barrett was being interviewed on a talk show. Why Bremer didn't report anything I'll never know: he had a bigger staff than John Meredith who was responsible for the whole curriculum division. What a mess! The minister knew she was going to get little sympathy from me and it had to be very embarrassing for her to have the premier fire the commissioner and, I believe, without her knowledge. I was with her in Montreal at the time the premier fired Bremer and our first knowledge of it was when the press was all over her wanting the details. She got to a phone as quickly as she could and found out what the press knew and she didn't . . .
>
> I wasn't privy to how they named the people for the research and development [branch]. By then, Jack Fleming was the deputy minister. But it turned out to be another disaster. They too were all fired after a short time. Dr. Stanley Knight headed up the research and development group and I think some of them were from Bremer's group. At any rate, they set up office and proceeded to try to take over the affairs of the ministry.[8]

1973: "The commissioner . . . has not altogether been successful"

Eileen Dailly

In a press release issued in Vancouver on Saturday, January 12, 1973, education minister Eileen Dailly attempted to save political face by explaining why Premier Dave Barrett publicly dismissed education commissioner John Bremer during a television interview two days earlier, returning control over the direction of public schooling to educational government officials in Victoria:

> Prior to my trip to Montreal for a meeting of the council of ministers, the Premier, the Honourable David Barrett, and myself reviewed the present status of the education commission and came to a number of mutual conclusions upon which I will elaborate shortly. I understand that Thursday evening Mr. Barrett expressed the view that the commissioner on education has not altogether been successful. I will try to now explain why we feel this is so.
>
> First of all let me review the objectives of the Bremer commission. Basically it was for Mr. Bremer to examine the present system in the province, through public discussions with all interested groups, and report to me on possible needed

changes. He was also asked by me to help set up, where necessary, special task forces to deal with specific problems. My intention was not to have one large report produced at the end of a certain period of time. Instead I wanted an informal and less structured type of commission with interim reports.

In moving through the province last year Mr. Bremer certainly stimulated public thinking on education, but also unfortunately in some statements did create some unrest and concern with certain groups who assumed because of his role as a one-man commissioner that these statements were predicting government policy. Our goals and objectives would have been better achieved if Mr. Bremer had assumed more of a listening, evaluating, and reporting role.

I have discussed this in a very frank manner with Mr. Bremer and have concluded that the role of the one-man commission as conceived by Mr. Bremer was not producing for me the necessary evaluation of our system and recommendations for change which I had hoped for.

I have reached the decision that educational change in this province can now best be served by having the newly-reconstructed department of education responsible for evaluation and recommendations to me for new directions in education in this province.[9]

1973: "This couldn't be the agenda"

Henry Armstrong

Henry Armstrong served as executive director of the BCSTA from 1973 to 1990, a period of immense political turbulence in public schooling. He recalls the lack of a steady hand at the tiller of educational government during Eileen Dailly's time as minister:

I remember Eileen Dailly calling us into a meeting in December of 1973 and she was putting together a committee comprised of representatives from the BCTF, the BCSTA, and the ministry, and our task was [to draft] a whole new school act. We were to meet two days a week for four weeks and, by the end of January, we were to have the genesis of a new school act. We arrived on a weekend in January to find a paper . . . [that] was to be a discussion paper for our meetings. In essence, it indicated that teacher-salary grids be done away with and that all teachers be paid the same salary regardless of qualifications and experience. And it recommended that we could cure all the ills of the system by having all administrators elected by their staffs. Our initial reaction to that was that this couldn't be the agenda. We figured this was a red herring, and we went looking for the agenda. In the third week, we found out that this was the agenda and at that point we withdrew from the meetings, and our president called a press conference, and expressed loss of confidence in the minister of education, Eileen Dailly.

We had a similar kind of situation [with Mrs. Dailly] when she called us in to consult with us when she announced that she had decided to reduce class size by two across the province and that this would involve a wholesale injection of new teachers . . . I said, 'Well, Mrs. Dailly, if you're going to reduce class size, where are the capital funds to build the additional classrooms? Because if you spend the money simply to hire additional teachers, you will not reduce class size unless you earmark the money specifically and unless you build the additional classrooms.' She immediately dismissed the fact that additional classrooms would be required. Our lobbyist at that time was Alan Nichol. When we came out of that meeting, he tried to teach me another political lesson that you never tell the emperor that he has no clothes.[10]

1973: "The most archaic management structure I had ever seen"

Jack Fleming

It was not just the minister's office that was turbulent during the NDP government's 1,000 days in office. In 1973, when Jack Fleming replaced Joe Phillipson as Mrs. Dailly's deputy minister of education, he found an education department that operated mostly out of its hip pocket, certainly when it came to budgetary estimates and matters of school finance:[11]

The Bremer commission was given the task of identifying the thrusts for the new government; the new boy in the ministry, myself, was given a rather confused role of assisting Bremer in his task where possible, but I was more seen having the responsibility to update the ministry in its relationship with the government . . . The Bremer commission was cut off at the end of the first year without having made a report to the minister. It is my guess that the premier and the minister became dissatisfied with the lack of progress of the commission. Perhaps there was a misunderstanding between the government and Bremer. One has to understand that governments have very short timelines; it seemed Bremer's timeline and theirs were different.

I thought the department of education was probably the most archaic management structure I had ever seen. It was literally a case study. The basic information systems and decision-making processes necessary in an organization did not exist. First, it was obvious that the department was oblivious to its own problems. The department's financial function was always centered around one man [Ed Espley] who was the premier's controlling agent. He was encouraged by the premier to maintain his isolation from other branches of the department. In fact, the financial agent in each government department was the pipeline to the premier in how to control expenditures in each department and the premier was a one-man decision-making government. The premier [W.A.C. Bennett] felt his most important function was to keep financial control of the province—far more so than this [NDP] government.

As far as I could tell, Ed Espley didn't even discuss financial matters with the deputy minister. For example, the 1972-1973 budget estimates were sent by Espley to treasury board without the deputy minister [Joe Phillipson] or the minister ever having seen them, to my knowledge. Because the thrust of the government of the late 1960s and early 1970s was to focus on financial matters, it seems they left educational issues to the bureaucracy to deal with. In essence, there was little policy development in that area even to the point of completing the recommendations of the Chant commission. Cabinet had not dealt with educational issues for some time. The senior officials of the ministry made decisions in their branches on educational matters quite divorced from the politicians and each other. The policies they operated under were in their minds, not on paper and adopted by legislature. In essence, senior officials were educational caretakers who dealt with issues as they saw fit, with little involvement of the political arms. I found in 1973 that it had been beyond the senior officials' memories when they had last sat down and discussed the total responsibilities of the department.

After the Bremer commission fell apart, the minister was under considerable pressure to give some statement as to where education in the province was going. The ministry inherited a number of people from the Bremer commission. One of these people was Marguerite Reid who was given the responsibility of completing the 'White Paper.' Writing a 'White Paper' is a very difficult task. After 50 drafts, it was acceptable, but probably said nothing but motherhood statements. It is easier to write a *School Act* than a four-page 'White Paper.' By the time it was circulated, it lacked any super-charged words that might be misinterpreted . . .

It was my advice to the minister that if she was going to bring change to the system she would have to involve the people in the system to bring about that change. I wasn't alone in this opinion. A study we had done said much the same thing. Therefore the minister was persuaded to establish an internal structure that would seek to involve the educational community in system goals clarification and implementation. As deputy minister, I informed the research and development staff that they were to involve superintendents and ministry officials in the formulation of initiatives and policy. However, by accident or design, the group that coalesced in the branch had a clear political agenda. They were on probation and [later] they were relieved of office.

When I arrived, it was obvious that for some time the ministry officials and the past governments had not seen the need or the responsibility to establish policy in a shared, consultative way with the public. The problem was that by the 1970s, the practices of the government and ministry were seen to be very outdated; that is, the practice of a person of influence speaking to a ministry official and getting a policy changed—keeping in mind that policies were really only personal practices of a ministry official, not the government—was seen by the larger public as totally unacceptable. Even though it was unacceptable, there needed to be a proper system devised to deal with policy as an alternative.[12]

1973: "Government and the BCTF have been accused of terrorist activities"

Henry Armstrong

In an interview, BCSTA's executive director Henry Armstrong described the immoderacy of school politics British Columbia-style and some of the reasons for the struggles between the BCTF, the BCSTA, and government in the 1980s:

The actions taken by the BCTF were not actions, they were reactions. They were reactions to an anti-intellectual, anti-educational government and they were taking the only course they saw open to them, which was a political route. I disagree with taking that political route. I disagree with educators entering into the political domain at all. I started this discussion by saying 'a pox on all their houses.' A pox on the house of the far right that was anti-intellectual, anti-education: a pox on the left that tried to counteract that by taking political action against it instead of taking educational action against it, and of course, my bias is that educators ought not to enter the political arena.

There are people in the BCTF who would disagree with that, and say, you know, that 'you've got to match terrorism with terrorism,' and to some extent, in both cases, the government and the BCTF have been accused of terrorist activities in education here. And no doubt both of them are committing terrorist activities in terms of the child in the classroom. But it's difficult to say just who's to blame and where the cycle starts. My point is that I . . . blame, in terms of the present circumstances, the provincial governments of the last decades. I . . . blame the politics of the BCTF. I . . . blame the politics of school boards, where school boards have allowed themselves to be drawn into this.

I had a big fight, back in the days of restraint, whenever members of my executive of certain political persuasion would say, 'Fine! The government wants to cut! Let's make sure we cut where the public will see it.' And I was arguing, 'No! Let's make sure we cut where it will do the least damage to the child in the classroom.' If you want to introduce a policy of making sure that the cuts are done in such a way that they will be shown to the public, then you are playing the government's game, and you're as much an educational terrorist as the government.

So there were those kinds of politics being played by school boards. There were the politics of the BCTF, there were the politics of the government, there was the politics of the minister of education within the ministry, and politics being played by some school administrators. Not to mention the day-to-day problems that were being created in the system that I've been talking about where superintendents were being paternalistic in their management style, couldn't figure out why in heaven's name they were breeding teacher militants. The whole thing has to come together and you have to look at the whole thing as a broad spectrum, and as to which one of those variables is the most important, God knows.[13]

1973: "Whitey says they are all failures!"

Frances Fleming

Here, Frances Fleming, the first woman to be appointed a school superintendent in post-World War II British Columbia, recounts two stories that illustrated the tensions between schools and the families they served in the north-central part of the province:

In 1973, while I was vice-principal of Magee Secondary in Vancouver, I was approached by Charles Ovans, general secretary of the BCTF, to see if I would let my name stand in the search for new district superintendents of schools. It was time the province had a woman in that position, Mr. Ovans argued.

In those days district superintendents outside metropolitan centres were appointed by the minister of education. To receive such an appointment, one had to be willing and able to relocate. It so happened that my husband Ray had taken early retirement that spring, and for the first time in my life I was free to move anywhere in the province. I applied and was appointed to Quesnel, and the district calmly took a bow and professed to be honoured to have the first woman superintendent.

The district was all set to go. My predecessor, Doug Fair, had organized it before he retired. Billy Hurst, secretary-treasurer was on the spot to assist and advise, and there was a strong central staff that knew the district well. Mr. Fair, who had seemed a rather austere chap to meet, had left a cartoon in the main drawer of the office desk, a drawing of a psychiatrist leaning over and saying to the mother of an obvious brat, 'Have you ever considered belting the little bugger?' It broke me up.

Pupil evaluation proved to be a particular problem in northern schools as I would learn in two instances. The first story concerns a little two-room school at Nazko that served some ranchers' children and those of the Nazko Indian Band. The embarrassed young teacher there had just launched into a dull lesson on the Parthenon. The gaps between this young man, the subject matter, and his class were almost insurmountable. After school I went over to the band offices and watched the same little children playing like young otters on some homemade rotating equipment made out of heavy timber that would have decapitated anyone less daring and agile.

'What do you think of our kids?' asked a big scar-faced man outside the office. I told him that they were wonderful, beautiful little kids. He spat. There was no friendship in his face.

'Huh! Whitey says they are all failures!' Their last teacher had written 'Fail' on every report card and quickly left the Valley. I could only warn the new young man to try to relate the curriculum to their daily lives, and to submit all report cards to the central office before he distributed them.[14]

School evaluation likewise proved a problem on another occasion—in this case because of an overzealous Cariboo principal. He had invited me with great urgency to come to view his wall charts of which he was obviously proud. Before I made time for this, I received a worried delegation from his school. I have never seen nicer, more dejected people. 'We know our kids are real inferior, real dumb,' said the spokesman, 'way below average in every way . . . low IQ's . . . the whole bit. Worse than any other kids in Canada, I guess. How can we get them to high school if they're so dumb?' Some of the women were sniffing back tears and the men were red-faced and totally angry. They assured me that they liked the school, liked the principal, who could not do any better than he was doing with the kids he had to work with. I promised to see what could be done.

An immediate visit to the school revealed the source of the principal's pride and the parents' despair. It was the charts. There were charts everywhere. One listed the names of the pupils and their IQs. Others showed Canadian norms for standardized tests and the lower achievements of the pupils in his school. Every comparison possible was posted in beautiful lettering and rainbow colour. The principal had exhausted the resource centre and spent a lot of his own money obtaining and administering standardized tests to his discouraged pupils. He was heart-broken when he was told to remove them forever from human sight and get on with the job of teaching these good average pupils, giving them encouragement and every assistance within his power. We assured the parents at a later meeting that all would be well, but I think those charts would haunt them all the days of their lives.[15]

1970s: "A B.C. school in the Alaska Panhandle"

Donald Campbell

In the following story, Stikine district superintendent, Donald Campbell, describes one of the most anomalous features of schooling in the province, a development prompted by the geographical proximity of a B.C. school to an American settlement in Alaska:

The Alaska Panhandle—that part of the State of Alaska reaching south from the eastern main body of the state for almost 1,000 miles to about Prince Rupert and separating the northern portion of British Columbia from the Pacific Ocean. It contains the small city of Juneau, the capital city of the state, which has no connection other than by sea and air to the rest of Alaska and the United States—no road connection at all. It is along the Panhandle also where the Stikine River comes roaring to the sea from its origins in British Columbia. The 1,200-mile long Chatham Channel and Lynn Canal lead northwards to the communities of Haines on the western side of the inlet and Skagway, seven miles further north on the eastern side at the very northernmost part of the inlet. Skagway of course is famous as the 1897 starting site of the gold rush trail to the Yukon and was the site of Soapy Smith's infamous saloons and gambling enterprises.

Much to my complete surprise there was a one-room, one-teacher British Columbia school two miles within the border of Canada [British Columbia] and three miles from Haines, USA, and thus it was in a part of the Alaska Panhandle. There was no phone connection nor did I ever see any mail communication although the district secretary-treasurer did tell me there was perhaps a request for some small supplies about once a year. Sure enough, on checking the records there was the school with 16 pupils registered. Being new to the job as district superintendent and an official trustee as well, this meant that a visit was needed to find out what it was all about and to meet with the teacher and students. Getting there though was a completely different matter and as I found out, not a trip to be taken lightly.

The first point of reference en route to Haines was Whitehorse in the Yukon Territory, located at Mile 917 of the Alaska Highway. After reaching this jumping-off place one started out on the road towards Dawson City, further west and north. After innumerable dreary miles the driver saw a building with the name of Haines Junction painted on it and a road leading off to the southwest. This road then continued over a high plateau with no vegetation or trees taller than three feet and having, every 100 yards, 15-foot high poles stuck in the side of the road with alternate red and white stripes painted on them. These poles marked the edge of the road when it was covered with snow during the winter when all vehicles in both directions were issued numbered tags and then led in convoy style by an RCMP patrol car. At the far western end of this sub-arctic plateau the road descended steeply and entered the warm, moist Pacific climate. What a change and relief!

The school appeared a number of miles southwards but since the day was now well spent it was best to proceed further on to the town of Haines and get a place to stay overnight. To get there one passed from Canada into the United States but there was nothing to mark the difference other than a painted post alongside the road, which was quite a change from other border crossings in southern British Columbia. Very comfortable quarters were easily obtained in Haines and good food available in a nice restaurant.

A very pleasant time was had at the school the following day for it was a happy school with an excellent teacher. One of the most amazing things of note was the abundance and quality of equipment and student supplies, both on the playground and in the classroom. This was best illustrated by noting that there were two state-of-the art motion picture projectors and a goodly supply of modern educational films. The same type of supply situation was evident everywhere one turned. I could not recall any of these items being supplied by the school district and paid for by the province. At the end of the school day I was invited for refreshments to the home of the teacher. I asked the question concerning the source of these supplies, as well as about the background of the school and the pupils.

What I learned was this—during World War II, when Russia joined forces with the Western Allies, airplanes were flown from the United States to Russia via Alaska, with fuel and repair stops provided at certain places along this route. Fairbanks, Alaska was one of the important fuel and repair stops but had no oil or means of getting it. Consequently, a program was developed whereby oil was shipped by sea to Haines, stored in huge tanks and then pumped through a pipeline up and over the mountains to Fairbanks. A powerful pumping station was built just inside the Canadian border with housing provided for any of the army staff and personnel having families. At the conclusion of the war the pumping of oil to Fairbanks continued, the staff became more civilian in status and lived there with their families, but American army officers held command and control. The parents among the pumping staff insisted that a school be provided for their children and since the location was on Canadian soil within British Columbia, a one-room school was established.

After learning this bit of northern history, the question of school supplies came up and it seems that this was a thorny problem indeed for some years because of extremely poor means of communication with the school district office 1,400 miles away. Relays were needed from, or through, Whitehorse and this system did not work well at all. To overcome this difficulty the current teacher, being a very resourceful teacher indeed, explained her problems to the U.S. commanding officer, a personal friend, and he immediately solved her problems. The solution was quite simple. He took her lists, picked up the phone, and ordered everything from Seattle. All supplies were delivered the very next day by plane, direct from Seattle, Washington to Haines, Alaska and then by truck to the school, with no records or costs involved. What a wonderful system this was, and it continued from that day forward.

The supply and delivery of the two motion picture projectors and attachments followed the same pattern as outlined above. The exception being that when the first machine was ordered, the commanding officer included an order for a second machine because it was easier and cheaper to supply this than to detach a worker from the pumping station crew to go to the school and repair the machine even if it was for as simple a job as replacing a burned-out light bulb.

The following day for the return trip to Whitehorse, rather than re-drive the weary miles, I attempted to board the ferry to Skagway. My plan was then to put the car on the train and ride in style up over the mountains on the White

Pass and Yukon narrow-gauge railroad following the route of the old gold seekers. The ferry captain objected to this though when he saw the official B.C. government decal on the side of the car. He just would not allow the car to board for some official reason or other. To try to get around this, the decal was splattered with mud so that it couldn't be seen but the ruse didn't work, the captain still wouldn't let the car aboard the ferry. So, back onto the dusty, dirty, gravel and mud road to Whitehorse.

Progress and automation eventually caught up with the pumping station at Haines, for the following year when the pumping station and its program became fully automatic, station personnel were released, the student population disappeared, and the school was closed. The teacher transferred to the Whitehorse school system where I am certain that she continued to do an excellent job of teaching, and became loved by students and parents alike.[16]

1970s: "Travelling in the north"

Barbara Naef

Barbara Naef graduated from Britannia High School in Vancouver and entered the "emergency" teacher preparation program in the late 1950s as teacher shortages mounted. Later, she went to Germany as a teacher for the Department of National Defense. In the 1970s, she served as a supervisor for the school district in Prince George. Getting around the province's interior and northern regions in winter sometimes proved challenging Naef recalled:

The school district in Prince George contracted with Indian Affairs to supply two supervisors to oversee a number of their schools in the lakes area west of Prince George. One of the schools to be visited was Tache and, although there was a gravel road in from Vanderhoof, the best way to get there was to charter a plane from Prince George. One early spring day another supervisor and I headed out in a small charter plane. As was usual at that time of year we left from the Prince George airport on wheels and the skis would be used to land on Stewart Lake. Circling the village of Tache there was no warning of the danger ahead. The weather was good and the lake was clear for landing. The pilot chose to land a fair distance out on the frozen lake. He started down and touched the surface while on board we started to get ready to pick up our gear and unload.

Suddenly things didn't feel right. We were not sliding over the ice as we should have been but after a momentary settling seemed to be sinking. The pilot said nothing but gunned the engine and we slowly and clumsily headed towards the shore. The path we took was anything but straight and although the pilot continued to gun the engine we felt as if we were barely moving. Besides the noise of the engine there were other noises coming from outside the plane that I couldn't identify. The other supervisor and I had no idea what was going on but we'd both done enough flying in similar conditions to know that something was not right.

The pilot managed to let us know as the plane careened towards the shore that we had broken through the ice when we landed and that we were trying to get to shore before the plane sank. What a shock! And yet there was nothing we could do. I think we held our breaths, probably believing it would make the plane lighter. The shore had never looked so far away and we suddenly understood why so many villagers were on the bank watching the plane. No thanks to us but thanks to an exceptional pilot we got to shore. The villagers told us that because of the weather there had been a thaw and then the lake had refrozen. That was the ice we had broken through when we landed. They told us that under about six feet of water there was another ice surface. We never did find out whether that would have helped us or made our situation worse if our pilot hadn't acted as quickly as he did.

I had other experiences with small planes, like getting out into the middle of Williston Lake at Finlay Forks on a plane and then having the engine not start. Again, thanks to a determined pilot who was not about to lose his plane or stay out there overnight we eventually got out. When he decided there was nothing he could do to start the engine he got out on the float and paddled us to shore. Once there he tinkered with the engine until it started and without further ado we flew back to Prince George.[17]

1973: "Which one would you like us to use on your little girl?"

Frances Fleming

Frances Fleming's experience as Quesnel superintendent had its lighter moments as she observed here:

Corporal punishment had been banned by Minister Eileen Dailly in the spring of 1973. It had not affected us at Magee Secondary in Vancouver because we had not used the strap for four years. The Cariboo, along with many other rural places, had not approved this legislation, and my director of instruction, who knew of what he spoke, confided that some principals were mightily tempted to utilize the occasional whomp with the strap with the full approval of parents. To remove this temptation I called in all the straps, all the corporal punishment record books, and advised the principals to find and read a copy of the *Public Schools Act.*

The admonition to read the school legislation was interpreted as an order to dig out their Bibles and start reading daily scripture. Word was out that I was a sort of religious zealot. At my first meeting with the principals this rumour was dispelled and interest in the *Public Schools Act* was somewhat refocused.

But those straps! We collected about 50 of them long, thin shiny ones, short fat thick ones, ones with rivets, one with ends slashed, straps of every shape and size. Because no standard had ever been set for the strap, anything went, and considerable originality had been used in their selection. I set up workshops, invited principals to send difficult pupils to my office, invoked parental assistance and in the spring, took part in a BCTF task force on alternatives to corporal punishment.

Shortly after school opened, I was visited by a young mother who dropped in to give me her views on corporal punishment. She refused to send her little girl to any school where the principal could not use the strap. She was very firm about this. I told her that girls were occasionally strapped as well as boys. That was fine with her. On sudden inspiration I reached down into my bottom drawer and lifted out the mess of straps. 'Which one would you like us to use on your little girl?' The woman turned pale. 'Are those straps?' she asked in a quavering voice. I assured her they were. She stood up. 'Mrs. Fleming, do you know my name?' she asked. I did not. 'I hope you never get to know it!' she exclaimed as she sped away down the long corridor.[18]

[On another occasion], a landlady came in seeking redress against a young teacher whom, she claimed, had defaced her property by drawing big red hearts on her shag carpets and put, she hissed conspiratorially, red initials in the middle of these hearts. Before she could give me the culprit's name, I told her that this was not the business of the education ministry and that I could not listen further. She left in a huff. There are things no superintendent should know. [The following] September I was asked to transfer to the special education branch in Victoria. My 13 months as a superintendent came to an unexpected and untimely end.[19]

1974: "I decided to leave the superintendency"

Harry Cullis

Former West Vancouver principal and district superintendent of schools for Lillooet and, later, Squamish, Harry Cullis resigned his position on August 31, 1974, after 15 years as a superintendent, for reasons he discloses here:

> The NDP were in power in Victoria for the first time and, expecting things would now improve in education, I found my hopes unfortunately and unexpectedly dashed. The NDP were making a gigantic mess out of education. They would not listen. So far as they were concerned, superintendents were suspect authority figures, who must be taught to listen to teachers—in this case often the second-rate but politically strong teachers. Before, fighting dragons had not been easy but on occasion one could do something worthwhile for children—but fighting well meaning but misguided, and often un-informed friends, was impossible. Never one to remain for long in a position I did not enjoy, I handed in my resignation. My peers and my bosses in Victoria appeared shocked. Superintendents did not resign. In many ways, I was not cut out to be a civil servant . . . Often at war with my principles, I found the decisions harder and harder to make. It was time for a move.[20]

1974: "Creation of the Nishga School District"

British Columbia Department of Education

Long defined educationally as wards of the federal government, aboriginal peoples sought greater control over their educational lives as the 1970s began. The first step in the educational emancipation of aboriginals in British Columbia was manifest in the establishment of the Nishga School District. Here, an education department bulletin reported developments to date and the activities of two of its senior managers, Joe Phillipson and John Walsh:

> A unique educational development in British Columbia, and one certainly worth noting in the bulletin, is the creation of the new Nishga School District, soon to be completed. It's in the Naas River Valley in the north-central interior, and is populated about 95 per cent by native Indians who, for the first time, will have what is for all practical purposes their own school district. Mr. Phillipson and Mr. Walsh, whose integrated and supportive services division is most

directly concerned with the education of Native Indians, went into the area a couple of months ago and met with about 100 citizens, mostly Native.

In the near future, Mr. Phillipson will return to the area to discuss the boundaries of the new district with S.D. 88 (Skeena-Cassiar) which will be effected, as well as the appointment of an official trustee and other related matters. Mr. Phillipson hopes that the new district may become operational in January 1975.[21]

1975: "A terrier for high standards"

Walter Hardwick

Walter Hardwick, a UBC geography professor served as deputy minister of education from 1975 until 1979, when he returned to his academic post. Here he discusses the confusion within the Social Credit government about public spending during the time of his appointment and the views of his strong-minded minister, Patrick McGeer:

The state of the school system was the single most talked-about issue in the hustings in the 1975 election and the cabinet was prepared to reinstitute compulsory exams, uniforms, or whatever they believed was eroded over the previous 20 years. I told [Minister Patrick} McGeer that he was going to have to accept the public's judgment on the system and that what we could and should do is to bring order and accountability to it. He basically accepted my judgment, although he was a terrier for high standards. I then set out to establish a measure of fiscal and educational accountability. When I started to look around the ministry, there were no measures of anything that would allow us to assess standards. My colleagues in the ministry were operating on years of experience but they were in a total information and data vacuum.

It ran on the old boys' network. They had their knowledge of the system, but it wasn't verifiable in any way. It was their opinion against someone else's and so we had a constant stream of delegations from school districts coming to the minister with their figures and perceptions about a situation.

McGeer was a hawk on restraint and believed in it. He saw the economic downturn in 1976, and believed there had to be a lid put on spending both on the capital and operating side. However, school boards and many of his colleagues in the cabinet did not see it as he did. If you look back on the pupil-teacher ratio issue, you'll find that the monies were raised locally by school boards to bring it down; it was not provincial money. McGeer stood firmly on the level of provincial expenditure in the school system. That's why the provincial share of the cost of education decreased in those years.

However, not the same can be said of all his colleagues in the government. In some ministries, and particularly in the health ministry, there was no management of the subsidiary organizations, hospitals and so on. Consequently, there were tremendous inflationary salary settlements and expenditures. I personally think that if the rest of the government was operating consistently with the policies of the ministry of education at that time, that by 1979 or so the boards would have made up their own minds as would have the arbitrators, to slow down the expenditures and lessen the salary settlements. But you can't have a couple or three ministries trying to curtail spending while others are spending like mad. You can't be building mega-projects on one hand, and think you can convince the public bodies that revenue has flattened.[22]

1976: "Larger than the country of France"

Alan Newberry

Alan Newberry was appointed superintendent of schools for the Fort Nelson and Stikine school districts in the mid-1970s. In the following story, he described the scope of his managerial responsibilities and the challenges of supervising schools in British Columbia's most northern region:

The uniqueness of my northern assignment is such that I find myself playing the role of district superintendent of schools, chairman of the school board, and vice-chairman of the community college. The division of field services has assigned me to the position of district superintendent of schools for Fort Nelson and Stikine school districts. There are 63 teachers in the Fort Nelson school system, and 31 teachers in the Stikine school system. The minister of education by order-in-council has appointed me official trustee of the Stikine school district. In this role I must perform all those functions normally assumed by a school board including board chairman, chairman of the salary committee, member of the liaison committee, and chairman of the education committee. Needless to say, the meetings of the Stikine school board and the minutes . . . are certainly unique in British Columbia record keeping. My third assignment which is dictated by the *Public Schools Act* is that of councillor of the Northern Lights College. Since the Stikine school district must be represented by a school trustee on the college council, there is no choice in who performs that role.

This describes some of the uniqueness and excitement of an assignment in British Columbia's far north—and in a small superintendency. Not exactly a small superintendency: these two school districts cover the northern third of the province of British Columbia. The geographic area of the assignment is larger than the country of France.

The travel budget for one year in both school districts is $11,000. This should indicate the astronomical distances between the central office and the schools in the field. For example the Atlin Elementary School is 750 miles from the school board office. The Telegraph Creek Elementary School is probably the most remote situation in British Columbia, accessible by plane during certain periods of favourable weather and at a cost of $350 for a chartered air trip from Cassiar.

To reach the schools in the Stikine school district. I must travel by CP Air from Fort Nelson to Watson Lake, then u-drive on northern roads for about two and a half hours to reach the community of Cassiar. From Cassiar, Good Hope Lake School is easily accessible. Dease Lake is accessible only by helicopter or other aircraft, or by a braver northern road driver than myself.

Telegraph Creek can be reached realistically only by chartered aircraft. If I wish to travel to Atlin, British Columbia, I must first take a plane first to Whitehorse in the Yukon Territory, and then take a u-drive to the community of Atlin. By the way, accommodation in some of these communities is non-existent. The usual visiting quarters for dignitaries from the school system in Telegraph Creek is the primary classroom for the district superintendent, and the floor of the intermediate classroom for the supervisor of instruction.[23]

1979: "The move from public education toward private schools is building"

Jim Carter

R.J. "Jim" Carter was a West Vancouver secondary principal and was appointed deputy minister in 1979. He served in that position for a decade during one of the most fractious periods in provincial school history. Here, he reflected on ministerial priorities and educational government's shift toward more demonstrable outcomes in the 1970s and 1980s:

McGeer had two thrusts when he became minister in 1975. First, he wanted to firm up the kindergarten to grade 12 system, and second, he wanted to introduce several new initiatives in the post-secondary system.

He attempted to firm up standards in kindergarten to 12 by establishing a core curriculum, English placement tests, achievement tests, and so forth. At the post-secondary level, during those years McGeer was minister, we opened the Open Learning Institute, the Knowledge Network, the Justice Institute, David Thompson University College, medical research labs, and expanded the community college system.

McGeer also tried to curb spending increases in the kindergarten to grade 12 system. Government grants to school districts increased marginally in those years and, in fact, there was a shift in spending towards the post-secondary system . . .

By 1980, the first signs of the conservative shift were being felt in England and the U.S. and, I believe, the government was aware of the mood of the voter. Initiatives, such as mainstreaming and wholesale changes in the *School Act*, were moved ahead with caution . . .

There's no doubt that a dramatic shift took place at that time . . . I assume that Vander Zalm was appointed as [education] minister because they wanted an outspoken person at the helm—and I believe that he was more outspoken than anybody bargained for . . .

One of the policy directions I saw the ministry moving toward was English placement tests and other initiatives to establish standards. We believed we could do something between government exams and what was going on. We'd hoped that it would achieve a fairly common standard from school to school, but it didn't. For example, in the Greater Victoria School District, mathematics standards varied from school to school so dramatically that an A in mathematics 12 in one school was equal to a C or C+ in another . . . Schools were not taking their achievement results seriously and dealing with them as one would have expected.

We had major wars within the ministry about government exams. I . . . held firmly to the notion of exams . . . My motivation [wasn't] deep, philosophically. To me, it [was] a practical thing to do to gain back support of public education.

The move away from public education toward private schools is building.[24] I believe public schools through government exams will dismiss the . . . notion that public schools are not doing a good job.

I think we have to change many of the historical relationships. The dramatic shift of 1980 to the conservative mode means a completely different approach must be taken—new skills, new abilities, a different attitude toward consultation and relationships.

The system must be given a chance to function through greater clarity in purposes and expectations. The governments of the past have been more guilty than school boards in creating a long list of expectations [for schools]. Now we'll work to confine and refine those expectations through . . . school-based management and deregulation.

The role of the superintendent is going to depend upon strategic considerations . . . If experience tells us that the most effective approach is to jump over the superintendent's office in order to effect things at the school level, we will do that.[25]

1980s: "From servants of the Crown to employees of the boards"

Peter McLoughlin

As far back as the 1930s, school inspectors had complained that, although they were senior in rank to school principals, their salaries were substantially lower. The salary problem persisted even after 1958 when the provincial inspectorate was closed and district superintendencies were established. The issue became more aggravated in the 1970s as salaries for teachers and principals in local school districts jumped substantially while the salaries of provincially-employed district superintendents remained tightly constrained by the civil service salary grid. Matters came to a head in the late 1970s when superintendents decided to leave government service and become employees of local school districts, largely for reasons to do with financial compensation.[26] For many, however, this change proved costly. Local boards did not offer the security of tenure associated with government. In the space of a decade, 1980 to 1990, 67 of the 129 men and women who served as superintendents of British Columbia's 75 school districts left the superintendency to find other positions in education in and outside the province. Here Mission and, later, Agassiz-Harrison school superintendent Peter McLoughlin reflects on their decision to leave government and the important consequences it had for superintendents professionally and for public education in general:

We had no one to blame but ourselves. We felt no pressure from our boards or from the provincial government. It was our decision and we actually voted by a show of hands that we were in favour of moving from our tenure with the ministry to the uncertainty and, for many, the humiliation of local employment. Those of us who were strongly opposed had made, we thought, strong rational argument against such unwise change in our employers and in the concomitant working conditions. And it wasn't that the proponents of the proposed change were stupid. It was the concept that was not only stupid but also seriously hazardous for many of our colleagues. I can recall one of the compelling arguments supporting the change made by one of our brightest colleagues. And his money argument won the day.

As field superintendents we were caught in the salary structure of the civil service in general and of our own ministry's personnel in particular. The deputy was doing his level best to correct the compensation package but to no avail. All of us were being paid salaries far below those of the secondary principals we were supervising. Elementary principals of large schools were also ahead of us. In Mission, for example, I was number five on the totem pole. In big districts it was significantly worse. In private conversations for months beforehand we would try to dissuade people. The salary problem would be sorted out in due course without having to go to local employment. I went so far as to say that there would be a heavy price to pay for this foolishness. I suggested that there would be a large number of abrupt and unplanned 'early retirements.' Education would suffer during this period of instability among the educational leaders.

I reminded my friends that we knew all about the salary problem when we joined the ministry staff. My own salary as principal of Kelowna Secondary School dropped by $6,000 when I became a superintendent. And, in 1971, that was a big chunk of money. But we did it. We knew the financial consequences. But we also knew that we could have a much greater influence on education in the province as superintendents of schools than we ever could as secondary principals.

There was a certain camaraderie among us as field superintendents . . . We were supportive of each other and we could go to bat for colleagues in difficulty. We could have a quiet chat with a neighbouring superintendent, get and give advice, and we knew it would be confidential. In those days we filed monthly reports with the superintendent of field services and we had other communications systems to give Victoria early alerts when trouble was brewing. But best of all we could, and did, spend most of our time working on educational development within our schools in our districts. We were 'visible.' We never felt we had a problem with having two sets of bosses. At times it even worked to our advantage being able to say, 'The ministry won't like that,' to the board and 'My board won't stand for that,' to the ministry.

We were there for the advancement of education and we had a degree of independence. Although we were ministry types we battled with the buildings people for capital for proposed new schools and the like. And while we were devoted to the educational welfare of our own districts, we also had the security of knowing that we could be independent of the whims of some school board members, and we could get away with it. But things changed. There was a noticeable change in the ministry personnel at the same time. Instead of having 'been there, done that' characters we had a series of political appointments and a virtual absence in Victoria of personnel with senior school district administration experience. Pity.

Not long after the rather stupid movement of superintendents to local short-term tenure we then had the next dumbest thing: the exclusion of principals and vice-principals from the BCTF. At one stroke of the political pen, the principal-teacher in every school was segregated from his or her colleagues on the staff. Relationships within schools deteriorated. In my view, and I speak as a former table officer of the BCTF, there has also been damage to that organization. It now lacks the sobering influence of the elders of the profession, the principal-teachers of the schools. Leadership at all levels has deteriorated. However, let's face it, we superintendents did ourselves in with local employment on that fateful day in the auditorium of the provincial museum in Victoria.[27]

1984: "I was asked . . . if I was a good dancer"

Barbara Naef

As the following story illustrates, the criteria used to select school superintendents by local boards after 1980, when they were empowered make such appointments, was sometimes questionable as Barb Naef recalls about her own applications for a superintendent's position:

During my interview for the superintendency in Mission in the fall of 1984 I was asked, as were all five candidates, if I was a good dancer. The question was asked by the one male board member who informed me that as all the other candidates, four males, had been asked that question he thought it only fair that I be asked also. There were four females on the board.

For that same selection process one male candidate was exchanged for another after short-listing because the board member on the selection committee decided, based on an attached photograph, that the second one was better looking that the first one selected. Once the selection was made the board chairperson, at the next in camera meeting, while discussing the selection said that once she'd seen his big feet she'd made the decision and went on to imply it suggested other parts of his anatomy might also be rather large.

In the selection process for the superintendency of Maple Ridge in spring 1987, the selection committee had taken a short list to the board, based on reference checking, the criteria and the applications, which included three females and three males plus one male who was apparently a maybe. The three females included myself, Dr. Carole Chandler of Sooke (an assistant superintendent) and Bev Buchanan (a principal in Abbotsford) . . . The three females were, on paper, as qualified, if not better qualified than the men. The board took all three females off the short-list. We actually investigated taking legal action but our lawyer advised us we couldn't win so we dropped it.

The following was another real question asked during panel interviews for my candidacy as a superintendent and an assistant superintendent. During one interview I was asked by an experienced and well-known male school trustee if I could bake a rhubarb pie. This was the reality of being a female contender. Often you could not get short-listed and when you did these were the type of questions you might have to answer. I was also denied a superintendency because I was married at the time and the board decided that it was not right for me to have a high-paying position when my husband already had one. This information was relayed to me by the consultant who was handling the search on behalf of the board.[28]

1984: "Heinrich rules out education probe"

The Victoria Times-Colonist

As the social mandate for schools was broadened in the 1970s and 1980s, and as public and parental concern with the academic quality of the public schools intensified, British Columbians in and outside the public education establishment began to clamour for greater clarity about what schools could and should do. The idea of a royal commission was bruited, in particular, by the BCTF and the BCSTA in the mid-1980s. Here, a Victoria newspaper reports on the government's response to the BCSTA's request for such a large-scale study:

Education Minister Jack Heinrich has rejected a request by the B.C. School Trustees Association for a royal commission into education. The minister said Tuesday that the trustees have been asking for such a commission every year for the last 10 or 15 years and 'I don't see any particular reason for it.'

'We've introduced examinations, and we've got crews going around examining curriculum for grades 11 and 12 which are strongly supported by the public.'

Heinrich said that all that happens to royal commission reports is that after two years 'they sit on the shelf and gather dust. I want to do something and the people want something done, and I think we are.' The trustees voted overwhelmingly on the weekend for a royal commission to get trustees, parents, teachers, and business involved in setting the future course of education in the province.[29]

1985: "School Wars"

Crawford Kilian

Community college teacher and *Vancouver Province* newspaper columnist, Crawford Kilian, was one of the most outspoken critics of the provincial government's public sector restraint program in the early to mid-1980s. His book, *School Wars: The Assault on B.C. Education*, outlined what he saw to be the root causes of the political conflict over schooling in the province:

B.C.'s school problems are unique only in their intensity . . . Many American states pay teachers abysmal salaries, far below the B.C. average; yet those states do not go out of their way to bash teachers or bully school trustees. I know of no jurisdiction other than B.C. where the elected representatives of the people have chosen not merely to neglect education, but to attack it. This is generally true of the Socreds, and rare elsewhere. Government ministers in service areas like education, health and human resources act less as advocates for their constituents, than as their public enemies.

The chance for a return to some idyllic status quo is zero . . . Change is inevitable, and it is just a question of whose changes will be implemented. If they are to be positive changes, they will come only after British Columbians have done some hard thinking about the schools and the three major factors that now cripple them.

First is a dismally lazy and anti-intellectual attitude held by a sizable part of the . . . public. Second is a government all too eager to pander to that attitude, which it largely shares, even when the result is irrational policy and administrative chaos. Third is a government bureaucracy unable or unwilling to persuade its masters of their folly and equally incapable of persuading educators to cooperate. Many anti-intellectual British Columbians hold stubbornly mistaken beliefs about the state of education in the province. These myths are numerous . . .[30]

1985: *Let's Talk About Schools*

Provincial School Review Committee

In an attempt to address mounting public concern about the quality of provincial schools that had first surfaced a decade before, Jack Heinrich, Social Credit education minister, established a provincial school review committee in 1985 to gauge community and professional sentiments about public education. After extensive surveys of the public and school professionals, backstopped by an independent survey conducted by the Gallup poll group, the committee reported their findings. The committee's report, *Let's Talk About Schools*, however, did little to stifle the demands of some special interest groups, notably the BCTF, for a royal commission to study the state of the schools. Although the committee's study was far smaller in scope to the royal commission's inquiry, the committee's findings proved remarkably similar to those of the 1987-1988 royal commission. Among other things, the review committee reported that the public felt the quality of schooling was declining and were considerably more alarmed about this than educators inside schools:

> British Columbians agreed on what the goals of schooling should be. They placed greatest emphasis on intellectual development but they did not ignore the importance of goals to do with social, human, and vocational development. [Both] public and professionals view the issue of quality in schooling as something that is closely related to intellectual development and to a school curriculum that is characterized by strong academic programs . . . Both the public and educators are fearful that the quality of schooling today is not what it should be and a majority of them, in fact, believe that the quality of schooling has deteriorated over the last five years. British Columbians now feel that the quality of provincial schooling is not equal to that of other provinces, and ranks even more poorly when compared to what is seen to exist in British Columbia's private or independent schools. In general . . . the public is more critical of school performance than are educators, and ranks the quality of schooling lower than do members of the education profession.

> Another theme . . . was the . . . call for greater community presence in the life of schools . . . More than 80 per cent of those who responded to *Let's Talk About Schools* indicated they wished to be involved in schooling either 'more than now,' or 'as much as possible.' Along with this call for participation, respondents also stressed the need for greater accountability in schooling. This . . . was made evident in public support for standards, examinations, and a desire to monitor pupil and teacher performance. It was illustrated in public and professional interest in new mechanisms for providing political accountability. It was manifested in other ways: for example, specifying how school budgets should be spent, making explicit the roles and responsibilities of those inside and outside schools, and upgrading teacher qualifications . . . More than 90 per cent of public and professional respondents to *Let's Talk About Schools* held that standards should be established for all forms of schooling, including home schooling and schools operating outside the public system.[31]

1988: *A Legacy for Learners*

Royal Commission on Education

Prompted by the NDP opposition, and for reasons that are still unclear, William Vander Zalm, Social Credit premier, agreed in the spring legislative session of 1987 to convene a royal commission on education. Chief among the commission's tasks was to define a new mandate for schools that had become swamped by an array of new social responsibilities assigned to them since the 1970s. Entrusted to conduct the enquiry was Barry Sullivan, a New Westminster Q.C. and a former UBC soccer star. Under Sullivan's direction, the commission produced its report in August 1988, *A Legacy for Learners*, a report supported in large part by both major political parties. The commission's report, among other things, called for balancing the principles of "liberty" and "equality" in schooling, along with establishing better communications structures to bring an end to the "school wars" that had badly divided British Columbians in the 1980s:

> This report has outlined a portrait of the school system envisioned by the commission. In the broadest sense, it is a system characterized by both 'loose' and 'tight' properties: 'loose,' in the sense that greater differentiation, greater choice, greater diversity, and greater freedoms exist for all individuals within the system than at present; 'tight' in the sense that there is closer articulation and cooperation among the components of the system, that basic systems of monitoring and accountability are strengthened, that funding levels are indexed and predictable, that assignments of roles and responsibilities are

better clarified and defined, that zones of authority and jurisdiction are more specifically delineated, and that more appropriate structures are in place for communication, control, and action. It is a system that seeks to free the great human resources found in and around schools from the weight of conflict and uncertainty. Yet, it is also a system that seeks to protect the public good through structures and processes designed to ensure that certain skills and bodies of knowledge are learned, and certain protections are afforded youngsters, parents, teachers, school personnel, and the community in general.

In recommending loose and tight properties for the system, we seek to create an educational climate in which freedom exists within structure, in which the system's need for conformity and standardization is balanced by no less important needs for diversity and individualization; such a climate will enable objectives, standards, and responsibilities to be cinched down, whenever necessary, without depressing the efforts of parents, pupils, teachers, or school officials to develop new strategies for success to make the system more responsive to those it serves. Within such a climate, we believe, individual initiative can flourish and be rewarded. That climate, too, we trust, will promote the overall stability of the system, yet allow for greater flexibility in meeting diverse needs and environmental demands.[32]

1995: Termination of the Year 2000 program

Mike Crawley

The report of the 1988 royal commission was well received and prompted government to launch an ambitious new school reform initiative in 1989 known as the "Year 2000" program, a program generally based on a constructivist view of learning unfamiliar to many parents and greatly at variance with what the royal commission proposed. Managed mostly by school professionals seconded to the education ministry, the chaotic implementation of Year 2000 activities turned out to be immensely unpopular with parents and a political disaster for the NDP government in power. In his volume, *Schoolyard Bullies: Messing with British Columbia's Education System*, journalist Mike Crawley describes how the program came to an abrupt halt four years and a series of mishaps later:

Our society is influenced by the school calendar . . . We all notice the start of school and the return of yellow buses to the roads . . . All this means it's an opportune time for a politician to catch the public's attention on issues related to education. That's what Premier Mike Harcourt did in September 1993. 'To

> put it bluntly, the report card on the Year 2000 is in and it's failed the grade,' said the premier in a front-page story in the *The Vancouver Sun* on September 4, the Saturday before classes resumed . . .
>
> Harcourt's justification for killing Year 2000 was a Decima Research poll commissioned by cabinet. Based on this poll, the premier cited widespread concern about the school system. 'It's a pretty overwhelming opinion out there,' he said. 'Those concerns are deeply felt and real, and I share them.'
>
> The poll indicated that 43 per cent of British Columbians felt the school system had 'become worse' in the previous five years. Two-thirds of respondents said there is a 'great need' to improve the school system and another 30 per cent said there is 'somewhat' of a need. The three elements most cited as needing improvement were: acquiring basic skills, meeting the needs of all students (not just those who go to university), and preparing kids for the twenty-first century . . . When Mike Harcourt shuffled his cabinet on September 15, no one was surprised to see Anita Hagen [the education minister] get the boot.[33]

1999: "Parents put heat on B.C. schools"

The Globe and Mail

As the twentieth century was about to end, a bitter debate broke out in the Greater Vancouver area about parents' rights to enroll their children in so-called "traditional schools." Parental displeasure with the quality of public schooling had increased since the 1960s and 1970s, prompting ever-increasing subscriptions to non-public sector schools. By the 1990s, British Columbia parents—many of Asian heritages—were demanding access to "traditional schools" within the public system. Here, *The Globe and Mail* reported on the situation in Richmond, where the school board was split on the issue of whether to provide such choice to parents:

> Controversy over the right of parents to shape their children's education is rocking school boards throughout the Lower Mainland. The increasingly loaded emotional issue is being fuelled by a powerful new force on the educational landscape; thousands of parents believe teaching in Canadian elementary schools is unstructured and inconsistent. They want their children taught in so-called traditional schools, which emphasize back-to-basics education, tight discipline, daily doses of homework in all grades, uniforms, and teacher-centred classrooms with single desks in neat rows.

So desperate is the desire that parents camp outside the existing Surrey Traditional School for days in advance, hoping to claim one of the few coveted spots for their youngsters when applications open up in the spring. 'From year to year, teacher to teacher, there is a lack of consistency in the public school system,' complained Coleen Gem, spokeswoman for the association pushing for a traditional school in Vancouver. 'Immigrants from Asia are used to a more structured learning environment. We think parents should have a choice in the type of education their children receive.' The Vancouver School Board is to vote tonight on a demand from Ms. Gem's group for a traditional school. Later this month, the matter comes before the school board in the sprawling suburb of Richmond, home to most recent Hong Kong immigrants. Similar campaigns are being launched in five other Greater Vancouver districts.

The determined drive by ethnic Chinese parents for traditional schools has sparked widespread concern among teachers, parent advisory groups and some school board members. They also accuse the crusading parents of seeking public funds to finance what would essentially be private schools. Nowhere is the debate more highly charged than in Richmond, where 70 per cent of the district's 24,000 students do not have English as their first language at home. A pro-traditional school petition was signed by more than 3,000 people, nearly all of Asian descent. Parents have packed public meetings and school board meetings on the issue. 'It's become emotional. There is real fear any school will be 99 per cent Chinese,' said Sandra Bourque, a member of the Richmond school board since 1990. 'The parents have made untrue statements about our teachers and their methods and about Canada and Canadian kids. They say our schools are too slack and lack discipline. Their comments are very hurtful.'

Proponents heatedly deny they want to restrict traditional schools to ethnic Chinese or dominate debate. But they point out they are as much a part of the community as anyone else. 'This is not a race driven thing. No one ever mentioned race when Caucasian parents were lobbying for traditional schools,' Ms. Gem said. Visible minorities make up one-third of the Lower Mainland. This is the community that's out there.

The Richmond board is split on the question, voting 4-3 last June to approve a traditional school in principle. The full evening will be set aside at the board's next meeting to make a final decision. 'Emotions are almost at the boil now and they are going to crescendo,' said chairwoman Chris Evans, who supports the proposal on the grounds of parent choice. At the moment there are just five publicly-financed traditional schools in all of B.C. The Surrey Traditional School, now in its fifth year, with more than 300 students from kindergarten to grade 8, is the most prominent showcase. Quiet reigns within the school. Desks are in rows. All students wear a type of uniform—green tops, skirts and pants in the lower grades, navy blue in the higher grades. Rookie principal Shelly Nightingale didn't know what to expect when she was appointed to the school in September. 'But for the most part, it's been wonderful. The kids are great, and they comes from homes and families where they really support education,' Ms. Nightingale said.[34]

2001: "B.C. introduces legislation limiting teachers' strikes"

National Union of Public and General Employees

The National Union of Public and General Employees (NUPGE) is one of Canada's largest unions and represents the interests of 11 Canadian public sector unions comprised of some 340,000 members. Here the NUPGE's website posts a bulletin sharply critical of the British Columbia government's 2001 decision to try to stabilize labour relations in schools by classifying education as an "essential service:"

> Premier Gordon Campbell's anti-labour government has stepped up its campaign against organized labour, introducing legislation declaring education an essential service. The practical impact of Bill 18, tabled Tuesday in the legislature, would force teachers to keep enough staff on duty to allow schools to remain open in the event of a strike.
>
> 'This bill puts children first,' Labour Minister Graham Bruce said. 'It will restore education as an essential service under the labour code to ensure that no child's right to education is denied during school strikes and lockouts.' B.C. is the only province to propose this type of legislation, although the rights of teachers are restricted in some provinces, and in two—P.E.I. and Manitoba—teachers are not allowed to strike at all.
>
> Bill 18 also follows through on Liberal campaign promises related to secret votes for union certification, mandatory sectoral bargaining in the unionized construction industry, and workers' pensions. NDP leader Joy MacPhail said the legislation tips the balance unfairly in favor of the government and against teachers in contract negotiations. B.C. teachers are to begin province-wide bargaining this fall. David Chudnovsky, president of the BCTF, called the move 'needlessly disruptive.'[35]

2004: "The result was a change in government"

Ken Novakowski, Teachers' Newsmagazine

A year before the BCTF's illegal October 2005 strike, the organization's executive director Ken Novakowski signalled that the federation was prepared to do political battle with the Liberal government in the 2005 election. Here, Novokowski reminded members of the political clout the federation had enjoyed in recent decades and warned of things to come:

> 'We won't live with it!' With those words in 1972 . . . President Adam Robertson heralded a new political stance for the B.C. Teachers' Federation. On behalf of all teachers, Robertson declared the BCTF's intention to fight to change the government of the day in the next provincial election. Teachers were angry with government legislation restricting a school district's ability to raise revenue, with government attempts to chip away at the tenure rights of teachers, and with the government-imposed ceilings for arbitrated teacher salary increases. All that came on the heels of the BCTF's first province-wide strike action in March of 1971, when teachers across the province shut down all schools to protest the government's unwillingness to improve pensions for retired teachers. The BCTF went on to play a major role in the August 30, 1972, election that defeated the W.A.C. Bennett Social Credit government.
>
> The success of the 1972 teacher involvement served notice to all political parties . . . This political-activist stance of the BCTF did not come about overnight. It was the result of many meetings and extensive debates by teachers within the organization over the five years leading up to the 1972 election . . .
>
> Not until the election of October 1991, did the organization [again] mount a full-scale initiative to defeat the government of the day . . . Teachers' involvement in the 1991 'Teachers make a difference' campaign was extensive. A survey of locals following the campaign showed that about 6,000 teachers were active in the election campaign. The result was a change in government. In the two elections (1972 and 1991) where the organization (BCTF) went all out to seek a change, there was a change . . .
>
> The current . . . Liberal government of B.C. has given the teachers of this province good cause to throw them out . . . The government has destroyed collective bargaining for teachers, removing the right to strike and legislatively imposing terms and conditions of employment that remove class-size limits and other teaching provisions long fought for and once won by B.C. teachers

> ... Given our history, given our grievances, given our options, why would anyone be surprised that the BCTF Annual General Meeting decided to make it a priority to get teachers involved in the next provincial election?[36]

2005: "The strike as kitsch"

Andrew Coyne

The Liberal government was returned to office in 2005 and, following the collapse of negotiations between the BCTF and the British Columbia Public Schools Employers' Association (BCPSEA), the government refused to negotiate directly with teachers, as the BCTF demanded. Instead, government imposed a second consecutive contract on teachers that extended the previous contract until June 2006. The BCTF held a vote in support of illegal strike action and reported a strike mandate of over 90 per cent. On October 7, teachers began a province-wide full-scale strike that continued for two weeks even though the British Columbia Labour Relations Board had issued a return to work order and the British Columbia Supreme Court had ruled that the union was in civil contempt. Not everyone was in sympathy with the BCTF's decision to strike, or its decision to defy the Supreme Court ruling. Here *National Post* columnist, Andrew Coyne, offers his view of events and the phenomenon of public sector strikes in Canada:

> In other news ... thousands of public school teachers across British Columbia are out on strike. They are striking in defiance of the law, as both the B.C. Labour Relations Board and the B.C. Supreme Court have ruled. Yet, even in the face of fines of as much as $150,000 per day, the teachers' union vows to stay out, leaving more than 600,000 students in the lurch ...
>
> It's a big story, and yet it isn't: Teachers are always out on strike somewhere, illegally or otherwise—if not in B.C., then in Ontario, or Quebec or some other locale. Teachers' strikes have become as much a part of the school year as prom night. That is, in the public school system that's true. But you rarely hear about a strike by private school teachers, do you?
>
> The common denominator in every case is the public sector. Strikes, once common across the economy, have become disproportionately a public sector phenomenon. Public employees account for 18 per cent of the workforce, but half or more of all days lost to strikes in a typical year. There's a simple enough explanation for this: Unions themselves are disproportionately a public sector phenomenon. Today, fewer than one in five private sector workers in Canada belong to a union. Three out of four public employees do.

And why is that? One word: competition. Strikes are rare wherever competition from rival providers makes such interruptions too costly, for management and labour alike. In the private sector, that is increasingly the case; the more competitive the industry, the less the incidence of either unions or strikes. But in the public sector, especially where it enjoys a monopoly or near-monopoly, unions are still a force, and the strike remains the weapon of choice . . .

The whole business has a strangely antiquated, cloth-cap feel to it. The strike evolved as the natural strategy of unskilled mass labour, at a time when workers were many in number but few in rights. Now it's the tool of television producers and tenured professors . . . It's all just a little bit kitsch.

The present dispute was triggered when the B.C. government imposed a two-year wage freeze on teachers. That's unpleasant, no doubt, though people put up with much worse in other lines of work. The difference is that teachers feel entitled to shut down the province's schools to make their point—even in defiance of the law. The teachers' leader calls it civil disobedience, and compares the union's situation with that of the suffragettes.

It's not that they're particularly hard done by (at $65,000 per, B.C.'s teachers are among the highest paid in the federation of Canadian teachers). It's just what they do. It's how they have learned to behave. I doubt it occurs to them that everyone else does not do the same.[37]

2005: "School boards plan appeal to highest courts"

The Globe and Mail

A hotly-debated issue that surfaced in 2005 was whether British Columbia teachers could use the parent-teacher interview as a forum for the discussion of class size or whether teachers should be prohibited from discussing public policy to do with conditions of employment with parents. An August 5, 2005 article in *The Globe and Mail* described developments concerning these matters before the courts:

The province's school boards, backed by the B.C. Ministry of Education, are planning an appeal to the Supreme Court of Canada after losing a court challenge to keep teachers from discussing government policy with parents. A B.C. Court of Appeal ruling this week found that the issues teachers want to raise, such as class size, were relevant to parents. Prohibiting any discussion was an overreaction, two of the three judges ruled, and had the potential to undermine teachers' dignity and professional status. In a dissenting opinion, however, Mr. Justice Peter Lowry wrote that in his view public schools are not the place for teachers to advance their political agendas.

Hugh Finlayson, CEO of the B.C. Public School Employers' Association, said the Court of Appeal ruling did not address what limits and parameters are allowed within a workplace. 'We will be asking the courts to grapple with that issue. It's a sensitive issue for parents and the school community. There is freedom of speech but the freedom of speech is not unlimited,' Mr. Finlayson said . . .

Teachers filed a grievance against the association after school boards prohibited them from posting documents on bulletin boards, distributing pamphlets to parents, and discussing bigger class sizes and cuts to services with parents during interviews . . .

The issue of freedom of expression has been debated at various levels but the B.C. case may be the first to be taken to the Supreme Court of Canada.[38]

Notes

1. The homeroom, "Eileen Dailly—Minister of Education, 1972-1975," retrieved 25 October 2009 from http://records.viu.ca/homeroom/content/topics/people/daily.htm.
2. Mrs. T.J. Rolston was the first woman to serve as education minister. She held the portfolio from 1952 to 1953.
3. The Honourable Eileen Dailly, Minister of Education, *The Public School System: Directions for Change* (Victoria: K.M. MacDonald, Queen's Printer), 1-4.
4. Johann "Joe" Phillipson was born near Prince Rupert, B.C. in 1916 and grew up and attended school in Sooke, outside Victoria. He attended Victoria High and boarded with Ira Dilworth, later to be principal and, still later, regional head of the CBC. He attended Victoria College, then located at Craigdarroch Castle, and from there went on to Normal School on Richmond Road. He took his first teaching assignment at Groundbirch Elementary School in the Peace River, a one-room school. Following this, he took a job at a four-room school at Pouce Coupé, on the understanding that he was "willing to teach French."
5. John Bremer was a self-styled "egalitarian progressive" known for his "school without walls" experiment in Philadelphia.
6. Interview with Joe Phillipson, Victoria 28 October 1983.
7. Correspondence, Terry McBurney to Thomas Fleming, 13 July 2009.
8. E.M. Carlin, "Excerpts of Interviews with Deputy Ministers of Education, 1970-1984," UBC unpublished report, 1984, 7, 8, 9 and 10.
9. Press release, "Bremer Commission on Education" issued by the Honourable Eileen Daily Minister of Education, Vancouver, 12 January 1973.
10. Interview with Henry Armstrong, Vancouver, 2 August 1989.
11. Jack Fleming is the son of Frances Fleming. Thomas Fleming is not related to them.
12. Carlin "Excerpts of Interviews," 19, 21-23, and 29-30.
13. Interview with Henry Armstrong.
14. Personal papers courtesy of Frances Fleming.
15. Ibid.
16. Donald Campbell's manuscript courtesy of Terry McBurney and Barbara Naef.
17. This story is courtesy of Barbara Naef.
18. Personal papers courtesy of Frances Fleming.
19. Ibid.
20. Harry Cullis' manuscript is courtesy of Terry McBurney and Barbara Naef.
21. British Columbia Department of Education, *Inter-Departmental Information Bulletin*, No. 5, 14 May 1974, 2.
22. Carlin, "Excerpts of Interviews," 34-35.
23. Alan J.H. Newberry, "Some Aspects of Uniqueness in the Small Superintendency in British Columbia: A Paper Presented to the Seminar of Instruction Sponsored by the Division of Field Personnel, Department of Education," 3-8 October 1976, the Village Green Inn, Duncan, 1-3.
24. Passage of Bill 33, the *Independent Schools Support Act*, provided public support for non-public schools up to 30 per cent of local district operating costs. This greatly changed the landscape of educational provision by making it possible for more parents to afford non-public sector schooling.

25. Carlin, "Excerpts of Interviews," 45-50 and 53.
26. In August 1980, the British Columbia government approved the local employment of school superintendents.
27. Peter McLoughlin's manuscript manuscript courtesy of Terry McBurney and Barbara Naef.
28. Manuscript courtesy of Barbara Naef.
29. *The Times Colonist*, "Hemrich rules out education probe," 2 May 1984, 1.
30. Crawford Kilian, *School Wars: The Assault on B.C. Education* (Vancouver: New Star Books, 1985), 218-233.
31. British Columbia Provincial School Review Committee, *Let's Talk About Schools: A Report to the Minister of Education and the People of British Columbia* (Victoria: Queen's Printer, 1985), 6-9.
32. British Columbia Royal Commission on Education, *A Legacy for Learners* (Victoria: Queen's Printer, 1988), 219-220.
33. Mike Crawley, *Schoolyard Bullies: Messing with British Columbia's Education System* (Victoria: Orca Books, 1995), 115-122.
34. *The Globe and Mail*, "Parents put heat on B.C. schools," 1 February 1999.
35. National Union of Public and General Employees, 15 (August 2001) retrieved 20 October 2008 from http://www.nupge.ca/default.htm
36. Ken Novakowski, "It's who we are," *Teachers' Newsmagazine*, Vol. 17, No. 1, September 2004, retrieved 25 October 2009 from http://bctf.ca/publications/NewsmagArticle.aspx?id=7772
37. Andrew Coyne, *The National Post*, 12 October 2005, retrieved 9 November 2009 from Andrew Coyne.com.
38. *The Globe and Mail*, "School boards plan appeal to highest court," Friday, 5 August 2005.

Index

Permissions

The following permissions to use copyrighted material are gratefully acknowledged:

Yale University Press for materials from James P. Spradley (Ed.), *Guests Never Leave Hungry: The Autobiography of James Sewid, A Kwakiutl Indian* (Montreal: McGill-Queen's University Press, 1969), 16, 21-27, 31, 45, 53-55, 63 and 191-192.

Dorothy Blakey Smith, *The Reminiscences of Doctor John Sebastian Helmcken* (Vancouver: University of British Columbia Press, 1975), 120-121.

Derek Pethick, *Victoria: The Fort* (Vancouver: Mitchell Press, 1968), 117.

The Richards family for permission to use material from Eric Roberts, *Salt Spring Saga* (Ganges, Salt Spring Island, B.C.: Driftwood Press, 1962), 16.

Jan Gould, *Women of British Columbia* (Saanichton, B.C.: Hancock House Publishers Ltd., 1975), 108.

Harry Assu and Joy Inglis, *Assu of Cape Mudge: Recollections of a Coastal Indian Chief* (Vancouver: University of British Columbia Press, 1989), 86-88, 90, 95-97.

Daphne Marlatt and Carole Itter, *Opening Doors: Vancouver's East End, Sound Heritage,* Vol. 8, No. 1 and 2, Aural History Program, British Columbia Archives, Victoria, British Columbia, 1979, 15-19 and 94.

Frances Decker, Margaret Fougberg, and Mary Ronayne, *Pemberton: The History of a Settlement* (Pemberton: Pemberton Pioneer Women, 1977), 153.

Alice Glanville, *Schools of the Boundary: 1891-1991* (Merritt, B.C.: Sonotek Publishing, 1991), 127.

John Calam, "Settling into the Teacherage," Copyright © 2001 by John Calam.

Nelson Publishing for use of materials from Hilda Neatby, *So Little for the Mind: An Indictment of Canadian Education* (Toronto: Clarke Irwin, 1953), 11-19.

E.M. Carlin, "Excerpts of Interviews with Deputy Ministers of Education, 1970-1984," University of British Columbia unpublished report, 1984, 7-10, 45-50, and 53.

Mike Crawley, *Schoolyard Bullies: Messing with British Columbia's Education System* (Victoria: Orca Books, 1995), 115-122.

Crawford Kilian, *School Wars: The Assault on B.C. Education* (Vancouver: New Star Books, 1985), 218-233.